A Life of Anne Tyler

ANNE WELLMAN

Table of Contents

Foreword

"My life has nothing to do with my writing," said Anne Tyler. If something happened in one of her books then it never happened to her, she maintained. If a character had a certain trait, it was not one of hers. Whenever she saw something wonderful happen in the real world, she was plunged into despair because that meant it could not be used in her novels. Writing and reality were "mutually exclusive." In any case, Anne claimed, she had led a life so conventional and free of incident that even her biographer would nod off in the middle of it, let alone any readers. It would be the dullest book ever written: "Happy, but dull." When she was writing her novels she was trying to lead *another* life, somebody else's, to see what it was like; so why would she contemplate leading the same existence over again and putting a person already in her life into her work? She also did not want her readers "stepping outside" her story to wonder if she was describing her own husband or her own experiences. Her characters had to shine straight through her as though she were invisible, and her readers had to be convinced they were living inside the world she had created; her purpose would be defeated if they started to wonder about the author instead.

But as time went on, Anne was to concede that stages of her own life *did* emerge within her work—for instance that she wrote more about small children when she had them, and more about the death of husbands when she had gone through it herself. Adolescent-rearing, empty-nesting, aging, all were just as mirrored in her novels, she admitted, although only after the period she needed for things to settle in her mind before she could write about them. While her life and its specifics were not connected to her books her preoccupations definitely were, Anne finally acknowledged, not all of which she had been fully aware of at the time. Anne also revealed that in many of the later novels her own children were deliberately inserted as minuscule, sometimes one-sentence cameo appearances, and, as they came onto the scene in real life, their spouses and offspring. (Her family did not object.) Even strands of her personality had, after all, found their way in:

> *If you read something in my book you can know it didn't happen because I would never want to take real life and just turn it into a novel, but on another level I think that maybe some of the preoccupations characters have, or the defects, or the shynesses they experience, are mine—that I can't help but let a little of myself bleed into them.*

This is the story of Anne's life (never as mundane as she made out) and the way her preoccupations and general experience surfaced in her writing, which comprised twenty-four acclaimed novels, at least fifty short stories, and a range of nonfiction. Her first novel was published in 1964 when she was twenty-three, and her most recent in 2022 at the age of eighty.

It reveals a woman of great charm, warmth, and humor, but a woman who spent many years secluded from the world in order to concentrate on her writing—and who was far bleaker in her estimation of the human race than might ever be guessed.

All statements, thoughts and opinions directly attributed to Anne are derived solely from her own words or writings, and are given as exact quotes or carefully paraphrased.

Childhood

When Anne Tyler was six, and already in school, her family moved to an isolated mountain commune in search of a simpler life.

Here they had their own home, a rough, clapboard house that had no electricity when they first moved in but was certainly better than the hole in the ground where a more eccentric neighbor was living. There was only one telephone in the whole community. Using organic farming techniques, Anne's parents produced much of what they ate from a small garden and shared in the eating of some of the neighbors' livestock ("Is this Nancy?" a neighbor would recall Anne asking one night over a roast beef dinner.) When one of her brothers proved to be allergic to cow's milk, the family's animals expanded to include a herd of goats, and even late in life Anne was able to tell the milks apart. Her mother made the family's shoes out of goat skin and also made all their clothes; they bought sugar and coffee, but were otherwise self-sufficient.

Anne's parents were Minnesotans, her father Lloyd an industrial chemist and her mother Phyllis a social worker. They first met at a Quaker meeting in the late 1930s when undergraduates at the University of Minnesota, both of them pacifists with strong ideals. Phyllis Mahon's belief in non-violence, and her compassionate concern for others, soon convinced Lloyd that he had found the woman he wanted to share his life with. Encouraged by Lloyd, born a Quaker, Phyllis converted to Quakerism and they married in 1940, determined to dedicate their lives to eradicating poverty, war and injustice. Phyllis worked in family services in Minneapolis before their first child, Anne Phyllis, was born there in October 1941. Three sons were to follow.

Anne's earliest memory occurred before she could speak. She was sitting on a sort of changing table and her mother was dressing her in a little quilted coat, which she hated because she couldn't bend her arms in it:

So I thought I told her that I don't like this coat and she just kept right on putting it on me, smiling at me...she said, when I told her this memory, you wore that coat between seven and ten months. I always look at babies now and think: they believe they're communicating.

Her new home in the summer of 1948 at the age of six, and that of her first little brother Stanley Lloyd (nicknamed Ty), was the Celo Community in the western mountains of North Carolina, still going strong today. The Tylers had been searching for some time for a better place to raise their family, somewhere more in line with their own ideals. In the years prior to World War II both had opposed the upcoming conflict, joining organizations helping to educate the public about alternatives to fighting such as non-combatant service. During the war itself Lloyd was a conscientious objector, and after the end of hostilities he felt that the world had gone to hell. This disenchantment led to the young couple seeking out a place where they could live separately from the world, a retreat, "a Utopian, Emersonian community," in Anne's later words. Before

4

the move to Celo they had already tried out a number of other alternative communities, leaving Minneapolis to begin the quest when Anne was only about eight months old.

Celo, pronounced see-loh, was a remote settlement of twelve hundred acres in the beautiful South Toe River valley of mountainous Yancey County, a gathering of like-minded people where the land was held in common. Its Constitution at the time declared that Celo represented an opportunity for members to enjoy a life offering personal expression, neighborly cooperation, and care of the environment. All were welcome, with none excluded on grounds of race, nationality or belief (and no particular belief or ideology was required). The Constitution also made clear that, to avoid profiteering and abuse of the environment, land would not be sold to members but only assigned, and money could be lent at low cost to those who showed promise of being able to improve their property while living in harmony with others. Everyone would share resources and live off the land, but there was also an emphasis on autonomy and individualism.

The Tylers hoped that the mainly agricultural life at the commune would instill in their children a firm foundation of good values and hard work, far removed from what they perceived as the intrinsic materialism of mainstream America. They may well have been influenced by a Celo pamphlet printed in about 1946 which described the settlement's purpose as being "to live and work in a small progressive community. To rear children in a wholesome environment where they could become acquainted with nature. To raise some of their own food. To work for themselves—or in small organizations—at callings that would provide simple but adequate living. To cooperate with friends and neighbors in creating a satisfying community life."

Commune members made money from various home-run enterprises, such as machine-knitting socks. Anne's father became one of three partners operating a mail-order business, Celo Laboratories, which developed and sold natural vitamins and drugs from the basement of the commune's newly built Health Center. Her mother Phyllis was fully occupied with household and family, including homeschooling: Anne and Ty were initially taught using the Calvert School correspondence system, meant for the children of diplomatic staff posted abroad. Phyllis would instruct the children with whatever materials were sent, which could sometimes be somewhat irrelevant for commune children, such as how to spell "hors d'oeuvre." It was good enough to keep the young Tylers permanently ahead of their grades but, looking back, Anne was less than enthusiastic:

I'm not a believer in homeschooling. If your mother is teaching you, and you don't get something, she takes it personally and I missed other kids.

For a brief time, when both Anne and Ty wanted company and their parents felt it was important for them to have other children as friends, they attended a three-room log schoolhouse in the nearby community of Harvard. There were eight grades in the school and fifth-grade Anne shared a room with the next two classes up; it worked well but was "pretty primitive," she remembered. In warm weather some of the children walked to school barefoot, bringing pint jars of milk to cool for lunch in a bubbling mountain spring. There were two outhouses, one for the boys and one for the girls. Inside, in cold weather, the children warmed themselves at the pot belly stove filled with coal that the pupils fetched in by bucket (competing for the honor). Those sitting nearest would end up with splotched legs. Anne felt like an outsider at the school because she recognized that the local Appalachian children, and their parents, saw the commune people as "just plain strange." She was to recall that as a child in this environment she evolved the ability to speak two languages—that of her highly educated family and their circle, and the more informal talk of her less privileged friends locally.

Instruction at the little school in Harvard was patchy and the teacher would sometimes abandon the class to see to his cows, leaving Anne or others to stand in front of the class calling out words to be spelled. Returning to dismiss the children he would slip Anne a nickel; Phyllis, also a writer, later published a story (under a pseudonym) that was told from the point of view of a child, called "The Year I Taught at Harvard." She did not consider the basic education there to be sufficient and in the end the children were withdrawn, although occasionally still sent along by Phyllis just to join the others at recess.

In addition to the homeschooling, and their time at Harvard, the Tyler children learned some practical arithmetic weighing out sugar and nuts at Celo's cooperative store, and were given carpentry, art, and cooking lessons by other members of the community; one remembered Anne and Ty turning up at his private art class as "guests." Both would simply knock on a neighbor's door and announce that they had come to learn something. "What do you want to teach me today?" Anne would ask.

Anne was eventually enrolled in another school when it opened nearby, South Toe Elementary, where she completed fifth grade and half of the sixth. The schools were wretched, Phyllis told a friend, and it was a wonder that Anne and Ty could read. "They talk like mountain kids and we can hardly understand them."

On Sundays all the children in the commune would be rounded up and taken to a log cabin near the meeting house to sing songs, staying outside in good weather on the faded old front steps. Anne would always remember sitting there at the bottom of the "beautiful green bowl" that was their valley, seeing the distant ring of purple mountains far in the distance and hearing the words of the hymn "This is My Father's World." For Anne, in later years, this music was not about God so much as the natural world she was living in.

Life seemed good at the commune and the Tylers persuaded both sets of grandparents—all mainly of British descent, a mix of Scots, Irish, English, and Welsh—to join them there. Anne's paternal grandfather Charles Tyler, a chicken farmer at the time of her birth, was kindly and very quiet, something she loved about him without knowing why. "He was very silent, very severe-looking, children all loved him," she remembered. Her maternal grandmother had been an English teacher, while her maternal grandpa was a poetry-writing mining engineer who was equally kindly and told a great many stories, including how his mother had died from childbed fever when he was only four years old. At a crucial moment during her illness he had been sent off to a nearby house to borrow some coffee, which the little boy understood to mean that coffee was the only thing that would keep her alive. He ran home as fast as he could —"with a steaming mug," as the young Anne pictured it—but when he got there she had died, which he thought was his fault. Anne was always to remember Grandpa Mahon using the exact same phrase every time he told the story over the years: "I ran as fast as my little legs could carry me." The tale eventually found its way into one of her novels.

But Celo was an isolated existence for Anne. She would be off in the woods, learning to be alone and to entertain herself by imagining. Pretending to be Dolores, a mother of eighteen children, she would walk from bush to bush—where they all lived—talking to the make-believe family and hearing about their dramas. At home, she described herself as "born watching and listening," hiding under the table and drawing as she listened to her mother chatting with friends (and picking up the undertones in the conversation, which she later saw had helped with her writing).

Starting as early as three years old, Anne also told herself stories in bed at night, carrying on with the Dolores saga or spinning another about a girl going west in a covered wagon. She would pretend she was a doctor, looking at her patients over her drawn-up knees as a desk, and listening as they explained how they got their broken arms and legs. Ty, sharing her room, would call out: "Mama, Anne's whispering again!" (She came to think of her writing as a continuation of that storytelling.) Her parents seemed to understand that it was her way of being creative and did not make a fuss, just asking her to be quieter about it. In the daytime she drew people on her blackboard and imagined what their lives were like and what brought them together. "It was a matter...of beginning to wonder what it would be like to be other people," Anne was to observe, looking back. The grown-ups would tell her to stop daydreaming or stop staring into space, and she later understood that writing was a way of disobeying those two major rules. For Anne, tapping her imagination to write was "really an extension of daydreaming."

Phyllis read to the children often, sometimes in the open on hot summer nights when the family all slept out under the stars. Anne credited her mother with helping her fall in love with books; as an adult she could still hear Phyllis' voice reading *Wind in the Willows* to her and Ty, and the sound of her brother's teeth chattering when they reached the "Wild Wood" chapter, in which Mole gets lost in a fearsome, eerie forest in the depths of winter. Ty's eyes would grow nearly black with fear, Anne recalled, and she was hardly comfortable herself. The children would sit closer and closer until their mother asked if they wanted to switch to something less upsetting, but they would shake their heads and beg for more. They chose to have it read aloud on Christmas Eve, because, as Anne pointed out as an adult, Mole was rescued and made safe in Badger's cozy burrow —a transition from snow-filled forest to warm, bright hearth that would make anyone supremely happy to be "snug at home, safe from the howling winter night, sitting close with his family," exactly the way you wanted to feel at Christmas.

But, of course, Anne wanted to be able to read by herself. Phyllis remembered that although she had felt some trepidation about embarking on the serious business of teaching a child to read, Anne had been so determined that she might have gone out and picked it up in the street. And, as soon as she could read and put pen to paper, Anne also began to write:

I feel as if I was writing before I could hold a pen...I was so relieved when I learned to read and could actually put stuff down.

At the age of seven she wrote her first story, in a notebook carefully labeled "Written and Illustrated by Anne Tyler," soon followed by dozens more. These were what she called "wishful thinking" stories, all about those lucky, lucky girls who got to go west in covered wagons—girls Anne desperately wanted to be. She was furious to have been born too late. She very much enjoyed the drawing part, and at this stage thought she might become an artist.

Seven was a crucial age for Anne. She had never been as intelligent as she was at seven, Anne smilingly declared as an adult, never as thoughtful or as introspective.

I remember when I was seven, making crucial decisions about the kind of person I was going to be. That's also the age when I figured out that, oh, someday I'm going to die, and the age when I decided I couldn't believe in God.

She had been trying very hard to be religious, and had suddenly realized she was simply not capable of it. She remembered thinking the actual words: "I guess I'm not a spiritual person." The family went to Quaker Meeting, a gathering for worship held in almost total silence, so that Anne as a child did not know what she was supposed to believe or not believe. You could come up with your own thoughts, she commented. As an adult, though, she was glad to have been raised a Quaker. Admittedly it had made her feel like an outsider, but she ultimately saw this as excellent for a writer. It was a "nice quiet religion," she was to say, and in the same way that people talked about secular Jews, she felt like a secular Quaker. Anne never returned to religion—professing no interest in finding out the meaning of life—but was always in harmony with Quaker ethics: peace and equality, and all that the Quakers stood for.

§

Books were hard to come by at Celo, although a community member who worked as a librarian would bring back books she thought people might like, dropping them off from house to house as she walked through the settlement on her way home. Anne, of course, adored reading. From a very early age she felt that the action in books was "much more reasonable, and interesting, and *real*," than in everyday life (although not fairy tales, which she positively hated, feeling insulted even then by the implausibilities and mistakes repeatedly made by the heroes). She read anything she could get her hands on, often many times over because there were so few children's books available to her. She was a continual, almost obsessive reader of absolutely anything in print, even appliance manuals:

When people spoke to me, I read their words running across a sort of ticker tape at the bottom of my mind's eye. (What had I seen there before I learned to read? I used to wonder.)...I longed for old age, when I would be allowed to stay sunk in a book for twelve hours straight, uninterrupted by grown-ups asking me to feed the chickens or set the table.

One book she was to return to frequently was Louisa May Alcott's *Little Women*, discovering it at the age of nine or ten and falling into it "heart and soul," as she put it. When Beth died Anne was so stunned that she simply did not believe it could have happened, reading and re-reading the passage and then looking around her trying to take it in. Each time she went back to the novel she felt the same shock and disbelief. (As a firmly non-religious adult, she resisted the temptation to read it yet again because she recalled "a certain note of piety" in the story and was reluctant to be disillusioned.)

But, well before that, she had been given a book for her fourth birthday that was to influence her for the rest of her life: *The Little House*, by Virginia Lee Burton.

Her parents read it to her first, and once she was able to Anne read it to herself, "sinking" into its colorful, complicated pictures all through her childhood and adolescence and even into adulthood. It was a simple story about a small house sitting on a hill among apple trees, the illustrations showing two symmetrical windows with their curtains looped back at the sides—like the forehead of a little girl with braids, Anne always thought. In the yard, children splash in the pond in the summer and go sledding in the winter. The lights of the city glow in the distance, and the little house sometimes wonders how it would feel to live there. Then the children grow up and leave, and things start to change. New homes and buildings and skyscrapers spring up around her, and the house can hardly be seen for elevated trains and speeding traffic. Her paint fades and her windows crack and she no longer knows whether it's summer or winter. But then the great-great-granddaughter of the man who built the house happens to pass by. She has the house moved to the country, to just the right spot, on a hill among apple trees where once more the little house has a family to care for her. She never again wonders how it would feel to live in the city.

At the age of four, all Anne knew was that she liked the book's tone of voice, the quiet rhythm of phrases repeated till they took on the inevitability of a melody. It made whichever voice was reading it become "hushed and gentle and sad," so that even the most fidgety of her little brothers gradually fell calm. As an adult, she could see there was more to the story. There was comfort in it, especially for children whose lives get rearranged in inexplicable, alarming ways. "Friends move out of their neighborhoods and never come back; baby brothers move into their bedrooms and never go away," she wrote in an essay about the book in 1986, in her mid-forties. It was reassuring that change could happen to a house, and the house could weather it and be just as good underneath—the change could be reversed. Or perhaps only partly reversed: the little house found a new hill with apple trees but in the final picture there was no pond, although Anne was never sure if this was intentional, some kind of lesson about not being able to go all the way back, or just an oversight by the illustrator. What she took from it, however, was a precocious understanding of change:

I took that very seriously. I thought you can try really hard to get something back, but it will never be exactly the same, so you shouldn't wish for things to change while you're going through them.

But the real point of *The Little House* for Anne was what it said about the passage of time, the way it introduced her four-year-old self to the feeling of nostalgia—the realization of what can be lost as time passes and the way all moments are joined, each linked inexorably to the next. Up till then she had experienced time unreflectively, with changes coming as sudden jolts in her existence. Now *The Little House* revealed to her all the successive stages, the rising and setting of the sun, the marching by of the seasons. And, once the little house is in the middle of the city she has yearned for, she finds that she misses the field of daisies and the apple trees dancing in the moonlight.

Reading these words as an adult Anne would recall the feeling of "elderly sorrow" that came over her at this very early age:

I had a sudden spell of...wisdom, I guess you could say. It seemed I'd been presented with a snapshot that showed me how the world worked: how the years flowed by and people altered and nothing could ever stay the same. Then the snapshot was taken away. Everything there is to know about time was revealed in that snapshot...

From then on, Anne had a constant awareness of the fact that nothing lasted forever, and that someday she would miss what she was now taking for granted—a valuable insight, she would come to feel, to take through life.

§

Celo was hard work for the adults but there were occasional relaxations. Crafts were an integral part of the way of life, with several residents belonging to the Southern Appalachian

Handicrafts Guild. There was also group entertainment when people would gather together in the evenings for square dancing and singing, or to read aloud and listen to records of classical music.

Anne's mother Phyllis later described Celo as wonderful, but also hard and "very difficult living." There were tensions in the settlement. Following its establishment in 1937, just over a decade before the Tylers' arrival, there had been frequent turnover among the members and difficulties in recruitment as the community struggled to establish its identity. Celo had been opposed to World War II (suffering attacks as a result) and during the war years the community's founder, Arthur Morgan, decided to seek new recruits among other conscientious objectors. Visiting a number of the Civilian Public Service camps where pacifists lived and worked as an alternative to military service or prison, Arthur talked about his community and issued invitations to settle there after the war. Several families did so, but according to Phyllis neither they nor the Tylers themselves had been made welcome by the existing residents: "...they really didn't accept us—most of us were Yankees—because we were also pacifist people who'd come from prison and from Civilian Public Service Camps to Celo." Local mountain folk had also objected to the influx of conscientious objectors, on one occasion turning up en masse at Celo to demand they be ejected. Generally they were suspicious of commune people anyway, Anne wrote later, "inclined to look at our feet and spit snuff when we talked to them."

Phyllis later commented that those who came to Celo were worried about returning to normal life after the rigors of prison or war and wanted healing, but once settled at the commune they discovered that difficulties arose when you were living very closely together. "So it was hard. I say it was hard." In an account written after leaving Celo, Phyllis described the initial buoyant optimism that had coursed through the members of the community as they attempted to create their own social environment and to live out Arthur Morgan's experiment: "It was the people who lived there…who made Celo a delightful place that first summer. There seemed to be no adequate way to make a living and yet far too much to do. No one had any money, nor was anyone much concerned about it." But by the end of her memoir Phyllis was talking sadly of "the gradual disillusionment and bitterness that overtook nearly every one of us. There was perhaps not a single community member who did not know at the end of his first year, that his private utopia would never work. Yet most of us stayed five years—some more —some less, for to leave was the bitterest defeat of all."

However, some of the troubles Phyllis encountered with the other settlers may have been of her own making. The adult Anne described her mother as a very difficult woman who did not get on with anyone, adding that she was sometimes scared of her; the comment of her character Willa in *Clock Dance*—that nothing was more terrifying than an angry woman—was her own thought, Anne admitted. Until she had a family herself, she said, she almost never had women friends and was "just a little scared of women." She saw her mother as the kind of person who always believed other people had it better than she did, looking sideways to see who was getting more cake or more love, and feeling that she was less loved than her siblings (although in Anne's view Phyllis' parents adored her).

There was a long gap between Anne and Ty and the two youngest brothers due to Phyllis' repeated miscarriages. Phyllis told a friend at the commune, Arthelia Brooks, that she suffered from Rhesus incompatibility, the condition that develops when a mother with Rh-negative blood becomes pregnant with a baby that has Rh-positive blood from an Rh-positive father. The first baby is unaffected, but the mother's immune system may then create antibodies that can cross through the placenta and go on to attack the red blood cells of her next Rh-positive baby. That baby may miscarry, be born with severe jaundice, or suffer life-threatening health problems. Once these antibodies have been made, the mother will retain them for life, with the antibodies growing more powerful with each Rh-positive pregnancy and causing ever worsening damage to the babies. Until a preventive injection was developed in the 1960s, many such babies simply died, although from about the late 1940s a complete blood transfusion for the newborn started to save more lives. Lloyd and his partners at Celo Laboratories were working to develop a drug that would combat the condition and reportedly succeeded, though production was said to have been halted when more cost-effective drugs began to be researched elsewhere.

Anne as a young child would be told that a baby was on the way and get very excited, and then be disappointed to learn that it wasn't happening after all. When Phyllis became pregnant again the year they moved to the commune, she confided to her new friend Arthelia that she had little hope of carrying it to term. There had already been the heartbreaking death of a Rhesus baby in the commune the summer after the Tylers arrived, the little body brought back to Celo from the hospital and buried close to the home of the devastated family. Arthelia, standing at the graveside as the stricken mother held her baby in her arms for the last time, thought she would "burst with grief," not only because of the baby's death but also because there was little hope the family could ever have any more children. There was a happier outcome for Phyllis, who must have been all too aware of the sad event. In 1949 she told Arthelia she was going to Chicago to be under the care of specialist doctors, and in due course returned with a baby boy, Anne's second brother John Seth, known just as Seth.

Anne used to wonder why her mother kept trying to have another baby when she seemed to be at her wits' end with her existing two children. She decided that when she became a mother herself, she would be calm and predictable. To Anne her much loved father was quite different: she described him as a quiet and patient man, extremely kind, who adored his tempestuous wife. "He thought she was wonderful. Sometimes when she had really been on the rampage, he would say, Oh, she's just overtired." Anne as a child felt furious that in the fairy tales she so disliked there would be a wand-waving solution, impossible to hope for in real life, to what she later called the "highly relevant problem" of a mean mother and a father who offered no protection. She was to view her father as a very interesting man who probably thought that he himself was just ordinary and humble, but that his wife was magnificent.

Her parents' relations with each other—in Anne's words, Phyllis stormy and Lloyd conciliatory—was a pattern that Anne at the crucial age of seven became determined to avoid when she grew up. At home with Lloyd while her mother was away in Chicago, Anne realized she was behaving like Phyllis, "kind of short-tempered and cross." Her father's reaction, again, was to be mollifying. Anne had the thought that if she married a man like her father then she would turn into Phyllis, so she needed to marry the opposite type. "Pretty clear thinking for a seven-year-old," she observed.

The scary woman of Anne's portrait does not altogether tally with other descriptions: Phyllis' friends spoke of her as a quiet and gentle person, and even Anne herself pointed to her mother's sympathetic and attentive ear for the problems of others. Phyllis kept an extremely detailed and loving baby book on Anne for at least her first four years, marveling at her daughter's growing independence, early reading skills and talent for drawing, and how Anne was initially jealous of Ty but later took affectionate care of him (including trying to get him to quieten down so she could tell him a story). Photographs pasted into the book show Phyllis gazing fondly at her child; for Phyllis, little Anne was "gentle, kind and sweet and has most unchildlike unselfishness." She did write in the book, though, that three-year-old Anne generally preferred her father because he was kinder.

In Anne's opinion Lloyd would happily have stayed his whole life at Celo, but when a job as a water quality chemist opened up in 1952 in Raleigh, North Carolina, the decision was made to leave. The mail-order drug and vitamin business had not proved that profitable and Lloyd was finding it increasingly difficult to provide for his growing family. (He once learned to operate a sock-knitting machine to earn some extra money when savings had run out, and became a good operator, but failed to make much at it.) And, despite Anne's belief that her father was happy there, if not her mother, by now both Lloyd and Phyllis were frustrated and disillusioned with commune life. A non-commune member had been placed in control of the Health Center, a matter of some concern to Lloyd and several others; as the dispute worsened he offered to resign his commune membership, but was refused. The controversy continued and eventually, after resigning from Celo's land association and even from Quaker Meeting, Lloyd asked for a two-year leave of absence to take up the post in Raleigh. When this period had elapsed he was declared a non-member, at which point he showed himself far more hard-headed than Anne was ever to paint him. He had left their holding there in the care of his parents but now demanded the lion's share of its value, apparently in defiance of the Celo rule that land was only assigned to members and did not actually belong to them (unless this stricture had been amended). A wearing, years-long dispute with the commune followed, with Lloyd emerging mostly the victor; the commune charged him with being materialistic and "a fanatic."

Others, too, were later to characterize Lloyd as "a very strong man" who would take Phyllis along with him. He certainly had the strength of his convictions about right and wrong. While at Celo he and Phyllis had suspected a family of abusing their adopted daughter and, highly indignant, had courageously raised the issue; they were subsequently proved right.

Both sets of grandparents stayed on at Celo, although in the end Lloyd's father did join the family in Raleigh. It must have been hard for Anne and her brothers to leave them all behind.

To others at Celo the young Anne had seemed very equable, remembered by her father's business partner in the drug and vitamin enterprise as a loving, lovable, calm, thoughtful, and private child. Another commune member described her as brilliant and imaginative.

It came as a surprise to their old neighbor Arthelia Brooks many years later when she began to see notices of novels by an Anne Tyler; is it *our* Anne Tyler? she asked her husband. The academic Elizabeth Evans later tracked down Arthelia to talk about her memories of Anne (and gave her a copy of *The Accidental Tourist*).

It is difficult to gauge just how happy or unhappy Anne may have been over the whole period, although it was clearly a lonely life for her. As an adult she described Celo as idyllic and peaceful, but also said that talking about her childhood depressed her. She had hated being a child, never knowing what to expect next, although later she was to realize that she remained more in touch with the emotions and physical sensations of childhood than with any other period of her life. But she couldn't wait to be a grown-up, and spent the passive, powerless time of being a child sitting behind a book and waiting for adulthood to arrive. Asked when older what she would tell her younger self, Anne replied:

That everything ends, eventually. This would serve both as a reassurance (I used to worry I would be stuck in childhood forever) and a warning: take proper note of all that's around you before it's gone for good.

But one thing is certain: what she also described as a fairly isolated existence had a considerable influence, conferring on her what she called "that slight distance," the ability to look at the world like a sociologist with an extra inch away from it. She believed that any kind of a "setting-apart situation" in the early years could provide this detachment:

In my case, it was emerging from that commune—really an experimental Quaker community in the wilderness—and trying to fit into the outside world. I was eleven. I had never used a telephone and could strike a match on the soles of my bare feet.

Growing Up

In yet another move for Anne in her short life, the family decamped to Raleigh, the capital city of North Carolina, sometime around Christmas 1953. She was to consider the frequent moves as a very young child a convenient explanation for her legendary ability to get lost, and for her "utter lack of a sense of place, which I bend over backwards to compensate for in my writing."

It was here in Raleigh that the youngest of Anne's brothers, Jonathan Mahon, completed the family in February 1954. The Tylers initially stayed on the outskirts of the city, where because their resources were exhausted from the years at Celo they lived in a series of rentals—including on a farm—before finally settling in their own home at 2512 Kenmore Drive, a traditional white two-story house in a quiet and leafy suburb.

Raleigh was not yet the large city it was to become, still retaining the small-town feel of an earlier era and a rural atmosphere from the surrounding tobacco farms. To Anne, it seemed to be a pleasant sort of place, with a tree-shaded square at its heart where a statue of a Confederate soldier stood guard on his pedestal. Small shops lined the adjoining streets. She could see a movie at the movie house for fifty cents, eat a pit-cooked-barbecue sandwich at the five-and-dime, and buy clothes at a department store from a clerk addressed as "Miss Mildred."

Anne was enrolled for a short spell at a Raleigh elementary school and when she first arrived, very young for her age, the other girls flocked around her. All of them wearing red jeans fashionably rolled up to the knee, they complimented Anne on her handmade smocked dress "in a very kind and solicitous way" that instantly conveyed she was dressed completely wrong.

One said, "Do you have a boyfriend?" And I said, "Oh, I'm only eleven." And she said, "I know, do you have a boyfriend?" And I thought, "Oh, I'm in another world here." It was very tough to figure out, and I remember it very clearly...

All the children in her new school looked very peculiar to her, Anne recalled, and felt she certainly must have looked peculiar to them. It had been a strange life at Celo, she would reflect as an adult, musing that it was better never to leave such a place if raised there because it was so different outside. Although she loved being out of the commune, and enjoyed the new experiences, it was hard to adjust; in her own words, it was almost like a Martian landing on Earth. She felt like an outsider, different from those around her not only on account of her commune upbringing but also because, born to a Minnesota family, she was of the North as opposed to the South—a sense of otherness that she had already experienced among the local mountain people back at Celo.

I did spend much of my older childhood and adolescence as a semi-outsider—a Northerner, commune-reared, looking wistfully at large Southern families around me.

Before long she started at the city's Needham B. Broughton High School, usually just known as Broughton High School and generally acknowledged to be the best public high school in the state. Here she did well, finding that her idiosyncratic education at Celo had actually placed her ahead of her contemporaries, although later quick to disclaim any special genius. (Her brother —who perhaps by now was starting to lose his nickname Ty, having asked to be called Israel instead of his birth name Stanley—arrived at the school not long after. He also shone academically, and played French horn in the school orchestra.) She was good at art and throughout her high-school years still planned to be an illustrator, not a writer. Her art teacher in grades ten through twelve, Alice Ehrlich, thought Anne definitely had a gift for painting, and remembered that she spent most of her time in the art room. The teacher learned not to push, or try to change her style, but to leave her alone, and then she would produce some "wonderful things." Anne would come in and go to the back of the room, sometimes not wanting to talk, and just sit reading or painting. The young girl was not very convivial, Alice recalled—amiable with everyone but keeping her distance, and with only one friend at the school. But she made her mark: people were "very much aware of her presence."

Alice assumed that on graduation Anne would do something in the art world, although also recalling that she was reluctant to display her work in public. The students occasionally held little art shows, and Alice was to regret not buying some of Anne's pieces as another faculty member did. Her style was very distinctive, the teacher remembered, generally depicting people rather than landscapes or specific scenes in nature. Sometimes it was a trilogy—mother, father, and child—usually a family, with the figures highly stylized. Alice described becoming "very, very close" to Anne; she thought *she* was the lucky one and that Anne was one of the most delightful people. (Alice Ehrlich eventually knew all four Tyler children and said of them that "brilliant is the only word that comes to mind."

Anne would later send her former teacher signed copies of her novels.)

Math was never a strong point and Anne occasionally prayed the school would burn down before a math test the next day. But, not surprisingly, she particularly shone at English and was much influenced by a superlative teacher, Phyllis Peacock, a tiny dynamo of a woman with immense energy and a flair for drama. Phyllis never sat down during her lessons and would dress up as Lady Macbeth to teach Shakespeare or fall to her knees to declaim the speech of a dying man. These dramatizations sometimes called forth a smirk from her teenaged students, Anne remembered, but they were invariably drawn in despite themselves. Phyllis Peacock was a teacher who demanded discipline and hard work from all her students, that they *think* while reading, and strictly adhere to the rules of good English when writing—she would demonstrate that "all right" was written as two separate words by racing to one end of the room, throwing up a window and yelling "all," then racing to the other end to throw up another window and shout "right." If a student's theme was too wordy, she stamped "Cut out the dead wood" across the paper. But at the same time she was immensely encouraging, also awarding an "Orchids to you!" whenever possible, sometimes accompanied by a flower. She encouraged Anne's involvement in the school's literary magazine, *Winged Words*, founded by Phyllis herself in 1950, and was doubtless the impetus for Anne's future pickiness about grammar and the string of similarly obsessed characters in her novels.

"Read, read, read," Mrs. Peacock used to tell her students, and Anne later concurred that this was the one absolute necessity as an education for writing. Several of those students went on to become writers and dedicate books to her, including Anne, and one of them later wrote the inscription to this magical teacher on a granite block placed in the plaza around the Education Building in Raleigh: that she had a "combination of effortless command of the subject, the discipline of a field marshal, the theatrical skills of classroom mastery and, most crucial, a fervent belief in the life-or-death importance of her subject."

Anne always sensed her teacher's true passion for literature and that she was never just a woman doing a job. The spirited Phyllis Peacock, for her part, recognized Anne's writing talent from the start. She was to remember her former student as always very sensitive, not only to people around her, but also to other writers, particularly the great writers: "She seemed to have an understanding of their purpose." Phyllis discounted her own influence on the fledgling author and pointed instead to the freedom of Anne's home life, which she believed had made Anne feel at liberty to write. The Tylers were a thinking family, in her opinion, interested in ideas, people and serious causes.

Phyllis Peacock's response to her work meant much to Anne:

I showed my writing to my parents and my mother, especially, was supportive but Mrs. Peacock got really excited and that made a huge difference...Mrs. Peacock just had something about her that encouraged imagination and experimentation; I can't explain what.

Anne's mother at this stage was mostly concentrating on raising her family, with the two youngest taking up much of her time, but was also busy in civic organizations such as the League of Women Voters. As practicing Quakers, both Phyllis and Lloyd were active in the Raleigh Friends (at that time absorbed into the United Church) and Anne, too, participated at least to some extent, taking part in a youth worship event at United Church in early 1956 when she was fifteen—perhaps unwillingly, given her stated renunciation of religion at age seven. As her teens progressed, what she really enjoyed was heading downtown with friends after school to listen to records for free in the booths of a music store, returning home afterward in the red and gray city buses that charged a nickel a ride. She had summer jobs including a stint on a local tobacco farm, going home each night with tar up to her elbows from her work "handing"—passing tobacco leaves to the stringer, the person who tied the leaves on sticks for curing (which Anne wanted to do and was jealous of). The skilled stringer was always a black woman, while the handers were mostly farm wives and a few teenaged girls like Anne. "And they talked, talked, talked. It was a real education." She was also noticing the way the people in her neighborhood would sit on their porches and tell stories.

Back at school, Anne's interest in English extended to theater and she eventually joined Broughton High's "Golden Masquers" dramatic society, playing a part in Thornton Wilder's *Our Town* in 1955 and getting her picture in Raleigh's *News and Observer* alongside two of the play's handsome young actors. She appeared in the society's group photo in the school's 1957 yearbook: a little plump, her short hair flicked up at the ends and, as yet, lacking her trademark fringe.

While still reading voraciously she had continued to think about a career in art, not writing: she assumed books had to be about major events, and none had ever happened to her. In school they were assigned works like *Julius Caesar* and George Eliot's *Silas Marner*, featuring what to Anne were "impossibly lofty and fine-spoken" characters, and even the books she read on her own were not about the kind of people who lived in North Carolina tobacco country. But one day in the school library, aged fourteen, Anne made a momentous discovery: a book of short stories by the celebrated Southern writer Eudora Welty. Her teachers had previously convinced her that the only life stories worth writing down were those like Silas Marner's, but Eudora's work said something completely different:

I was absolutely dumbfounded one day to come upon a sentence in Eudora Welty's "The Wide Net" about how Edna Earle was so slow-witted that she could ponder all day on how the tail of the C got through the loop of the L on the Coca-Cola sign. I realize this would rank rather low on any list of great revelations, but what she was saying to me was that literature could be made out of the ordinary things of life—Coca-Cola signs, and crêpe-de-chine bras, and all those other little objects George Eliot never heard of.

Reading Eudora Welty's story, she realized she knew women like Edna Earle, that it was possible to *write* about such people. She was to remember the experience as a "revelation—almost literally a flash of light." Eudora was writing about country people just like those Anne had been handing tobacco with, and not in Shakespearean English: she was telling what was real out there. From that point on, Eudora's work was to be a massive influence on Anne. Reading Eudora Welty taught her that there were stories to be written about the mundane life around her, not just heroic people, and how "very small things are often really larger than the large things." She saw that using the smallest details made a story come alive, and became convinced that she should put them in her own work. There was another quality, too, which Anne was to draw upon even more than the attention to the small stuff: Eudora's attitude toward her characters, "her sympathy, her kindness, her keen and amused but forgiving eye."

Eudora's stories also enlightened Anne about the South. For a Northerner now growing up there, "longingly gazing over the fence at the rich, tangled lives of the Southern neighbors," Eudora was a window on that world.

If I wondered what went on in the country churches and "Colored Only" cafes, her writing showed me, as clearly as if I'd been invited inside.

She also enjoyed reading the usual adolescent favorites like her grandmother's copy of Betty Smith's *A Tree Grows in Brooklyn*, about an impoverished young girl in New York. Living in North Carolina tobacco country, Anne later reflected, was about as far from the Brooklyn tenements as she could get, but she remembered being completely caught up in young Frankie's world and feeling nostalgic when the little girl grew out of her hardscrabble childhood and went on to better things. Heavier classics, presumably in her later teens, included Dostoevsky's *The Brothers Karamazov*. Reading J.D. Salinger, author of *The Catcher in the Rye*, was another joy. When Anne was sixteen and finally asked to the senior prom by the boy she had been hoping for, the world caved in when she suddenly fell ill and was unable to go. Her mother, in sympathy, brought her the family's prized *New Yorker* magazine the moment it arrived. When the boy came by to see how she was and to give her the corsage, Anne was deep in a new story by Salinger. She declined to see him, saying she was busy and did not want to be disturbed. It was a happy chance to read in peace. "There I was, in bed, alone, on the very day that the *New Yorker* published *Zooey*."

Anne did extremely well at Broughton, gaining a certificate of merit for outstanding performance as part of the National Merit Scholarship Program in 1958, and, as one of the school's winners in the statewide Good Writing Contest for high-school students the year before, perhaps beginning to feel her way as a potential writer. But art was still more on her mind. Graduating at the age of only sixteen in 1958, she was tagged "Artist" in the text accompanying her yearbook photo.

Her characteristic phrase, surprisingly, was "What's for Eats?"

§

Anne was accepted at Swarthmore College in Pennsylvania, an institution with Quaker roots. However, when offered a generous scholarship by Duke University in nearby Durham, North Carolina—likewise founded by Quakers—she decided to accept. Her parents were anxious to save money for the education of their sons, which Anne's mother told her was more important than for girls. The scholarship was just too good not to take, Phyllis insisted (and, as a senior, Anne had joined every committee going in an effort to secure such a scholarship).

I remember feeling an initial inner pinch of protest, but then I reflected that really she was right, which wasn't all that unusual a conclusion back in 1958.

Anne later wrote that this was the first and only time her being female was ever a serious issue in the family. Although her life wasn't ruined, she commented, the injustice and unfairness of it rankled. (Her brother Ty was awarded a Swarthmore scholarship —entering at the very early age of fifteen—and brothers Seth and Jonathan were to go too.) But for the most part, Anne always felt that her parents treated them all equally. She cited her father in particular as not only extremely kind but also "fair-minded," thus contributing to her "complete unawareness" of gender inequality, both growing up and later on in life.

Still under seventeen, in the fall of 1958 Anne left home to start at Duke as an Angier B. Duke Scholar, a scholarship paying full tuition for young people showing exceptional promise of achievement. Eager to begin college and a new life (even if initially miserable about being at Duke), she had no qualms about leaving home so early—although she did not entirely break free. Her mother continued to make all of Anne's clothes throughout her time at university, and Anne claimed that after she started buying her own clothes she discovered she was two sizes smaller than the outfits Phyllis had been sewing for her all that time. (More likely, Anne had finally lost her youthful plumpness and assumed the slender figure she was to retain for the rest of her life.)

Still possessed of a strong urge to draw and paint, Anne initially had trouble deciding what to study. According to her mother she took an aptitude test at Duke that indicated she might not make it as a painter, but could as a writer. She opted to major in Russian literature—chosen for a not very good reason, as Anne put it. When she set off for Duke she wanted to do something outrageous and different from her parents. "There was a period in my life, starting at seventeen or eighteen, when I seemed determined to do whatever seemed the most contrary thing," she was to say, joking on another occasion that if she could have majored in outer space she would have done so.

I seemed to worry that I would totally repeat the humdrum qualities of my family life, not any terrible sins, but just...am I going to grow up and lead the same lives as they? And so I would every now and then make these sudden, left-hand wrenching turns.

The Cold War with the Soviet Union was then in full swing, so it seemed to Anne that studying Russian language and literature would be sufficiently unusual, enough away from the pattern of her family's life. She also thought that the best literature—Dostoevsky, Chekhov—was in Russian. The head of the department told her he had been tailed for years by an FBI agent and that maybe it would happen to her too. "Of course I was thrilled with the idea," Anne recalled, although as far as she knew nobody ever did. Anne's parents, meanwhile, were worried about their daughter's choice of major, but without letting Anne see it. Phyllis, wringing her hands, would sit with a friend and ask "How is Anne ever going to make a living? She's majoring in Russian literature!"

As well as Russian, Anne took courses in Italian and comparative literature, and of course English. She studied creative writing with the charismatic Professor William Blackburn, who made his students feel that their work—both their study of literature and their attempts to create literature—was profound and meaningful. "He never taught writing merely as writing," remembered a former student, the celebrated North Carolina poet Fred Chappell. "He taught writing as literature, as part of a civilized discourse that always had been and always would be going on. When you wrote a story, no matter how naïve or clumsy, he made you feel that you had contributed to that great conversation."

But the most influential instructor at Duke for Anne as a developing writer was the young Reynolds Price, an author and future Professor of English who, coincidentally, was another former student of the inspiring Mrs. Peacock at Broughton High School. It was Reynolds who would write the eulogy to Phyllis Peacock inscribed in stone at Raleigh's Education Building, and in his later reminiscences he listed everything that she had taught him about writing (and must also have taught Anne): clarity of style, respect for one's readers, and, if it is to succeed, a narrative that takes unseen pains to make its story as visible to the audience as a good clear movie. She had insisted on "straightforward American English, stripped of shorthand, jargon and code and as lucid and entertaining as the complexity of the subject allowed," Reynolds wrote about Phyllis Peacock, and she had always maintained that enduring literature was made by individual men and women much like themselves.

Anne first met Reynolds when she was registering for freshman English in the university gymnasium soon after her arrival. When the instructor wasn't sure she could fit Anne in, a young teacher seated nearby—in Anne's words, "distinctly exotic-looking, at least to a North Carolina girl who had never been anywhere"—offered to have her in his class instead.

 Taking his very first creative writing class at the age of twenty-five, Reynolds tried to look severe and authoritative as he surveyed the room full of young women. (Almost all freshman classes at the time were segregated by gender, only converging later.) He claimed to have particularly noticed Anne from the moment he was seated at his desk. She sat at the head of the row on his right, facing him with the same grave self-possession he was struggling to show the class himself. She had a "beautiful clear face, long black hair, and dark eyes...The imposing girl responded to the name Anne Tyler with a surprising blush." Asked along with the other girls to state how her name was pronounced and to say a little about

herself, she declared that Anne was pronounced Anne and that she had lived in Raleigh since she was a child.

Reynolds' first assignment to his students was to write on the subject of their very earliest memory, describing it as honestly and pictorially as possible, in however many words proved necessary. The majority brought him descriptions of incidents from around age three, which Reynolds knew was about the norm for memory. Anne handed in just one hundred and fifty words describing a shaft of light that fell on her crib when she was still under one, and how she thought she was explaining to her mother that she didn't like the padded jacket she was being dressed in because she couldn't bend her arms in it.

Her brief description struck him, not so much for its "few clear words of evocative prose," but for the remarkable earliness of her small scrap of memory. His next assignment to the students was to produce a short essay about their first encounter with death, such as the funeral of a grandparent. Later he was unable to remember a single item from the crop of thirty-six essays he received but could certainly recall Anne Tyler's. Called "The Galax," it was an account of a hike up a steep ridge near Celo that Anne had made at the age of ten. In the narrative, she has been invited by a local mountain woman to join a group gathering wild galax, a waxy-leaved evergreen plant which they would stay up all night tying into bunches to sell to the cities as funeral decoration, making a cent for every ten bunches. The woman is kind to her, but Anne is aware of the contempt she and the other locals (described by Anne in the story as "weasley-faced mountain children, stooped overalled men, bony women") have usually evinced for members of "the Community." On the way home in the twilight, after hours of picking, Anne calculates that the fastest worker has only about sixty cents' worth of bunches in her basket and remarks out loud that it doesn't seem worth it. Nobody answers her, and at the foot of the ridge they leave her to find her own way home, in the dark, by following the sound of the river.

With remarkable subtlety for such a young writer, Reynolds observed, and with so few words allowed, Anne had conveyed how profoundly she differed from the mountain dwellers around her. On an impulse he told her that from then on, whenever he assigned themes to the other class members, Anne could secretly write whatever she wanted. "It was my first impulsive move as a teacher and one that, most obviously, I've never regretted," Reynolds was to comment. All her subsequent papers were perfect, in his estimation. For Reynolds, she was "the most prematurely skilled" of all the young authors he came to know, almost as good a writer when in his classes as she was later (and he thought her one of the best novelists alive in the world). In those early days he would tell her how good she was and how she ought to be a writer, but Anne would just respond with an OK. To be an artist was still her main ambition.

He regretted never keeping copies of Anne's work, which he later saw could have supplied a compelling portrayal of a gifted apprentice writer's rapid growth and self-discovery. And had he thought to photograph her, he would have had "another picture of the engaging woman Anne Tyler was becoming." Instead, he attempted to preserve his memories in a poem that he wrote after a visit to Anne decades on:

> *Thirty-seven years ago this month,*
> *You entered the first class I ever taught—*
> *The gray-eyed Athena, straight as a poplar.*
> *Tall, dark-haired and far more gifted*
> *Than a tasteful billionaire's Christmas tree...*

He could not have known what a vivid stroke of beginner's luck he had been dealt in having Anne in that very first class, Reynolds later reflected. To have the pleasure of such a presence, and mind, had seemed to him then to be almost normal. He only discovered afterward that it wouldn't happen often: time would teach him what an initial godsend Anne had been, "a gift of sufficient richness" to keep him a part of each year at a teacher's desk for the rest of his life. He was also to regret not seeing more of Anne during the college summers, as her family home in Raleigh was near his mother's and he had a brother the same age as her, but as an apprentice teacher he had been very mindful of advice from the more senior Professor

Blackburn to be extremely circumspect in his dealings with young female students.

To the very youthful Anne, still only sixteen when she started his classes, Reynolds seemed older than God. She loved it when he sat cross-legged on his desk and read out his latest story "in a great gust of boyish zest," inspiring Anne and the rest of the class to want to rush back to their rooms that very minute and write something just as mesmerizing. She loved the way he dashed around the campus with his draped navy blue jacket swirling behind him (misremembered by Anne in subsequent years as a romantic black cape with a scarlet lining); she loved his funny, incisive discussions, his practical, concrete advice for getting on with the job of writing, and his affectionate tales of a childhood in the backwater town of Macon, North Carolina. "Most of us were from Macons of our own," Anne remarked, "and we were astonished to hear that they were fit subjects for storytelling."

Reynolds also doled out the occasional criticism, however, which Anne said could seem shocking, yet oddly exhilarating to bright students from small-town high schools where they had routinely been made much of. At the end of her freshman year she wrote a story about a poverty-stricken black woman lying ill in hospital and reflecting that her hands on top of the sheet looked like an India-ink drawing. "That wouldn't happen," Reynolds told her firmly. "A thing like an India-ink drawing wouldn't cross that woman's mind." He was right, Anne admitted to herself, with a feeling akin to relief. His criticisms were a matter of respect, she decided: he took the class seriously enough to tell them the truth. She saw how genuinely appreciative he was of his students' original perceptions, which led her to understand that they had something to offer too, and were not just the blank slates they had thought they were in high school.

In her sophomore year Anne became a member of a more advanced writing class comprising students Reynolds had deliberately selected as especially promising, with Anne in his view prime amongst them. This class in short story writing met one evening each week at the apartment of fellow student Fred Chappell to read and discuss their own work as well as a set text, a volume of Eudora Welty's short stories. (Anne remembered that the students' writing styles at this point, including her own, could sometimes be a mix of the then highly popular J.D. Salinger and Reynolds Price himself. Another professor at Duke told her that her work would have a great deal more value if it had a little less Price in it, a comment that became seared into Anne's memory.) During the class Reynolds was particularly struck by one of Anne's stories, the biblically titled "The Saints in Caesar's Household," about a girl whose friend has a nervous breakdown. He read it at home with mounting excitement: he had known that Anne was good, but to him the new story represented a "long stride onward." Anne read it aloud herself at the next class meeting and her classmates granted its strength but, in Reynolds' opinion, were not prepared to acknowledge it as the first-rate achievement— by any standards—he knew it to be. Although a very raw teacher, he was sage enough not to press the point with them, understanding that it might be discouraging. Instead, he told Anne privately what he thought, and asked if he could do for her what Eudora Welty herself had once done for him: submit the story to an agent. Some four years earlier, when Eudora was at Duke University to give a lecture, she had read Reynolds' work and passed it to her agent Diarmuid Russell, of Russell and Volkening, who took Reynolds on. Anne agreed to the proposal with a simple yes, Reynolds related, remarking on her "sometimes unnerving self-possession—or was it genuine shyness?" In the event Diarmuid Russell, although impressed with "The Saints in Caesar's Household," did not succeed in finding a publisher. Anne thanked him politely for his efforts. In those days she barely knew what an agent did, she was to recall —and forgot all about him until much later, when she had a "novel to peddle."

For Reynolds "The Saints in Caesar's Household" was the "most finished, most accomplished short story I've ever received from an undergraduate in all my thirty years of teaching," and every year he would read it to his classes. It was eventually published in 1961 in the Duke literary magazine *Archive*—where

35

Anne herself became an assistant editor in 1960—and then printed again in two collections of the work of young writers.

Anne's first piece in the same magazine in March 1959 had been "Laura," a story narrated by an eleven-year-old living in a place again simply called "the Community" who inadvertently laughs when she hears of the death of Laura, an older woman whose conservative religious views had set her apart from the other members. Only later does the young girl realize that she laughed because she had no other way of expressing her loss. In all, five of Anne's pieces were to appear in *Archive* magazine during her time at Duke. A biographical note preceding one of her stories in 1959 read, presciently: "Anne Tyler sits quietly but attractively in most of her courses, saying little to demonstrate her intellectual and emotional depth. She is the kind of person who would be lost to all but her closest friends if it were not for her writing."

In 1960 Anne won the university's Anne Flexner Memorial Award for Creative Writing with the first two chapters of a novel, and subsequently won the same award a second time with "The Saints in Caesar's Household." Her novel, a mother-and-daughter story, was apparently never finished, but Anne soon completed another: *I Know You Rider*, a title taken from an old blues song. The tale of various misfits in a small North Carolina city similar to Raleigh, the book was rejected by several publishers as too reminiscent of Southern writers like Carson McCullers and Flannery O'Connor. Anne always denied their influence, although conceding that she had read both authors by the time she wrote the novel (and was to observe, much later, that she thought Flannery unkind to her characters). A far greater influence, in her opinion, had been the music she was listening to at the time: blues guitar and folk songs, both of which feature in the book. The novel was never published and the manuscript is now in the Duke University archives. Some of the words of the old blues number later appeared in Anne's novel *Morgan's Passing*.

But as well as her classes and writing Anne had the usual experiences at college—including an intense love affair, perhaps her first. She fell heavily for the son of a very rich family from Mobile, Alabama (probably the dark and handsome future author Thomas R. Atkins). Her parents disliked him and were unimpressed with his affluence, believing as they did that wealth should be shared. Anne was deeply enamored and very upset by her family's hostility; she told her former high-school art teacher Alice Ehrlich, to whom she was still close, that she would rather have him than anything in the world. It was the first time, Alice recalled, that she had ever seen Anne openly rebellious.

 The affair must have ended and Anne survived, finishing at Duke seemingly without further serious entanglements. The stage had continued to be an interest. She joined the Duke Players, taking on a number of significant roles: the female lead in an original play by a fellow student, Mrs. Gibbs in Thornton Wilder's *Our Town*, and Laura in *The Glass Menagerie*. Reynolds summed Anne up in those college years as "self-possessed, witty, communicative"—and also "frighteningly mature." Conferences with his other freshmen students could be fraught with dread and regret for Reynolds, but always good with Anne, who would hand in perfect papers. In 1961 she graduated at age nineteen with mostly A's, twenty-sixth in a class of 271; she was elected into Phi Beta Kappa, America's most prestigious academic honor society.

Reynolds Price's encouragement and enthusiasm during her time at Duke had been a special gift to her, Anne was to acknowledge. They kept in touch after Anne left, and ultimately Reynolds became a wellspring of encouragement and support in her writing career—once even suggesting that she introduce more intellectual characters into her novels, and advising that she should smile in her jacket photos. He thought she had been far more outgoing as a college student, and involved with her contemporaries, than she was in later life—to the point that he became worried about how far she had withdrawn from the world. In Reynolds' opinion she was a wise and benign person, but with a quality of deep melancholy in her work—a combination which rendered it anything *but* sunny and sentimental. He believed there was "some family unhappiness, never talked about. "

Over time Anne forgot all her Russian and regretted doing so, although admitting she had never quite mastered speaking it. But she was grateful that she had majored in the Russian classics. Every summer for some years after leaving college, when it was possible to slow down and appreciate it, she made a point of re-reading *War and Peace* (sometimes making the same claim of *Anna Karenina*, which Anne believed to be "about the best book ever written"). She had learned much about the Russian writers' specific techniques and craftsmanship, which she later saw emerging in her own work; she loved the "purity and clarity" of both Tolstoy and Chekhov, and cited the latter as a particular influence (detected as such by more than one critic in the years to come). What struck Anne about Chekhov's work was its economy, the fact that he trusted the reader to understand, from just a few lines, the greater story underneath, when in her view so much of the literature she had been assigned in school was wordy and ornate and overstated:

...the eye-opener was Chekhov—his ability to imply heart-wrenching emotion without giving his readers more than a few bare details. Among all those extravagant, complicated stylists, Chekhov's simplicity made a lasting impression on me.

She was also thankful, ultimately, that because of her parents' slender funds she had ended up at Duke and not Swarthmore:

After all, Duke had Reynolds Price who turned out to be the only person I ever knew who could actually teach writing. It all worked out in the end.

§

While Anne was studying at Duke her parents were becoming ever more active in the cause of pacifism, with Lloyd writing to Raleigh's *News and Observer* to defend the right of citizens to protest nuclear testing and highlighting the silence of the American press in the face of international actions against such tests, or to point out biased American reporting on the crisis with Cuba. From the late 1950s and early '60s both he and

Phyllis became increasingly vocal on these and other issues, particularly civil rights as the movement gained momentum: in 1962 they signed an open letter in the press calling for desegregation in Raleigh. Anne, away at college, appears to have been mainly focused on her writing and studies, but also took political action in support of civil rights. According to Phyllis, her daughter was the only white woman to attend Durham's sit-ins in 1960—protests that had spread from the city of Greensboro, where black students had insisted on their right to be served at a Woolworth's lunch room. Concerned about Anne's safety after the action some of her fellow protestors tried to accompany her back to Duke, but were warned against it. The university was very upset about the situation, Phyllis recalled, and they told Anne that she must never walk home with a black man—not because of any danger to Anne, but because of the danger to her black companions if seen with a white woman. "I...participated in my share of civil rights marches and anti-war protests," Anne was to remark in later life.

Anne's brother Ty had also been involved in protests, reported by Phyllis to be the first white male to join in the sit-ins. One night the Ku Klux Klan white supremacist group called her to say they had taken her son and that she would never see him again. Distraught, Phyllis then happened to pass Ty's open bedroom door and realized that he was actually there in bed. It had been nothing but a scare tactic.

Phyllis herself was writing during these years. At the time of Anne's birth, while professing to have no talents or accomplishments, she had nevertheless declared a wish to write a "bunch of books." Now, under the pseudonym Anna Greenbough, she produced an account of a childhood at Celo—calling it "Winterstar"—which was published in 1959 in the left-leaning magazine *Liberation*. Despite the pseudonym it caused such consternation at Celo, according to Phyllis, that she soon had to abandon any thoughts of another piece on the same subject. The doctor at the Celo Health Center had written to the magazine in protest, threatening to sue.

She also started writing book reviews and non-political articles for the *News and Observer* in Raleigh, including an item on America's Peace Corps volunteer organization in 1961. She eventually wrote a regular column for the local press called "Beautiful Lofty People" (presumably after the W.B. Yeats poem *Beautiful Lofty Things*).

After graduation Anne did not return home to live in Raleigh with her busy parents but instead went off to Columbia University in New York, having been awarded a National Defense Foreign Language Fellowship. She chose Slavic Studies as her subject. But she was uncertain about her future, perhaps entertaining doubts as regards a career in academia. There was clearly a degree of frustration, but, as Anne later reflected, because she felt so vague about what she wanted to do she could "hardly chafe at not yet doing it."

Living in New York, Anne developed what she called an addiction to riding the city's trains and subways—turning into an enormous eye as she rode, taking things in and turning them over and sorting them out:

> *But who would I tell them to, once I'd sorted them? I have never had more than three or four close friends, at any period of my life; and anyway, I don't talk well...For me, writing something down was the only road out.*

A year later—possibly not completing her studies—Anne "fell prey to an impulse" to go to Camden, Maine, a small coastal town where she worked the summer of 1962 scrubbing the decks of a schooner and proofreading for the local newspaper. The town seemed unusual to her; for one thing, she was struck by the fact that "no one, not even the young people, appeared to want to leave." Most of them seemed bound to that one place forever, something Anne felt she wanted to write about.

What may have been a lonely summer in Maine suggests some kind of crisis for Anne—probably, turmoil about what path she should take in life. She was to recognize in time that it was not necessary to go to graduate school the minute after leaving college. In the end, she took a job back at Duke, working in the university's Perkins Library as a Russian bibliographer. It was a step that was to lead to a momentous meeting.

Taghi

Working at the library at Duke was very boring, Anne found, but realized she actually liked doing dull things that did not overly drain her. Her duties included ordering books from the Soviet Union and other undemanding tasks as she listened to the talk of the other librarians around her. But it was a humdrum existence, and she felt her mind needed to "take a little more wing." She tried some writing in the evenings, although tired from the nine-to-five and feeling that her brain was not functioning so late in the day.

On a night out for dinner with friends in October 1962 Anne was surprised to find they had brought along a stranger, a tall, handsome man some years older than herself. This was Taghi Mohammad Modarressi, an Iranian on a psychiatry residency at Duke. Expecting just a cozy evening out with an old friend and his new wife, Anne was not pleased, and even less so when her friends told her that Taghi would pay for her meal as if they were out on a date. "I was just outraged by the whole thing," she remembered, but then Taghi came out with a sentence in his still imperfect English that she was never to forget: "It wonders me why you are so hostile." It was irresistible, Anne confessed. She discovered that Taghi was a published novelist and a warm and happy person who just truly enjoyed life. A romance began.

Taghi was in fact nearly ten years older than Anne, in his early thirties—which seemed "ancient" to Anne in her early twenties—and only relatively recently arrived in the US. His interest in writing had begun as a boy after his lawyer father died while Taghi was still in elementary school, and his mother took her three sons back to live with her family in Tehran. Here Taghi was exposed to a rich intellectual and literary world and a feast of books in his grandfather's library. It was also a secret gathering place for opponents of the Shah's oppressive regime, and the young boy would often sit up listening to them talking until he fell asleep.

41

In high school Taghi had a collection of short stories published—with the happy title *Perpetually Drunk*—and wanted to go on to study literature. Instead, perhaps to help the family finances, he entered the medical faculty at Tehran University. He published his first novel in 1953, while still a student and supporting himself by working at a bank. The book was awarded a prize by a literary magazine, and was later acknowledged by critics as one of the few original works of literature to appear at a time when there was fear of censorship and most prose fiction took the form of translations of foreign works. In fact Taghi had cleverly taken a Biblical theme for his novel, thus giving it a remoteness that allowed him to write about fundamental human problems in a non-political way.

He developed a fascination with psychiatry when a close friend and fellow student suffered a psychosis, and he began to see a connection between writing and psychiatry. He was drawn to go and research traditional means of treating mental health disorders in the Persian Gulf region. But, while visiting villages there to collect material for his thesis, an incident occurred that set him on a new path. Suspecting Taghi of revolutionary and leftist motives, the Shah's secret police detained him for questioning and confiscated all his notes and tape recordings. "It was a very bad experience, one that left me with a sense of rage and humiliation," Taghi recalled, and after graduating in 1959 he decided to leave his native country for an internship in the US. Arriving in Wichita, Kansas, to take up a post there, he had only $15 to his name (and promptly spent $5 of it on a bottle of Hennessy cognac at the airport). During the internship Taghi lived with his brother, also a doctor, and found time to write another novel. After about eighteen months he left for the residency at Duke University School of Medicine in Durham and his crucial meeting with the young Anne.

It was not love at first sight, according to Anne, but clearly the relationship deepened and after a few months Taghi proposed. Anne was engaged to someone else at the time who was away in New York at drama school—"I was always getting engaged"—but her response was "Oh, well, why not?" (One of her characters was to respond to a marriage proposal with the very same words.) Doubtless there was much more to it but for

Anne, choosing to marry an Iranian was definitely part of her campaign to be as different as she could, to do the "contrary thing." It turned out to be a very good decision but only by luck, she said, given that it was actually one of her deliberate wrenching swerves away from the pattern of her family.

I was saying, "What can I do that is most outside the mold of a librarian puttering around?"...every now and then I say, "Wait, I don't want to go gently here. I'd like to take a sharp right-hand turn."

Miss Anne Tyler

A pensively posed Anne, along with other newly engaged Raleigh maidens, appeared on the society page of the *News and Observer* in April 1963, tagged as the imminent bride of "Dr Taghi Modarressi of Durham." Anne's mother felt very uncertain about it all, constantly telling her daughter that Taghi could take many wives. ("Tell her you'll always be my favorite one," Taghi would quip in response.) Anne, too, could see that it was "an unlikely sort of marriage," a proposed lifelong union with an Iranian when to start with she hadn't even been too sure where Iran was. When Phyllis warned her daughter of the perils of a cross-cultural marriage Anne countered with evidence of how much they had in common—how at a concert she and Taghi had both suddenly been gripped by the dramatic shadow of the conductor on the ceiling of the concert hall when everyone else was deep in the music. She later recognized this as a naïve thing to have put forward in support of a cross-cultural alliance, but still felt she had a point. In the end her mother came to adore Taghi—"more than she loved me," Anne once joked.

Duke Graduate Weds Iranian, reported the *News and Observer*. The wedding on 3 May 1963 took place at United Church, as did the reception, hosted by Anne's parents and members of the Raleigh Quaker Meeting. It was a simple affair. Anne's former art teacher Alice Ehrlich attended, commenting later that Anne looked like alabaster next to Taghi with his much darker coloring. After a honeymoon in Charleston, South Carolina, the *News and Observer* stated, the couple would reside in Durham.

Anne was now twenty-one and continuing her attempts to write but, probably distracted by her new marriage, not feeling particularly moved to do so. There had been at least a year and a half after leaving Duke when nothing came to her "automatically by inspiration." After completing her education she had felt "just tossed out" as regards writing. "You don't know what's expected of you next and suddenly there's nobody to discipline you from above." Because her professors were no longer there telling her to have something in by Monday, she did nothing (although likely receiving some of Professor Blackburn's regular "reminders" to ex-students to keep on writing).

And it seemed to me, as time passed, I just decided, well, that was a stage in my life and I guess it was for nothing and now I'm going to be something else.

She might never have taken up writing again, Anne believed, had Taghi's visa to stay in the US not expired and forced a move to Canada. By July 1963 the couple were living in Montreal (initially in an apartment swarming with cockroaches), where Taghi had found a residency at the Allan Memorial Institute on the campus of McGill University. But Anne was at a loose end. For about six months she was unable to find a job and thrown on her own resources, knowing nobody in the city and once again feeling like an outsider, the Canadian culture "half foreign, half familiar," the cold winter weather a shock. Her family did not visit until Thanksgiving of 1964. There was literally nothing else to do and so all the time she had, Anne just wrote, having now apparently abandoned any idea of art as a career (later granting that "the world did not lose a great artist when I decided not to do it").

Prior to her marriage and the move to Montreal she had already achieved her first story in a national publication, a tale called, prophetically, "The Baltimore Birth Certificate." In

August 1963 she published a further story in *Seventeen* magazine and yet another in the prestigious magazine *Saturday Evening Post*—"A Street of Bugles," about the launch of a boat in a small coastal town. The idea for it had grown out of the summer Anne spent by the sea in Maine.

But she was also writing her first published novel, *If Morning Ever Comes*, issued by the publisher Knopf in October 1964 and dedicated to Mrs. Peacock. Her editor at Knopf was Judith Jones, Anne's senior by seventeen years, who had already distinguished herself when working in Paris by rescuing Anne Frank's *The Diary of A Young Girl* out of a pile of rejects and insisting it be published. Judith said she fell in love with Anne's work right from the start. She was to remain Anne's sole editor for the next forty-seven years.

§

If Morning Ever Comes, the first of three novels set in North Carolina, is the story of law student Ben Joe and his six sisters, one of whom has left her husband and taken her child back to the family home in a small town. Imagining himself responsible for his sisters as the head of the clan, Ben Joe leaves his studies at Columbia University to come home and investigate, only to face untold complexities: his widowed mother's chilliness, his sisters' self-reliance, his painful memories of an alcoholic father

—and a renewed relationship with his first girlfriend Shelley. Emergent in the novel were Anne's characteristic humor and the themes that were to occupy her throughout a lifetime of writing: the passing of time, the isolation of the individual within the family, the impossibility of change, and the difficulties of human communication.

Anne had already used Ben Joe and his family in two stories, "I Never Saw Morning" and "Nobody Answers the Door," with different plotlines but the same issues—family members closed off from each other, lonely and frustrated. The novel is written from Ben Joe's viewpoint, a deliberate choice of the male angle. Reynolds Price had once announced to his roomful of female students at Duke that men could write about women because they had been raised by women and so had an intimate knowledge of their lives, but that women could not write about men because they did not have the same experience. Anne found this "very galling," and looking back later was sure she had consciously thought, when planning this novel, "well, we'll show you, Reynolds." She was to declare many times how much she loved the men she had grown up with, feeling lucky to have been given such a wonderful picture of the male species by her father, grandfathers, and three brothers. It was the best experience of men she could have had, she would say, and she always wanted to know what they were thinking because they were good and interesting people. Men made Anne feel comfortable, and she could see they were not so different from herself.

Some incidents and scenes in the novel are likely reflective of recent events in Anne's own life. Ben Joe shivers on the campus at Columbia in New York, the wind from the river cutting clean through his clothes and leaving him gasping, no doubt as suffered by Anne herself when studying there for her Ph.D. Like Anne, Ben Joe's girlfriend once spent a summer proofreading; like Anne's mother Phyllis, his mother attended League of Women Voters meetings.

Still concentrating on short story writing, and feeling that this was really what she wanted to do, Anne's attitude toward the novel had been ambivalent—she had forced herself into it on learning from her agent that publishers would only buy short story collections if the writer was already an established novelist. She had once accidentally left the first half of the only copy of the manuscript, in a little green vinyl suitcase that was part of a set her grandmother had given her for college, at Montreal Airport:

When I realized later I said oh, well, no great loss, and didn't bother going all the way out to the airport to get it. I think it was a month or so before Taghi picked it up on his own initiative while he was out at the airport on some other errand. I didn't have any particular feelings about it then, but I was glad to have it later when it took so long to find work and I needed something to do with my time.

Working through the very minor editorial changes with her new editor Judith in an exchange of letters, Anne revealed her youthful inexperience in the world of publishing—admitting that she had kept no copy of the manuscript, and was therefore uncertain which pages Judith was referring to. Her replies to the various points raised by Judith were nevertheless thoughtful and meticulous, Anne sticking to her guns in some areas but giving way in others where Judith had made valid arguments, and asking advice on new questions now occurring to her. She had had no idea that permissions would be required to quote from songs (and, in responding to a request for a listing of the sources for the quotes she had initially included, demonstrated a casual familiarity with the likes of blues singers Lead Belly and Blind Lemon Jefferson).

Judith had been impressed not only by the quality of Anne's

 writing, but by Anne herself. Meeting Anne for the first time in person in Montreal in September 1964, Judith in a private memo described her as a particularly genuine young writer, caught up in the exciting business of publishing a first novel rather than concerned about how much attention she would get. Judith suspected, accurately, that "this girl is a real pro

with lots of material in her and a very healthy objective critical sense about herself."

The mature Anne never liked *If Morning Ever Comes*—in fact said it ought to be burned. She had just been winging it, without a plan (and would observe that the same was true of her next work). It had also been written, in a way, out of curiosity: she wanted to see what it felt like to be part of a huge Southern family, as the four Tyler offspring had been so spread out in years. She had always envied Southerners and felt isolated from them. But she viewed the resultant work as bland, formless and wandering, her hero Ben Joe "just a likable guy; that's all you can say about him." One reviewer commented that Ben Joe was about as interesting as a cucumber sandwich, and Anne thought they were right. She wished the manuscript *had* been left at the airport.

Nevertheless, critics at the time were astonished by how good the book was. A "brilliant first novel," said the *New York Times*— exceedingly good, so mature, so gently wise and brightly amusing that it was hard to believe the author was only twenty-two. Anne's touch was deft, her ear for the rhythms and irrelevancies of small-town Southern colloquial speech phenomenal; only a rarely talented novelist could have written such a fine book, the critic declared. A second review in the paper did complain of far too slow a pace and nothing momentous ever happening, although concurring that Anne Tyler had written a subtle and meaningful book for one so young. Other critics bemoaned the lack of plot, with the *Virginia Quarterly Review* dismissing the book as little more than a series of character sketches. Reviews abroad were positive. A charming tale, said the *Times* in Britain, "mild and softly flowing." For Britain's *Times Literary Supplement* Anne's debt to J.D. Salinger was "considerable" but small-town Carolina was superbly described, and Miss Tyler would likely go beyond her youthful attempts to provide big answers and allow her talent for dialogue and comedy to produce a very good novel indeed.

Anne's mother Phyllis, on the other hand, merely described the book as "interesting," according to Anne's account at least. "I thought mothers were supposed to like *anything*," she wrote drily to Judith.

Judith Jones credited the *New York Times* review with giving the book its send-off, and, boosted by the paper's plaudits, it sold well for a first novel at 13,000 copies (though far less well in Britain). Bantam bought the paperback rights the following year. For the first time in her life, but not the last, Anne felt the spotlight of media attention.

An Author At 22

By JOAN FORSEY

GO TO INTERVIEW A LIBRARIAN who has just published her first novel and you half expect to find someone who for years has been languishing among the bookstalls thinking 'maybe I could do it too.' Or someone who even looks rather bookish —hard-covered, stolid, grey.

Not so Anne Modarressi, whose first novel, "If morning Ever Comes," will be on the bookshelves Oct. 19. The tall, slim, 22 - year - old Southerner (who writes under her maiden name — Anne Tyler) brightens up the law library at McGill.

A native of Raleigh, North Carolina, Mrs. Modarressi hasn't exactly been languishing anywhere.

In her 22 years she has managed to graduate from Duke University in Durham, N.C. (majoring in Russian), do post-graduate work in Russian at Duke and at Columbia University in New

her writing in the evenings and on weekends. She finds writing "agonizing" but by far the harder part, she says, is to read it in print.

"You think you have an idea but when you sit down to write you discover it's not as developed as you think it is. But the harder part is to read it in print—that's usually about a year later. By that time you hate it because it's too long ago, and you're too embarrassed about the whole thing. I think that's much harder than writing."

Encouragement, however, comes from her husband "He writes himself, in his own language, so I think that makes him that much more under-

Interviewed at home in Montreal by journalist Jorie Lueloff, "slim brunette" Anne was reported to consider the South her true home and herself "a Southerner through and through," one of the many women writers of the region. She believed that unlike some novels, hers gave a true picture of the South, which she described with youthful enthusiasm (using the accepted terminology of the times):

I love the South. I could sit all day and listen to the people talking. It would be hard to listen to a conversation in Raleigh for instance, and write it without putting in color. And they tell stories constantly! I love the poor white trash—they're fascinating and everything about them is so distinct. And I love the average Southern Negro—they speak a language all their own. A Southern conversation is pure metaphor and the lower you get in the class structure, the more it's true. Up North they speak in prose, and the conversation doesn't have as much color.

There were many freaks in Southern literature, Anne had continued in the interview: terrifying, violent, almost bloody people, but another sort of character written about by Southern writers tended to get forgotten, "quiet, gentle, tactful, basically good people." Ben Joe, she believed, was a Southern character, the most Southern thing about him being his "inability to realize that time is changing"—to her mind a very typical Southern fault. Like all men, in Anne's opinion, he was more easily fooled by what is on the surface, whereas women can detect what goes on underneath, and, as writers, examine the difference between the two. Southern writers concentrated on the little threads of connection between people, and she thought that she might always write the same kind of novel—even if she herself might sometimes want to get away from being constantly in a "small, red clay town."

§

In 1964 Anne had found another job as a librarian, this time in the McGill University Law Library (where one of her co-workers, a painfully shy man, became the inspiration for a future character). She continued writing; it was something that had "crept in around the edges," she was to say. In February 1965 came "Will This Seem Ridiculous?," an essay published in *Vogue* about the process of growing up. In this, twenty-three-year-old Anne recalled her family's old Model A Ford that they used to drive through the mountains when she was a child, getting laughed at by other drivers when they had to use a watering can to fill up the leaky radiator at roadside waterfalls. As they drove, the car made a noise like a lawn-mower and on bad days emitted sounds like pistol shots from its rear tires. Anne could hear the swishing sound made by newer, fancier cars passing by and wished they had one too. When the day came that she finally rode in a better car she realized the swishing sound could only be heard from the outside. Her expectation had not been met, she wrote in the essay—and neither had her belief that on reaching the age of twenty she would be "old and certain of things." She was not—she seemed still to be changing, and wondered if the changes she was constantly undergoing would ever make it possible to understand life completely. She would rather be "young and *sure* of things," Anne declared in the essay, while also recognizing with her more objective and slightly older perspective that in a few years she would view her youth as "a perfect, separate island in time" and forget what she was thinking now, that youth was no distinct time at all. She would remember things differently:

I'll look at it, maybe, the way I look at that Model A—picturing my parents, young and dressed up, sitting erect on the seats in front, and my brothers pressing their noses to the cloudy back windows. I'll forget all about the lawn-mower noise and the pistol shots from the tires.

By March 1965 Anne was pregnant—sickness making her feel rotten, and so treating herself like a "Southern lady" (presumably, languishing on a couch)—but she had already delivered her second novel to Knopf: *The Tin Can Tree*, published in October 1965 only one year after the first. The fourth chapter appeared in a periodical one month beforehand as a standalone story entitled "Everything But Roses."

The Pikes, a country family living on the outskirts of a small town in North Carolina, have lost their little daughter Janie Rose in a tractor accident, and *The Tin Can Tree* deals with the effects of the tragedy on both her family and close neighbors—

in particular Simon, the dead child's now neglected and troubled ten-year-old brother. Hanging in the air is the future of the relationship between the children's adult cousin Joan, who lives with them, and their neighbor James, who feels he cannot abandon his self-centered and (maybe) chronically ill brother. Once again there is sadness but also humor in the need for family—flawed as they may be—and yet at the same time the desire to escape. Present, too, as in the first novel, is the focus on the nature of time, and the slightly magical world created by Anne that is akin to real life but not quite of it. The difficulty of communicating with others is also present, although Anne was ultimately to resent the fact that blurbs on her books always said she was concerned with lack of communication: "I don't think communication is really all that hot between people. I don't think it's necessary or desirable in a lot of cases."

The novel had been inspired by Anne hearing about a little girl who liked to pile on several layers of underwear (as Janie Rose did) and about a woman with two children whose favorite had died. Anne also called on her teenage job as a tobacco worker in North Carolina: just as Anne had done, Joan helps out as a hander on a local tobacco farm, sorting and arranging leaves to pass to the stringer tying the leaves on sticks for curing. Anne describes from experience how the leaves are brought from the fields by mule and how hot it is, sweat trickling down between Joan's shoulder blades. Two of the stringers compete with each other to be the fastest and most efficient, and all the while, as the black tobacco gum forms thick layers on hands and forearms and works itself between their toes and into their shoes, the women talk: meandering, gossipy, inconsequential, sometimes immensely significant. "Bravest thing about people," says Missouri, one of the workers, "...is how they go on loving mortal beings after finding out there's such a thing as dying." The rhythms Anne reproduced in their talk were culled directly from the time she first heard local speech patterns as a young teen.

The jacket of the first edition highlighted the fact that Anne considered herself a Southerner, and the very regional flavor of the tobacco-tying scene was duly noted by critics. She "neatly captures the casual yet complex movement of Southern rural speech with its indirections and interruptions, its reticences and awkwardnesses which manage to express emotion," approved the *New York Times*. Yet rurality and Southernism were not Miss Tyler's chief interest, the review perceptively continued. Southern Gothic was missing, and the book was really about the human tendency to stay frozen in place, in postures we choose for ourselves. For other critics, Anne's youth was again a point of interest, with the *Saturday Review* commenting that on page after page of the novel she offered proof of a maturity and a compassion to be expected only from a more seasoned heart. But, despite the good reviews, the book did not fare as well as her first, selling only 8,500 hardback copies. Bantam again picked up the paperback rights.

Anne considered *The Tin Can Tree* a more consequential novel because in her first she had been "afraid to be too serious," but she was later to dismiss it just as she had dismissed *If Morning Ever Comes*:

I wrote them because I wanted to write books. There's no flame in them. They're of little value. There's no real trip, no investment in them. I'd like to be rich and eccentric enough to buy all the copies.

In December 1965, after two very impressive debut novels, Anne was granted one of four annual *Mademoiselle* magazine Merit Awards for the nation's four most promising career women (the others going to an actress, a ballerina, and a civil rights lawyer.) Anne was not persuaded to come for the honor in person.

§

With the coming baby in mind Anne and Taghi moved to a bigger apartment in Montreal. Their daughter Tezh was born in October 1965, much overdue and weighing in at nine and a half pounds. Anne had continued working at the library till a month before the birth, which took place the day before her twenty-fourth birthday. She was shocked to have delivered a girl; she had never even *seen* a baby girl close up, she wrote in a letter, and had somehow assumed all babies were purely a male species. But it had been a pleasant shock, even if she kept wondering how they were going to raise her. Little Tezh—pronounced to rhyme with the first syllable of "measure"—was a very sociable baby who kept adult hours and required lots of conversation (an "insomniac," in another description) and Anne found she had her work cut out. She did not return to work but instead walked her new daughter up and down all night and cared for her all day, with little time left for anything else. When she was not wringing her hands over whether Tezh was all right, Anne sat staring at the baby "stupidly trying to convince myself she's real." Anne's mother had come to help out and, when a reporter from *Mademoiselle* magazine arrived for an interview very soon after Anne had left hospital and ended up staying too long, Phyllis forthrightly kicked the woman out.

The third novel Anne had been working on was laid aside, but Anne's decision to be a stay-at-home mother meant that ultimately she also became a career author.

I never really planned to be a writer; I just didn't know what else to do. And writing full-time wasn't actually a decision at all—I had quit my library job to have a baby, and never went back to it but did go on writing. So you can see it didn't take much courage.

Another change in Anne's circumstances soon followed: a return to the US. They had originally planned that when Taghi completed his residency in Canada they would make a permanent move to Iran, where Taghi wanted to start up a psychiatric clinic and training center. Anne and Taghi had visited the country a year after their marriage to meet his family, which she had prepared for by secretly learning some of their language, Farsi. (On the plane on the way over she casually made a remark in Farsi to Taghi, to his great delight. Earlier, he had discouraged her from trying to learn because it was so difficult.) At the airport, a huge crowd of people were there to meet them—Taghi had warned her in advance about his hundreds of relatives, but she had assumed he was exaggerating. They were all cheering and clapping and laughing and waving giant bouquets of flowers; it was "the most welcoming arrival I've ever been through," Anne would recall. She realized later that his family must have had to make some mental adjustments when a non-Muslim American bride suddenly arrived in their midst, but all were immediately warm and welcoming.

Iran, during the month that Anne spent there, was just as exotic as she had imagined: muezzins calling the faithful to prayer, bazaars full of gold and silver, and peddlers singing in the streets. Taghi's multitudinous family—who all took turns hosting the newlyweds for dinners, teas, and picnics—were exotic too, eating a midday banquet off a tablecloth laid on the ground. Then the aunts would unpack the uncles' striped silk pajamas from embroidered bags for a nap in a corner of the cool stone floor while they, wrapped in their prayer veils, slept in another. But at the same time they were just like any other family:

They'd wake late in the afternoon and sit drinking tea from tiny glasses while they sifted through the family news: marriages and births and deaths, little scandals, feuds that had lasted twenty years and would probably continue for another twenty.

As their time in Canada drew to an end, Anne imagined that once they moved to Iran she would carry on writing about the American South: she couldn't picture herself writing about exotic market places. But in 1967, after four years in Montreal, Taghi was offered a job at the University of Maryland Medical School and instead they moved to the city with which Anne Tyler would forever be identified: Baltimore.

Wife and Mother

A populous place of hot humid summers and cold winters, Baltimore in Maryland lies some forty miles northeast of Washington, DC. During the Civil War, slave-owning Maryland did not secede from the Union like other Southern states but many of its citizens had Southern sympathies, and when Anne moved there in the 1960s most old-line Marylanders still considered themselves to be Southerners. The city's industrial history now lay mostly in the past but after hundreds of years as a major port, ships were still sailing from the wide harbor opening to the sea through beautiful Chesapeake Bay.

But in inner-city Baltimore at this time things were tense, and just about to hit tipping point. Heroin use in both black and white communities had doubled in the previous decade, with drug use the prime reason for an escalation in robberies. Violence increased and there were also soaring numbers of broken homes amid an economy in decline, adding to existing tensions caused by the city's inequalities and long history of segregation. In 1968, a year after Anne arrived, unrest in black areas exploded with the news of the assassination of Martin Luther King. Protests at the murder included the torching of white-owned properties, looting, and attacks on police, leaving six people dead and thousands injured or arrested. The Governor of Maryland imposed a curfew and sent in 5,000 National Guardsmen, and, at the Governor's request, President Lyndon Johnson also dispatched 6,000 US Army combat troops to fully restore order. The hundreds of businesses that had been ransacked or burned never reopened, leaving whole districts permanently bereft of retail stores. White city dwellers fled to the suburbs.

By then, the suburbs to the north of Baltimore were already Anne's new home. Her second daughter, Mitra, was born in the city in November 1967 and the growing family eventually found the perfect place to live in Homeland, a prosperous, leafy suburb close to upscale Roland Park (where Anne was always reported to live, but never did). Below Homeland lay a series of adjoining neighborhoods, each with its own individual character and whose residents, in the later words of one local author, got darker in skin tone the further South toward the inner city.

The Modarressis' shuttered, gray and white stone house at 222 Tunbridge Road was French country style, one of many similar homes in an area of pleasant tree-shaded streets and some pretty duck ponds known as "The Lakes." At number 222, light poured through the large bay window into the step-down living room with its open fireplace. In matters of décor Anne preferred a simple look, a scattering of Persian rugs and just a few pieces of furniture and items of pottery. The family's floor-to-ceiling bookcases were full but always neatly organized, never overflowing (when someone gave Anne a new book, she would give one away). The kitchen was cheerful and spacious, a little old-fashioned. There were five bedrooms and three bathrooms, and Anne fixed on an upstairs room for her writing —choosing the second floor rather than the third, so that she could be "at least nominally" in touch with the rest of the house. This was to be her home for the next thirty-eight years.

The house was just right but Anne thought Baltimore "a very hard city to break into."

People here have been here forever. If they go away they come back. It's certainly a gritty city and not all beautiful, but people seem to feel they belong and then when you move in...

Anne once remarked to an old lady from exclusive Roland Park that her daughter Mitra was the only Baltimorean in the family because she had been born there. The lady replied, "Oh my dear, that does not make her a Baltimorean." It was tough going, in Anne's words like "breaking through the crust of something."

§

Back in Raleigh, Anne's parents Phyllis and Lloyd were still campaigning on the issues of the day. For Phyllis, who at the age of fourteen had picketed mines in Minnesota in support of a strike against poor conditions, humanitarian protest was in the blood. As her children grew up and started to leave home she had set about furthering her own education, gaining her master's degree in June 1964 at the University of North Carolina School of Social Work and then finding work as a probation counselor for the Wake County Domestic Relations Court, where she dealt with cases of neglected and delinquent children. Lloyd by this point had become chief chemist at the North Carolina Board of Water Resources. Despite these busy lives, both Phyllis and Lloyd remained deeply committed to furthering civil rights.

In 1963 they signed a pledge printed in Raleigh's *News and Observer* undertaking to patronize businesses that refused to practice segregation. Phyllis had been incensed when, in about 1962, a university student helping out in the family was ill in hospital and Phyllis had not been allowed to donate blood because the young woman was black. She had been very excited when Martin Luther King came to speak in Raleigh as part of a program at United Church, and during the event got to know the local black activist Vivian Irving. When the League of Women Voters committed to integration and Raleigh members didn't want to know, Vivian and other campaigners deliberately joined the organization and Phyllis courageously attended a meeting at Vivian's home. She went on to join in the fight for integration in schools and in theaters, where she would accompany Vivian and other black friends who would be refused tickets if it was a day for whites only. The campaign finally succeeded, and Vivian became the first black woman to gain entry to a Raleigh theater on a "white" day, a historic achievement—although Phyllis had sometimes worried that with all Vivian's brave activism her home might be set fire to. Lloyd, meanwhile, was helping to build integrated communities. Black guests were often invited to their home, and the Tylers sometimes found themselves ostracized in the neighborhood as a result.

As the decade progressed, both also wrote frequently to the *News and Observer* to protest American involvement in Vietnam and the sacrifice of American youth in what they labeled a "futile and hopeless war." From 1965 until 1969 they took part in a weekly silent vigil outside Wake County Post Office under the banner "Until Americans Stop Killing and Being Killed in Vietnam," and in 1966 they were reported in the *News and Observer* as intending to refuse to pay their federal income taxes in protest against the war. "We're Quakers," Phyllis told the paper in explanation of their action, going on to accuse the US government of crimes against humanity. Later, Lloyd would write to both Presidents Johnson and Nixon about the use of troops and the delay in bringing them home.

Anne's youngest brother Jonathan also became involved in anti-war protest, and according to Phyllis was the instigator of resistance to the draft at Broughton High School. One day as he was leaving the school he was assaulted by masked members of the Ku Klux Klan and arrived home severely beaten up. Phyllis felt destroyed. That same night two black men came to the house and insisted she get Jonathan up to be told "how to survive." They instructed him never to turn a corner without knowing what lay beyond and never to go any place without a friend, not even the restrooms at school. They alerted the janitors at Broughton High to look out for him (which Jonathan found very embarrassing). The principal told Phyllis that Jonathan had brought it on himself by agitating against the draft, and that there was nothing he could do, so the Tylers took steps to get their son away and managed to find him a place at a Quaker boarding school. His older brother Seth opted to stay on, wanting to finish his time at Broughton.

In 1969 the family lost Anne's beloved paternal grandfather, who had been living with them in Raleigh.

§

In Baltimore, an established writer at the age of just twenty-six, Anne now found herself the busy mother of a new baby and a two-year-old. She had always counted on having a husband and children, she said, "and here they are."

If you'd asked me when I was growing up what I wanted to do, I'd have said get married and have children...I was a product of the '50s. I never planned to be a writer. And, when you think about it, it is a very odd way to make a living. Just telling lies.

Her marriage was proving very happy. "I chose with amazing wisdom," Anne was to reflect. "It was pure, astounding good luck that it turned out to be the right person." More of her experience now found its way into her writing: in her later story

"Linguistics," American college student Claire falls for a foreign graduate student she meets at a party. She is particularly fascinated by the foreignness of his language. They marry, despite her family's worries that the couple have no shared history, and Claire gives birth to twins. Her husband slowly becomes more Americanized and less at home in his native country when he goes to visit, and Claire finds the marriage has developed its own shorthand vocabulary and shared history that seemed to be missing at the beginning.

Anne's extended Iranian family—Taghi's widowed mother, and various cousins and uncles—would often come and stay with them in Baltimore. Anne could still speak the Farsi she had learned in order to communicate with her new relatives, and really loved them: they were "just full of life and enjoyment and very warm," she said affectionately. But in "Your Place is Empty," a short story about the visit of an Iranian mother to her Americanized doctor son and his wife Elizabeth in Baltimore, there are signs of the cross-cultural difficulties Anne doubtless experienced. In the story Mrs. Ardavi's religious zeal disrupts the household: she refuses to eat bacon at breakfast because it is unclean, her son Hassan has to buy a pocket compass for her so that she can face Mecca during her daily prayers, and her laundry cannot be done with the family's because Elizabeth is a Christian and therefore the washer and dryer are unclean—having "contained, at some point, a Christian's underwear," wrote Anne in the narrative. Too impatient to learn English, Mrs. Ardavi is bewildered by the American way of life and, disliking American food, takes over the kitchen to prepare Iranian meals instead. When Elizabeth tries to reclaim her home the tensions come to a head and Mrs. Ardavi curtails her visit, having been unable to communicate with either her son or Elizabeth; she has lost her son to America, and his place at home in Iran will remain empty. In another story featuring the same family, "Uncle Ahmad," an overbearing, very non-traditional uncle dominates the household during his visit from Iran, dragging Elizabeth on insatiable shopping sprees and issuing invitations to other relatives to come and stay without asking his hosts.

Both stories are of course fictional, and Anne seemed genuinely fond of Taghi's family, but she did confess that her Iranian mother-in-law Razieh provided the "seed" for the first story.

§

As the girls learned to talk, Anne and Taghi made no attempt to teach them Farsi as well as English. The thinking at the time was that bringing up children to be bilingual could lead to difficulties mastering English, and Taghi had also been told that bilingual children could never use either language creatively, such as in writing poetry. None of this has been shown to be the case, and Tezh and Mitra came to regret not being given the chance to speak the language of their heritage.

Both the girls had inherited their mother's artistic bent. Tezh's first creative memory was of sitting in Quaker Meeting next to an artist family friend who was drawing, and passed her the sketch so that the little girl could copy it. Time flew as Tezh worked and she remembered thinking how great it was and how she would ask for more paper when they got home. Mitra, too, liked art. She was "the most resolute, private and self-possessed of children," said Anne, finding her daughter to be someone who always seemed absolutely clear about who she was, even from infancy, but at the same time was very sunny and peaceful. Mitra would drape her bunk bed so that the lower bunk became a kind of cave in which she could do her drawings or read, another favorite activity. Anne used to take the girls on regular visits to the local branch of Baltimore's Enoch Pratt Free Library for a regular supply of books, often Laura Ingalls Wilder or Maurice Sendak.

As for Anne's writing, it had to take a back seat.

"I thought I would have babies and write when they slept, which was a joke," Anne recalled. Even if she had had the time to write, she would not have had what she described as "the insides." She felt drained; too much "care and feeling" were being drawn out of her. The inspiration deriving from a working life had also disappeared. Now she only spoke to people at dinner parties, where conversation was intentional and deliberate: gone was the "easy-going, on-again-off-again gossipy murmurs of people working alongside each other all day," the sort of talk that stimulated her. She enjoyed tending the girls as babies—if sometimes anxious that she might die while they were still tiny and helpless, and finding that she much preferred the later stages—but it was hard to be solely, completely in their company and unable to write. And she couldn't think of any alternative, such as employing someone in the house. Children reared by domestic help seemed to her to be "diluted" and unable to use words well. Anne understood that she had to just get on with it, even having thoughts like "Well, I guess that's it—no more writing, ever."

In the end, of course, it was only five years between the birth of her first daughter and the point when the second started nursery school and left her free in the mornings. At the time, though, it seemed a great deal longer, and Anne couldn't imagine any end to it.

I felt that everything I wanted to write was somehow coagulating in my veins and making me fidgety and slow. Then after a while I didn't have anything to write anyhow, but I still had the fidgets. I felt useless, no matter how many diapers I washed or strollers I pushed.

The only way she could rationalize her life was to imagine she was living in a very small commune, with the divisions of labor she was used to from her childhood at Celo. It was a perfectly sensible arrangement, Anne told herself: one member of the commune was the outside liaison, bringing in money, while the other was the caretaker, repairing the electrical switches and reading to the children (including, of course, her increasingly threadbare copy of *The Little House*). There might be less physical freedom for the second member of the commune, but at least she had much more freedom to arrange her own work schedule. Anne was constantly going over all this in her mind and trying to convince herself that she really was pulling her weight.

One thing she did understand, if not immediately, was that having children made her grow richer and deeper. They slowed down her writing for a while, but when she did write, she had "more of a self to speak from." Unconditional love had been required of her, and life seemed more intricate—and also "dangerous" (perhaps meaning her concern for the children's well-being).

As Anne struggled with the demands of young motherhood it was clear that the next full novel would have to wait. The beautifully named *Winter Birds, Winter Apples*, started after *The Tin Can Tree*, had been Anne's first attempt at writing at night, but she found she was incapable of thinking past 3 p.m. and in her own opinion the work "never really gelled." Knopf, too, had had reservations. Judith Jones let Anne down as gently as she could, pointing to the absence in the novel of the dramatic staying power and gradual revelation of purpose that had so distinguished the first two works. She worried that it would receive a critical reception damaging to sales and to Anne's future career. Although undertaking to publish anyway if Anne felt strongly—stating that Knopf believed in her and did not want to risk losing her—Judith advised against it: in her view it would be wiser either to put the novel aside, or completely rework it.

Anne, at that point still in Montreal, had agreed. She felt it made sense "just to drop the whole thing" and—outwardly accepting, at least—told Judith that she would chalk it up as so much typewriter practice and start looking round for another plot. The abandoned manuscript is now with other Anne Tyler papers at Duke University Library.

It would not be the only draft to get dumped. Seemingly undaunted, however, Anne continued to write, despite the description of those early years of rearing children as a creative wasteland. She applied for a writing grant from the National Foundation on the Arts and Humanities and managed a string of short stories for prestigious magazines such as *The Southern Review*, the *New Yorker, Mademoiselle, Ladies' Home Journal* and *McCall's*. She was anxious not to forget how to write short stories, having found that the initial few she wrote after her first novel were much too long. Because of what she called her one-track mind, it had become difficult to do both kinds of writing—short stories and novels—at the same time.

But as the girls grew and Anne found more freedom, a third novel finally made its debut following a full five-year gap. The slender *A Slipping-Down Life* came out in 1970, after first appearing in condensed form in *Redbook* magazine. It was the last of the early novels to be set in North Carolina, despite Anne's stated intention after the beginning two to get away from the South in order to avoid it turning into a crutch. But she was still there, this time in the invented towns of Pulqua and Farinia, based on the real-life Fuquay-Varina in Anne's girlhood locality of Wake County. While the first two novels were somewhat out of time, this latest was set firmly against the cultural backdrop of small-town America in the 1960s: unpainted stores, rusty soft-drink signs and single paved streets —but also rock and pop music, the Beatles, and teen fan magazines.

Evie Decker is a podgy, lonely, hopeless teenager who lives with her remote father; they have a brutally rude maid, Clotelia, who skimps her way through the domestic work in the house. Evie becomes obsessed with cool local rock singer Drumstrings Casey, and to get his attention she carves his surname onto her forehead with nail scissors (backward, from doing it facing the mirror). The action was based on a real event that Anne had read about, a Texas teenager slashing her forehead with the word "Elvis." When Drum's manager realizes the resultant publicity could be good for business he invites the now infamous Evie to attend Drum's performances as his number one fan, and a relationship slowly develops between Evie and the singer. When things eventually go downhill with Drum's career and he feels he is already, at the age of only nineteen, beginning to lead a "slipping-down life," it is not her father but the careless, lazy and soap opera-obsessed maid Clotelia who is there for Evie. Once again, Anne examines the loneliness of the individual and the lack of real communication between people living closely together.

For Anne's mentor Reynolds Price, Evie and Drum became what he suspected to be "unevictable tenants of my head." The *New York Times*, however, was unimpressed. From the novel's attention-getting start with the nail scissors, wrote the reviewer dismissively, "there develops a wry little fable that plumbs the limited depths of Drum and Evie, and takes the measure of their social climate." In Britain, the novel was not accepted for publication until many years later, when Anne had a much higher profile, at which point the *Times* found it "wickedly clever, and perceptive about what makes people tick."

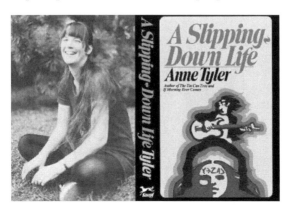

Sales were slow, the novel earning even less than *The Tin Can Tree*, only 7,800 copies in hardcover. It was mistaken as a work for teenagers, the American Library Association once even naming it as one of the "Best Books for Young Adults" for 1970, and as a result reviews were fewer and scantier. But Bantam again bought the paperback rights.

Anne herself later referred to *A Slipping-Down Life* as "flawed," lumping it in with the other two North Carolina novels as better burned; all three, she felt, suffered from a youthful attitude of "Let me tell you what my view of the world is." But she also professed some tenderness for it, feeling it represented "a certain brave stepping forth." She liked it because it was the one book of the three in which the characters do change, a process she had an utter lack of faith in and did not really believe people were capable of. It was a different kind of book from the first two, Anne observed, one that she felt more courageous for writing. Her earlier novels had been so similar and she had gotten tired of her own voice, but she had a special affection for lean, denim-dressed Drumstrings Casey, his family and everything about him: she felt he was the "direct inheritance" of her time as a tobacco hander. (Evie, too, has roots in Anne's own experience: she takes a job at the local library and greatly enjoys alphabetizing cards and stacking them in neat little piles for hours on end.)

The film rights to the novel were optioned by actor Paul Newman, with Anne lined up to write the screenplay, but the option was dropped when financing proved difficult and Paul felt he was investing in an unknown quantity. Anne in any case thought it would make a "terrible" movie. Some three decades later the story did finally hit the screen when it was made with Lili Taylor as (a very slim) Evie and Guy Pearce as Drum. The director of the film, Toni Kalem, first read *A Slipping-Down Life* when working as a secretary in the 1970s. She went on to become an actress and was eventually in a position to afford the now not very expensive rights to the work, which she had always dreamed of turning into a movie and directing it herself. She kept trying to interest producers in the idea over the years and, as Anne's reputation slowly grew, it went from people thinking she was talking about Ann Taylor the clothing store to everyone wondering how Toni ever got the option for an Anne Tyler book. After *The Accidental Tourist* was published to great acclaim in 1985, big-name producers suddenly started taking an interest, and Toni started to worry. She and Anne began corresponding. "The letters I received from her felt like one of her characters writing to me—they were quirky and beautiful," Toni said. "And every time, it was always Anne that stepped in and saved it."

The movie, somewhat changed from the novel—Evie's job is serving hot dogs at a grubby amusement park, dressed as a bunny—was nominated for the Grand Jury Prize at the 1999 Sundance Festival, and in 2004 won the Special Jury Prize at the Indianapolis International Film Festival. Lili Taylor as Evie also won an Achievement Award at the Newport Beach Film Festival.

Anne had no problem with the slender Lili playing a character she had written as very overweight. For her, director

Toni had kept the spirit of the book, as had all the actors—especially Lili and Guy playing the lead roles, both of whom in her view had treated the characters with respect and what Anne saw as "inspired understanding." The changes had not bothered her for this reason, even when Toni left the ending far more ambiguous, leaving it open as to whether Evie and Drum would reconcile. She had been given a draft of the script to read and Toni had been perfectly ready to make alterations had Anne felt her work to be compromised; instead, Anne felt her characters had been loved and comprehended.

Toni Kalem finally met Anne in person when the film was eventually screened at Baltimore's Charles Theatre in 2004, a delay of five years because of post-production disputes. Toni was excited and thrilled to learn that Anne would be present, but very nervous. Anne subsequently sent her a glowing email about the film, much appreciated by Toni. "I revere Anne's work so much. To have her be willing to speak out on behalf of the film when I know that she's such a private person is incredibly meaningful to me."

§

After *A Slipping-Down Life* all the rest of Anne's novels were set in Baltimore. She was to remark in the decades to come that the strongest influence on her writing about Baltimore was the city's own unique atmosphere, soaked up from myriad fleeting impressions: overheard conversations, the mood at her favorite crab house or at an Orioles baseball game on a summer evening, or most of all from the trance she fell into when driving past a string of row houses with everyone perched outside on their stoops.

Her imagination had once been caught by a picture in the newspaper of a grumpy-looking street cleaner in the city's historic district, doggedly pushing his broom past a statue of a little sprite dancing on one toe. For Anne it seemed to sum Baltimore up: a combination of blue-collar grittiness—"grit" becoming a word she would often apply to the city—with an abounding capacity for enjoyment.

She and Taghi were getting used to the place. In 1971 Taghi was granted a license to practice medicine and surgery in the state of Maryland. The girls were happily enrolled in Friends School of Baltimore, a private Quaker school only a few blocks from home. Life seemed very settled in the comfortable house on shady Tunbridge Road. But for Anne, learning to like her new home town was to be a slow process.

For the first two years we were saying, "We made a mistake, let's go back." But then you sink in, little by little.

Baltimore was slowly recovering from the troubles of the previous decade, although white flight away from the center continued, with the population there declining and still suffering from the after-effects of the riots. Around this time Anne wrote an uncharacteristically shocking story about the rape of a Baltimore teenager who surprises a burglar in her home: "A Misstep of the Mind," published in *Seventeen* magazine in 1972. What the central character, Julie, remembers after everything is over is "the capacity for betrayal in a cheerful world where dust floats lazily in sunbeams," the fact that the safety she had assumed in her neighborhood could crumble in a second. Leaving the police station after an identification line-up Julie has to pass "a black family all dressed up and sternly erect"—probably the family of her attacker, presenting a sad picture of pain and dignity far removed from the crime that has been committed.

But the city was also regenerating. Baltimoreans had already organized to protect historical areas of the city like the inner harbor from being razed for highway construction. While two hundred historic properties were still lost and hundreds of others sat vacant after being condemned for the proposed expressway, much had luckily been saved, including many of Baltimore's handsome old row houses that were to be such a feature in Anne's novels. For her fourth novel, however, the first to be set in her new home city, Anne chose as backdrop her more immediate environs: swanky Roland Park.

Here, she wrote in 1972's *The Clock Winder*, the young women wear their clothes with a "sloping, casual elegance" and their hair is smoother and hangs gleaming to one side; rich husbands buy their wives lingerie shops on Roland Avenue where they sit all day drinking gin and writing up the losses for income tax. The central character, Mrs. Emerson, is a moneyed widow and former Roland Park debutante, always immaculately dressed in matching skirts and sweaters and a string of pearls and spiky heels. She lives alone in one of the large houses of the area "far enough from downtown Baltimore to escape the ashy smell of the factories." When her daughter asks the black maid for her gravy recipe, she adds : "Is this something you get from your people?"

Mrs. Emerson engages as her live-in handyman a young drifter called Elizabeth, a college dropout in dungarees and no makeup who has a knack for mending things and also for attracting her employer's sons when they come to visit. Gradually Mrs. Emerson becomes more and more reliant on the cool and seemingly self-possessed Elizabeth, while two of her sons become downright obsessed, but for a long time Elizabeth stubbornly resists being sucked into fixing all their lives the way she rewinds the many clocks in the house. They act as a constant reminder that time is slipping by, and it is time, in the end, that effects a change: ultimately, she gives in to the Emersons' need for her to put things right for them. Anne commented about the novel that she felt "terribly strongly" that everyone should keep their hands out of other people's business, and that the ending had been intended as a sad one; she was surprised that others didn't see it that way.

Despite the Baltimore backdrop Anne had not quite finished with the parched red earth of her youth. Elizabeth comes from North Carolina, and went for a time to the imaginary Sandhill College attended by Ben Joe in *If Morning Ever Comes*. A section of the novel is set in Elizabeth's rural home town when for a while she goes back to live with her family. Here Elizabeth is quietly at odds with her preacher father about his deeply felt religion, and sees her mother as only superficially the perfect minister's wife, offering proper sympathy to the bereaved in the proper soft voice, while underneath she is all bustle and practicality as she freezes meals for people before anyone has actually died. Even the preacher suspects that his wife views God as his imaginary playmate.

The book was originally to be entitled *The Button Mender* (in reference to a dream in the book) but Anne's publisher Knopf disapproved of the title and instead suggested *A Help to the Family*, which Anne in her turn disliked because it made her think of a first-aid book for novice babysitters. Before Anne could submit *The Clock Winder* as her alternative, Knopf went ahead and released *A Help to the Family* as the forthcoming title, so that the work appears under both titles in the reference lists of the time.

The *New York Times* found it Chekhovian, with the richly idiosyncratic characters—and the structure—tending to amble about. "Gentle charm is the author's stock in trade," the review observed. "Her characters have so much of it one wishes their story had more substance." The *Saturday Review* was in agreement, seeing the novel as wandering aimlessly along with the author not quite knowing what to do with her characters. The *Times* in Britain disliked the too redemptive ending, but deemed Anne one of those professional American authors who made a good many British novelists look amateurish. A very feminine work, weighed in Britain's *Daily Telegraph*, "delicate, unpretentious, and highly enjoyable." Hardback sales of the book were on a par with Anne's previous titles, a total of just 10,600; once again, Bantam bought the paperback rights, in July 1973. Some ten years later, when Anne was far more famous, there was a flurry of interest from the movie industry but the project never got off the ground: the novel contained insufficient action to "captivate," one production company judged.

As for the new setting, Anne clearly still entertained mixed feelings. "We don't find Baltimore very friendly," says a character in *The Clock Winder* who has just moved to the city.

Another character makes brief mention of the senseless violence that occurs there daily and Anne also included a reference to the riots after the assassination of Martin Luther King—the august Mrs. Emerson donating a can of black olives for the victims, and, with similar obliviousness, writing to her soldier son in Vietnam asking if he has been to any tourist sights and to bring home some native crafts to solve her Christmas present problems.

There may be dawning affection for Baltimore in Anne's vivid description of a ride downtown past dark narrow buildings that suddenly brighten in the spring sunlight, with old ladies taking the air on crumbling front stoops while children roller-skate. "In the heart of the city, in a tangle of taverns and pawnshops and cut-rate jewelers, black-jacketed men stood on the sidewalks selling paper cones of daffodils," she wrote with a seeming degree of fondness for her new city. But later in the novel the mood again darkens, as the same downtown area is seen from the point of view of an Emerson son driving through it toward the greener and cooler streets leading up to Roland Park:

Row houses slipped past him in endless chains, with clusters of women slumped on all the stoops, fans turning lazily behind lace curtains, parlor windows full of madonnas and globe lamps and plastic flowers alternating with windows boarded up and CONDEMNED signs on the doors...Men scuttled out from package stores with brown paper bags clutched to their chests.

(The Clock Winder, 1972)

Baltimore's reputation was certainly low enough at the time. Mayor William Donald Schaefer wanted to do something for its image: working with ad agencies, he agreed to promote the idea that the city had appeal by encouraging visitors to collect charms for a charm bracelet at each of the few attractions the city then possessed. The campaign, declaring that Baltimore would henceforth be known as "Charm City, USA" was launched in July 1974—just days into a garbage collection strike that left piles of refuse all over the streets.

The strategy failed, but the nickname stuck.

§

With reluctance, Anne agreed to a press interview after *The Clock Winder*. She told journalist Clifford Ridley of the now defunct *National Observer* that she used to give interviews but had been misquoted a few times, most recently by that very paper. She was busy, she said, and her personal life was her own affair, but in the end she had given in. Clifford was invited to the house and the interview took place in the sunken living room, each furnished with coffee and cigarette, a protective collie wandering in and out. Anne talked of her novels and how she disliked writers who wrote about characters they didn't care for, and how she herself enjoyed writing about old people: "I'd like to spend the rest of my life writing about old men." She also mentioned her growing willingness to expose more of herself with each book:

There's more of _me_ *in The Clock Winder—not autobiography, but more that I feel.*

That was almost painless, Anne said to Clifford as he left, but she was increasingly to display the same strongly felt disinclination to talk to the press.

Her comment that there was more of herself in the book may perhaps have related to Elizabeth's wary relationship with her deeply religious father and busy, efficient mother. Anne was shortly to see more of her own parents than she had in a number of years.

In 1970 Anne's middle brother Seth had married a fellow graduate of Swarthmore, opting for an Episcopal wedding "with Quaker overtones" that was held on an island in Ontario paddled over to in canoes by the guests. Her parents, and youngest brother Jonathan, had continued their protests against the Vietnam war and were also lending their support to new issues: that year Phyllis wrote a funny newspaper article about the difficulty of boycotting lettuce picked by workers living in bad conditions when union-picked lettuce was so hard to find. (Some of the dialogue in the piece could have come from her daughter's pen: the "nice produce man" in the neighborhood store, asked by Phyllis if his lettuce is union-picked, replies "Well, now, I don't rightly know. They never tell us stuff like that." When Phyllis asks him to check the boxes, he responds in complete non-comprehension, "Honey, I wouldn't know what to look for down in all that fine print. This is real pretty lettuce and if it is union-picked, it didn't seem to hurt it none.")

Then, in 1973, Phyllis and Lloyd, now in their fifties, took the momentous decision to leave their country and live in Gaza for two years helping refugees.

Phyllis went out there in February to reconnoiter, finding thousands of Arab refugees living in miserable camps and a legacy of much "anger and hate" in the wake of so many years of Arab-Israeli conflict. Lloyd resigned from his work as a chemist at North Carolina's Department of Water and Air Resources and they prepared for their new duties administering daycare centers for the children of the refugees, a project operated by the Quaker-run American Friends Service Committee. Now that their own four children were grown, they told the local paper in an interview, they wanted to be of service to others. They would take an Arabic course in Jerusalem first and then settle in a modern house in Gaza.

 It had been a lifelong dream of Lloyd's to do something with the American Friends Service Committee and he had been actively preparing for it for years. But almost as soon as they arrived, Phyllis fell ill with a fever that neither the Arab nor the Israeli hospitals seemed able to diagnose. They returned to the US for Phyllis to get treatment and, because the house in Raleigh was sublet, needed to stay with Anne in Baltimore. In the end they were there for four months, if only on a week-to-week basis, as it remained unclear exactly what Phyllis was suffering from, whether it was serious, and if they would ever get back to the Middle East.

It was hard for her mother, Anne recognized, but she could see too that it might be especially hard in another way on her father, living in a state of uncertainty as his wife was whisked in and out of hospitals.

However, I believe he was as pleased with life as he always is. He whistled Mozart and puttered around insulating our windows. He went on long walks collecting firewood. He strolled over to the meetinghouse and gave a talk on the plight of the Arab refugees."Now that we seem to have a little time," he told my mother, "why not visit the boys?" and during one of her outpatient periods he took her on a gigantic cross-country trip to see all my brothers and any other relatives they happened upon.

Finally Phyllis, desperate enough to do something she would not ordinarily contemplate, decided to see a faith healer. Anne's father went along with it, whistling all the way. When the faith healer didn't work, Phyllis decided her illness was psychosomatic and that they should just go back to Gaza, which they did. The following summer Anne took the girls there for a visit: her mother's fever had totally disappeared, and Lloyd drove them down the Gaza Strip cheerfully whistling Mozart as his little Renault weaved among the tents and camels.

Several years later Anne still held this whole rambling episode in her head as a sort of lesson, reminding herself of it almost daily:

It seems to me that the way my father lives (infinitely adapting, and looking around him with a smile to say "Oh! So this is where I am!") is also the way to slip gracefully through a choppy life of writing novels, plastering the dining room ceiling, and presiding at slumber parties.

After struggling with the competing demands of being a wife and mother and at the same time a writer, Anne realized that her father's accepting attitude toward whatever life flung at him was now pointing the way. She was slowly learning to accept that the girls being home from school on a snow day was an unexpected holiday from writing, an excuse to play card games with them rather than typing up a short story. When Taghi's uncles visited from Iran, "hordes of great, bald, yellow men"—

just like the uncle in Anne's story "Uncle Ahmad"—all calling for their glasses of tea and sleeping all over the house on couches and armchairs, Anne saw that she might as well listen to what they had to say and work on her novel the next day instead. Having accepted that her time must always be divided, she could smile at the uncles out of a sort of "clear, swept space inside me."

§

In November 1974 Anne spent a week on campus back at Duke University, taking part in a creative writing program for the students, giving a reading, and participating in a panel discussion chaired by her old friend Reynolds Price.

When she was creating, Anne said about her writing practices during the discussion, she would protect herself from "experiences," not liking to see people—even though it always seemed to her that surely she should want to, if she was writing about them. It was just that she did not want to be influenced by the outside in any way, feeling that part of writing was putting on paper some of the privacy that had been kept bounded in, and therefore privacy had to be maintained while she was doing it. And what she wrote was like olives out of a bottle, she explained: whatever came out had to come before the next thing, like a necessary progression—there was no choice, and so what she wrote was not a waste even if rejected by publishers.

If Anne was writing a novel she also found it dangerous to read any books, especially at the planning stage or at a stage when she was not sure about what she was doing. Again, it was a matter of protecting herself, this time from being influenced and unconsciously imitating what she was reading, just as in her fiction courses at college she had written like J.D. Salinger. (As Anne grew more experienced the possibility of unconscious imitation was to become less of a problem—she was more swayed by what she overheard a cashier say in the grocery store.) In any case, her mind wandered and she couldn't take books in. Only once she was well launched could she go back to reading fiction.

Each novel now took about a month of meticulous notes and planning resulting in around ten little headings on a single sheet of paper, one or more of which she knew would be altered along the way and were therefore flexible. (Her first two novels, *If Morning Ever Comes* and *The Tin Can Tree,* had not been planned in this way, which Anne felt accounted for the "sense of vagueness" when she re-read them.) Once the book got going there was little rewriting, at least at this early stage in her career, since after all the outlining she was always fairly sure about the direction from beginning to end—except for the endings themselves, in fact, which Anne professed always to be wrong about. Chapter structure could be difficult: starting a new one was the hardest part of writing a novel. If a chapter was too long, she would carve it up and create another. Actual output varied from day to day, but could be as much as fifteen pages of very small writing or as little as a single page. She wrote longhand, sometimes printing; if Anne typed, she was unable to "hear" as well, and in any case often had the sense that everything flowed directly from her right hand—what she called "knitting a novel." The rhythm of typewriter keys also irritated her, and being a very poor typist she used to get angry with herself. Each chapter was typed up as it was finished, and then after more editing—some juggling and crossings out, but usually no completely new second draft—she would finally retype the lot into a neat manuscript.

Working hard depleted Anne, making her feel "used up and burnt out," so that between novels she had to accumulate a lot of experiences to make up. She accepted any invitations that came her way, any kind of odd jaunt that might get her "filled up again." Or she would write short stories to achieve the same effect, as stories were not exhausting to write and she could be "sort of playful" in them and not feel they would take up a year of her life. She could never write short stories at the same time as a novel, only in between. (Two had been published already that year.) They were her "dessert" after a novel, Anne had told the journalist Clifford Ridley, where she could say something exactly as long as it pleased her and then drop it.

Talking at Duke about her evolution as a writer, Anne observed that with each succeeding book she had trusted readers a little more:

First of all, I've trusted that they might possibly be intelligent and I don't have to explain everything, but more important, I've entrusted myself to them. I don't feel that I have to be on guard quite as much. I think that a lot of the vagueness that I see now in the early books was just wrapping cotton wadding so that no one could see me in the book in any way. And now, I figure, well it won't matter all that much after all.

As to why she liked to write, Anne joked that she liked to lie and it was an acceptable way of lying. But she also resented only having one life. As she was happily married she wanted to find out what it was like to be unhappily married ("I spend a great deal of time mentally living with incompatible husbands") or to go and live in a boathouse, and writing was a way to do what she could not do in reality. At first she had been writing more for an audience, but now it was to lead other lives.

Anne knew even then that she would never stop writing. She had tried, vowing after finishing one novel never to write another, but it was no good. After about a month she would be feeling more or less useless. "There's nothing for whatever it is in me, no place for it to go."

However, Anne knew that her concentration on writing meant that she probably shut off a good deal of her "wifely attention." She took less interest in her children, she admitted, if she was at a really pressing point in a novel, although she did not believe they were yet aware of it. "I could use a wife," she quipped, but added that in fact she would never want to lean on anyone that much for support. She took pride in solving her own novelistic problems, and did not want to talk it through with anyone else or even get sympathy. Anne wanted to think at the end that she did it all herself:

Anything I've ever written I've wanted to know how much dependency is allowed between people, how much right people have to want to change other people.

Gathering Pace

Anne had mentioned on the Duke panel that she could no longer write a Southern novel. She was later to date ceasing to be a Southern writer from when she moved to Baltimore, when she "came over to another geography"—at that point clearly not considering Baltimore a Southern city. She was in any case out of touch with North Carolina; her visit to the university was the first time she had been back in years, she told the audience. It would be presumptuous now, Anne felt, to set a novel in North Carolina unless she had spent time there to re-acclimatize, and if a writer really didn't know a place it would show through. Despite her continuing reservations about Charm City, therefore, it was again the setting for Anne's fifth novel, *Celestial Navigation*, published in 1974. It's a mostly bleak Baltimore this time, a place of crumples in the sidewalk, spindly trees, "endless dismal row houses." The middle of the city, in the throes of being rebuilt, is depicted as the site of some sort of bomb damage:

Whole blocks were leveled; nothing but rubble remained. Beyond were caved-in tenements showing yellowed wallpaper, tangles of pipe, crumbled understructures of something like chicken wire.

(Celestial Navigation, 1974)

It was a hard novel to write. "It took two years and it made me sick all the way through," said Anne (although she was also to say how very fond of it she was). By her own admission these were psychosomatic illnesses that apparently included a spell of agoraphobia, a condition suffered by her main character. She had also found it difficult to concentrate. With the children in school, she was now in a position to write as much as she wanted for the greater part of the day, but was nevertheless prevaricating, "constantly fighting the urge to remain in retreat" and finding feeble excuses for not knuckling down. She would go into her study and think, I really need shoelaces. Then she would get into the car and drive five miles to buy them.

The book came together in the end, with the help of a detailed floor plan Anne made of the house in the novel and a drawing of its front so she could keep track of who occupied which bedroom, plus records of the characters' ages in specific years throughout the work.

The main character, Jeremy Pauling, was based on the fragile person Anne had met when working as a librarian:

I was once supposed to supervise the library training of a very pale, pudgy, frightened man who had just been released from a mental hospital, and I was disturbed because no matter how gently I spoke to him, he was overwhelmed and would back off, stammering. He only lasted a day and then vanished forever, but five years of thinking about him produced Jeremy.

In the novel, abstracted artist Jeremy lives with his elderly mother in a narrow, dark, three-story row house smack in the middle of Baltimore. Utterly focused on his art—collages and figures made from random objects—pale, anxious, agoraphobic Jeremy is barely able to function in real life and relies on his mother, who takes in boarders; when she dies, the boarders stay on and Jeremy continues his former existence. Then a new lodger arrives, beautiful, down-to-earth Mary, who has run away from her husband with her young daughter and tries to make money by machine-knitting socks (like the commune people in Anne's childhood). Jeremy is transfixed by Mary's beauty; they form a relationship and produce a multitude of children who fill the house.

It's an unlikely union between two very different people, a practical, motherly woman and a highly focused artist who becomes increasingly distracted by the clamor and demands of domestic life, and is also angered when Mary starts treating him as just another child. Mary, in her turn, wants more commitment from the remote Jeremy and is eventually driven to a desperate step. The very different natures of the two are captured in the way each sees a bunch of wild flowers that

Jeremy gathers for Mary: for him, a beautiful intermingling of green and a glossy blue that reminds him of the blue of a madonna's robe, and for Mary, the reality—the reader is casually informed much later in the novel—a clump of chicory and poison ivy.

Celestial Navigation has been seen as an examination of Anne's own artistic dilemma, with Mary and Jeremy representing the two opposing sides of her nature: one side loving and caring for her family, the other obsessed about the art of writing. There are certainly similarities between Anne and Jeremy. When over-focused on an artistic "piece," Jeremy wanders into the kitchen and eats whatever takes the least trouble, a box of day-old doughnuts or a can of cold soup; in the same way, Anne's family could always tell when she was well into a novel because by her own admission she lost all interest in cooking and the meals would get "very crummy." There are the shared habits of listening for a little click in the head to indicate the right creative track, with Anne finding it by sifting through her copious preparatory notes; their closing themselves off from the world when in the throes of creation; their preference for seeing the world from a distance, Anne self-confessedly "looking from a window at something" but not willing to actually go over and see, preferring to remain behind the window and just write about it. Like Anne, Jeremy never simply goes from one piece to the next: "It was necessary to have a regathering period, an idle space sometimes stretching into weeks." And, like Anne, "he seemed to think pieces came out of him like olives out of a bottle, and he had no choice but to let the first one out before he could get to the second."

Celestial Navigation was a very "musing" kind of book for Anne, one in which she thought about a lot of things that interested her, particularly the creative process. She admitted that she identified with Jeremy, but insisted that while she understood him, she was not really like him. It was true that she had "sneakily" donated to Jeremy what she called little pieces of herself, including her habit of seeing the detail but not the bigger picture, "the slits in the screws of the electrical outlet but not the room as a whole." Feeling so close to her subject, Anne had even been respectful of Jeremy's privacy, cutting one sentence for every two she kept in. Creating Jeremy, said Anne, was a way of examining her own "tendency to turn more and more inward," although she also said that Jeremy took distancing too far. She was "outwardly more balanced" than Jeremy, managing to cope and get things done. "He's isolated, I'm isolated, but he's more so."

The novel also reflects other aspects of Anne's thinking at the time. Mary rationalizes the abandonment of her husband by her urge to try out different lives, to cheat on the rule that you can only lead just one: she wanted to climb into other people and be carried off to some new and foreign existence, to see "how they arranged their furniture and who their friends were, what they fought about, what made them cry, where they went for fun and what they ate for breakfast and how they got to sleep at night and what they dreamed of…I wanted to marry a mad genius and then a lumberman and then somebody very rich and cold and then a poet…" Anne also stated that she identified "enormously" with Miss Vinton, one of the boarders, who is a firm believer in not interfering and allowing everyone to take their own leaps, although conceding how very difficult it is to live among people you love and hold back from offering them advice. (Miss Vinton's vision of the future when young, her favorite daydream, was doubtless Anne's too: to be reading a book alone in her room, with no one ever, ever interrupting.)

Bemused reviewers saw Jeremy through a variety of lenses, some taking him as a fictional depiction of the American artist Joseph Cornell, a celebrated pioneer of the arts of assemblage and collage who lived an isolated life at home caring for his mother and disabled brother (a suggestion never obviously confirmed by Anne, who mentioned only the pale, frightened man she had met at the library). In the *New York Times* respected writer Gail Godwin saw Jeremy's agoraphobia as a reaction to the complexity and untidiness and depressing aspects of humanity; one *Times* reviewer in Britain saw Jeremy as ineffectual, woman-dominated and beset by fiends, and another as "semi-retarded." Some critics were bewildered by him, skeptical that such a maimed individual could persuade a beautiful woman like Mary to marry him, let alone father a brood of children. But there was general admiration for the craft of the book. Miss Tyler wrote with "virtuosity and perfect confidence, insight and compassion," said the *Times*; Anne Tyler had created two characters at once entirely original and entirely convincing, approved Britain's *Sunday Telegraph*, while for the *National Observer* in the US this latest novel was "altogether stunning" and Anne's richest book to date. "A work of literature. A work of art," enthused the *Washington Post*.

Anne's editor at Knopf, Judith Jones, saw *Celestial Navigation* as her first great novel. However, Anne's difficulties with the book had included a struggle with Judith about its very short last chapter, which the editor wanted to cut because she felt that everyone would instinctively understand what happened to Jeremy in the end; Anne insisted on keeping it in because *she* wouldn't understand. Anne also came to see that readers must find it hard to credit Jeremy with any sexual capability, and that really she owed it to them to "show how he managed it." As he was a character she felt very protective of, she acknowledged that she had failed to do this: "I let the book down on that account." The ending of the novel also proved unpopular with readers. Anne received several angry letters and calls from people who wanted it to go a different way, which Anne had wanted herself, and thought she would be able to achieve but couldn't:

I kept pushing toward it, but that writing felt wooden: my sentences were jerky when I looked back at them. In a way I felt I was trying to cover up a lie, and then I thought, I may as well tell the truth...

She always wanted a happy ending for her books (and preferred a book she was reading herself to be at least tied up at its conclusion, although because everything was blurry and muddled in real life she was suspicious of books where "everything is one-way"), but she was unable to do so if it meant being untrue to the characters. Anne acknowledged *Celestial Navigation* as "sort of sad, people had to keep on going the way they were going." She felt bad about it, but the characters were telling her "I can't go there, I can't do this, you're just going to have to accept the fact that we can't live happily ever after."

Sales were disappointing. Only 6,300 hardback copies were sold, and Bantam did not pick up the paperback rights until July 1976. Filmmaker Frederick Wiseman was very interested in making the movie—buying the option and writing a script—but eventually had to give up when unable to raise the money.

Commercial success was proving elusive; Anne was left owing money to her publisher. Serious money was still several novels ahead. Anne professed not to mind:

It doesn't bother me...It kind of gets on my husband's nerves, though, I guess he thinks my hourly wage is pretty low.

§

Anne's sense of place, and particular espousal of Baltimore, was starting to get noticed. She was the nearest thing there was to an urban Southern novelist, Reynolds Price declared. But by now of course Anne was not so sure that she *was* a Southern novelist, despite her youthfully extravagant claim after the publication of *If Morning Ever Comes*, with its strong Carolina setting, to be a Southerner through and through. Now, in a strongly worded interview on the subject for *Saturday Review* in September 1976, she commented that she did not actually consider herself Southern, although conceding she was perhaps more that than anything else. She certainly felt no sense of identification with archetypal Southern novelist William Faulkner, and was anxious to make clear that by the time she got around to reading him she was already embarked upon her own writing. He was an "extremely masculine" writer and his whole approach—"knitting off in all directions"—was wrong for her, and if it was possible to write like him, she wouldn't. She disagreed with him, Anne insisted: her strongest influence was Eudora Welty.

To her, in fact, Baltimore was the North, she told journalist and author Bruce Cook at *Saturday Review*, while acknowledging that there were ladies in the old houses in Roland Park who were like caricatures of the Old South and that whatever it was in her that remained "undeniably Southern" had made it easy to switch to Baltimore. Despite her four years in Canada, she had been able to write practically nothing about it at all, Anne observed. It had taken her a while to settle in Baltimore, to get in a comfortable groove, but now she felt right with it.

Anne's reputation was growing in general. In 1975 she was invited to become a regular reviewer for the *National Observer*, and continued to contribute about once a month until the paper folded in 1977. The editors of the paper considered her primarily a writer of short stories, and her first five reviews were of short story collections. But perceptions changed in line with Anne's developing stature, and her reviewing soon expanded to include novels. As time went on she reviewed for the *New York Times Book Review*, the *Washington Post*, the *Baltimore Sun* and the *New Republic*, among others. She did the reviews because "the various publications asked me to," but also because the extra income helped pay for the girls' fees at their private school. Between 1972, when the first of Anne's reviews appeared, and 1991, she produced more than two hundred and fifty.

Some review requests she turned down, in one case out of self-confessed repugnance at the subject matter. She told author Jay Neugeboren that she would be unable to review his novel *Before My Life Began* because of a "major shortcoming as a reader: squeamishness."

I have trouble reading about rapes and castrations and such. I'm not proud of that; I know, for instance, that it gets in the way of my being a good reviewer.

Anne was perceptive but gentle in her reviewing, seemingly loath to give offense and no doubt mindful of the occasionally hurtful nature of reviews when she had been on the receiving end. She always hoped there would be several opinions on a work: "I would never, ever, want to have the last word on anybody's book." Characteristically, she was very thorough, reading the book in question through more than once and placing it in context by reading all of the author's other works she could find. Where Anne loved a book, she said so enthusiastically, urging readers to buy a copy rather than borrow one. As for criticism, she felt that readers had a sort of contract with the author and if the author had failed his or her part of the bargain—weaknesses of plot or narrative, obscure, long-winded or turgid prose, poor dialogue—she would softly point it out. Fiction should be written to engage readers, Anne also believed, making them react and connect with what they were reading, and not merely be diverted or entertained. Characters needed to be *likable* to make you care about them, or at least ring true or demonstrate some kind of worth. However, this view did not preclude experimentation on the part of the author—as long as they succeeded in drawing the reader in. If a book she was reading was very obscure, Anne would think: talk to me, I'm sitting right here.

She felt the reviewing was of personal benefit:

I do believe reviewing has sharpened my thought processes. I used to read books like eating chocolates—I like it, I don't like it, toss it aside and reach for the next—but reviewing has forced me to stop and analyze what makes a book work or not work.

She was to review some of the most celebrated names in contemporary literature—Joan Didion, Vladimir Nabokov, Eudora Welty, Gabriel García Márquez, Margaret Drabble, Margaret Atwood—but equally, newcomers who could rouse her to similar enthusiasm and probably owed her their readership. One exception, however, was Marilyn French, whose feminist novel *The Women's Room* appeared at the height of the women's liberation movement in the 1970s and was eventually a *New York Times* bestseller. Anne in her frank review apparently remained unconvinced by its feminist intent, although managing both a positive beginning (Marilyn's fine writing) and a positive conclusion (Marilyn's abilities). For the rest, she did not mince words.

Forget all the other books about women's liberation, her review ordered: it was not Marilyn French's fault that preceding writers had gone "on and on" about the same subject. Marilyn's novel was about the progression of the central character Mira from childhood to independence—starting out submissive and repressed, and ending up liberated but lonely—and in all of this Mira felt herself to be a victim, Anne wrote:

Everything that happens—marriage, pregnancy, childbirth, the most mixed and mingled of occasions—seems almost purely negative, viewed with the glassy eye of belated resentment. There is no "equal time" offered; the men are given no chance to tell their side of the story. Compared to the women—each separate and distinct, each rich in character—the men tend to blur together. They're all villains, and cardboard villains at that.

The bias against men was of course intentional, Anne recognized: the author held that white middle-class males were hollow and posturing, and therefore hard to describe. Marilyn's character Mira perceived men and women to be separated by a gulf of "mistrust, incomprehension and exploitation." When the divorced Mira's friends discuss the injustices done to women, each character contributes her philosophy in what Anne described as "great chunky paragraphs." Marilyn French had written a collective biography of a large group of American citizens, she continued, "expectant in the '40s, submissive in the '50s, enraged in the '60s, they have arrived in the '70s independent but somehow unstrung, not yet fully composed after all they've been through." For Anne, *The Women's Room* was like an exhausting Russian novel full of quarrelsome, demanding families: it strained the patience and wore the reader down.

Anne clearly disliked the book, not only for its chunky great paragraphs of polemic but also, seemingly, for its message. For Anne, it was a narrow novel written with resentment, all men viewed as villains, the sexes seen as utterly divided; implicit in the words she uses is her own apparent dissociation from any such stance—although recognizing it as "a stage that a multitude of women are certainly experiencing." Her further reviews in the 1980s of feminist books by Andrea Dworkin and Kate Millett likewise disagreed with, in the first case, Andrea's overall sense of life as an "unremitting tooth-and-nail relationship" between the sexes, and in the second with what she saw as Kate's superfluous "feminist polemics." Anne's view was that men and women were human beings first, male and female second, with her own books generally laying little emphasis on gender differences and being written equally happily from either a male or female point of view. She saw her people as just individuals with "some bad traits, some good ones." Only a portion of her life, and almost none of her writing life, was much affected by what sex she happened to be, Anne declared, and even that portion of it would vary depending on the individual.

Some of Anne's reviews, however, did evince a more feminist awareness. Responding to a sexist description in one novel of a woman with "legs beginning at the hips," she asked drily where else they would begin. Reviewing a nineteenth-century cookbook she pointed to the female drudgery that would have been required to produce the food—"for it was never men." In reviews of children's books she applauded positive depictions of female characters, noting in one a doctor who happened to be a woman, and in another, female characters shown in "productive, unstereotyped roles."

Nevertheless, writing earlier in the decade in the *National Observer* about "novels by liberated women," Anne made a clear statement: "I hate 'em all." This she later qualified:

Certainly I don't hate liberated women as such...I assume I'm one myself, if you can call someone liberated who was never imprisoned.

As for the differences between male and female writers, Anne remarked, men tended to tackle bigger subjects, and while women were capable of the same thing, she thought them more interested in what lay within a small unit of people. For her own part, Anne had a self-imposed glass ceiling: it was who she was, and she was never going to write the great war novel. "There's my ceiling, and I'm pretty happy with it."

She continued to live her life the way she wanted to, striving always to put her husband and children first and fit her writing in around them; her female characters were to remain mostly untouched by feminism, deep in domesticity and, it would seem, enjoying it.

§

Anne's own reading tastes were wide ranging, although with definite boundaries. She generally avoided nonfiction, admitting for example that she had never read Edward Gibbon's *The History of the Decline and Fall of the Roman Empire*, despite shaking her head and bringing it up whenever there was mention of some modern example of self-indulgent excess (and not daring to actually read the book for fear of finding out that self-indulgent excess never came into it). She also shunned memoir, biography, collections of letters, and journals—keeping no journal herself, as she found it difficult to write one without sounding self-centered, and because it would "use up" her words. It was fiction, of course, that most gripped Anne, particularly the latest novels, excluding genres such as mystery and works of dystopia or science fiction. One of her later characters was to comment that they didn't like murder mysteries because they didn't care whodunnit, and Anne wholeheartedly agreed. "It happened. What can I say? They're dead!"

Classics like *Anna Karenina* she continued to read regularly, forever finding herself still bowled over by its immediacy and freshness, although she did not read Emily Brontë's *Wuthering Heights* until quite late—when "my luck ran out in my thirties." Discovering that several of her women friends considered the novel's central character Heathcliff their all-time favorite romantic hero, she felt she had to read it, but got only about three-quarters of the way through: it struck her as silly, Emily's writing style feverish and Heathcliff "an evil-tempered, spiteful lout without a shred of kindness, snarling away at a sweetheart almost equally viperish." She had immediately developed some serious concerns about the mental health of her friends, Anne joked. If Heathcliff was romantic, imagine the possibilities in Jack the Ripper, she remarked sardonically in the *New York Times* (perhaps at some risk of alienating the legions of Brontë fans).

One particular obsession for many years was Colombian author Gabriel García Márquez. Once, when the girls were ten or so and the family was at the beach, Anne went to a produce stand while wearing a T-shirt emblazoned with the title of Márquez' famous novel *One Hundred Years of Solitude*, her favorite book at the time. She was waiting in the cashier's line when a woman said to her, "I would love that."

Considering she was surrounded by children, all of them clamoring for different flavors of Sno-Cones, I knew right away what she was referring to. It wasn't my cantaloupe, or even the book; it was the hundred years of solitude…

At the point it was still her favorite novel Anne was astonished when she gave it to one of her brothers to read, confident of the "enraptured expression" that would surely come over his face, only to find him tossing it aside with the remark that he had once started it at an airport. "He could start it and not finish it? And then forget the whole experience?" For Anne, the novel was a deeply felt encounter that she could not imagine anyone failing to embrace. Márquez was intensely interesting to her in light of her own fascination with the passage of time and the changes it brings, and she loved him because he had somehow figured out how to describe time in literature as it is in life, "unpredictable, sometimes circular, looped, doubling back, rushing through sixty years and then doddering over an afternoon, with glimmers of the past and future just beneath the surface." She also loved how he had respect for the prosaic, but never seemed bound by it: after a tedious day spent marching her own characters from living room to kitchen, yawning as she tried to remember who took cream and who didn't, she found it "a great joy" to fling them all aside and read Márquez' description of a dead man's blood magically wandering around and hugging the walls so as not to stain the rugs. Most of all, though, Anne saw in everything he wrote the "assurance that we live among a wealth of possibilities, and are foolish to fear that they will ever thin out or dry up." (Much later, she was to admit she had overdosed on Márquez' brand of magic realism.)

Anne's next novel, *Searching for Caleb*, appeared in 1976, just one year after the previous work. Partly set in the 1970s and partly going back to the beginning of the twentieth century, the story revolves around a rich, snobbish, self-absorbed family living in Roland Park. The head of the family, elderly Daniel Peck, has left the others to go and live with his feckless grandchildren Justine and Duncan, Peck cousins who have married each other. Justine is an amateur fortune teller who advises her clients always to go with change, even though she herself remains in thrall to her own childhood. She accompanies her grandfather Daniel as he travels about the country in search of his younger brother Caleb, who took off in 1912. Eventually the stultified, disapproving family in Roland Park pay for a private detective to find the runaway, instigating a series of far-reaching events that leave the freewheeling Duncan and Justine facing a dramatic new stage in their lives.

There seemed to be a sudden explosion of reaction following the publication of *Searching for Caleb*, almost as if that magical thing, an Anne Tyler novel, had made its first real appearance (and "magic" was now a word that was starting to appear). Most notably, the respected author John Updike wrote a three-page review in the *New Yorker* describing the work as "funny and lyric and true-seeming, exquisite in its details and ambitious in its design." The Peck clan's conservatism and longevity both defied and embodied time, he said, listing too the number of Pecks who had nevertheless made their escape: not only Caleb, but his mother after giving birth to six children, Daniel himself to search for his brother, Duncan and Justine, and even their daughter Meg, who marries a prissy young preacher to get away from her parents' scrappy, nomadic existence. Although objecting to the odd touch of "Southern Gothic," such as the Pecks' maid knowing the whereabouts of Caleb for sixty years but declining to tell because she was never asked, John Updike's review offered virtually nothing but superlatives. Anne Tyler had the rare gift of coherence, of tipping observations in a direction, and of keeping track of what she has set down, he declared. "This writer is not merely good, she is *wickedly* good."

His enthusiasm was reflected elsewhere. Anne Tyler was a hard author to classify, wrote the *New York Times*, not traditionally Southern and somewhat out of time so that her books might have been set in any decade. The feminism of contemporary novels had seemingly passed her by, the review continued: her women were strong, often stronger than the men in their lives, but solidly grounded in traditional roles. Anne occupied a rather lonely place, it was observed, "polishing brighter and brighter a craft many novelists no longer deem essential to their purpose: the unfolding of character through brilliantly imagined and absolutely accurate detail." The *Philadelphia Inquirer* felt that the central concern of Anne's books was "the simultaneous lust to wander and to take root...Anne Tyler has made something magical out of common life." Magic and true, dazzling and wise, came from the *Boston Globe*. "Wonderful book. Wonderful novelist," announced the *Washington Post*. For the *Times* in Britain the novel was "strange and enchanting," a work about chasing rainbows; for the *Times Literary Supplement* it was a robust, witty novel concerned with an existential examination of freedom. The choices of staying put or running away, conforming or rebelling, were not as simple as they seemed, the reviewer wrote, and perhaps not important in themselves but more for the uses made of them, and Anne Tyler's cool handling of her material was original and exceptionally funny.

John Updike's comment that Anne was "*wickedly* good" was thereafter widely quoted in reviews and articles, and still is; his influence brought her national and worldwide attention, helped by his reviewing five more of her books in succession (if not always quite so enthusiastically).

The novel was a little more successful in terms of sales, selling 9,600 copies in hardback and later attracting offers for foreign-language editions from abroad. This time the paperback rights were bought by the Popular Library, which also picked up the renewals for most of her previous work and started publishing them in 1977. Having the paperbacks newly available just as the hardcovers were going out of print due to slow sales was a help in maintaining and extending Anne's audience, as well as her literary reputation. Editor Judith Jones also credited the new paperback editions with helping Anne's breakthrough into higher sales of hardcover: her audience became so substantial through the paperbacks, said Judith, that devoted readers couldn't wait to lay their hands on the next Anne Tyler and would buy the hardcover to get it quickly.

Anne declared *Searching for Caleb* not her best book, but the "most fun" to write of all her novels up to that point. She had loved writing about a huge family, describing it as like being at a big, marvelous party. If she could somehow arrange it so that for the rest of her life all she was doing was writing that book, she would be delighted. She had greatly enjoyed "being" Justine: "I was so reckless! So adventurous! Nothing like my true self." The less attractive characters, like Justine's selfish mother, did not appear unpleasant to her—as their creator, she had control over how far she ventured into them. She could feel "quite affectionate" toward people on paper that she couldn't stand to be in a room with, she commented.

She had made Justine the kind of fortune teller who used cards, but Anne hated doing research and felt it might kill it off instantly to go and see an actual fortune teller, so she just bought a little dime-store book to pick up some of the card formations. "It's a lot more fun to make things up," she declared. However, she had clearly taken the trouble to unearth plenty of obscure historical detail for this saga spanning five generations. The patriarch of the family at the turn of the century attempts to cure his ills by replacing the panes in the windows with amethyst glass, at that time believed to promote healing, and for the same reason wears a revitalizing electric battery on a chain around his neck; a 1908 Ford has a left-hand steering wheel (the year of the switchover from right-hand driving) and splashless flower vases; women of the 1900s wear Pompeiian Bloom rouge, and the streets of the old downtown Baltimore were paved with Belgian blocks (a detail Anne had found in a memoir).

She had considered several different titles for the novel— *Predictable Changes*, *Careless Losses*, *A Change of Fortune*, *Sudden Departures*, *Missing From the Family Album*, *Looking for Caleb*— before finally settling on *Hunting for Caleb*, but Judith thought this sounded too much like the movie *Deliverance* and convinced Anne to tweak the title to its present form.

The only "germ of truth" in the novel, Anne claimed, was the photo of Caleb playing a cello in the doorway of a stable hayloft twenty feet off the ground, which was based on a similar photo of her Great-Grandfather Tyler. However, there are indications that she may also have based Daniel Peck on one of her immediate grandfathers, and there are other occasional echoes of her own life. Anne suffered from insomnia, and so does Justine, who pickets a whites-only movie theater just as Anne's mother had done. Justine takes Daniel to Quaker Meeting, with its rows of "straight-backed radiant adults and fidgety children lining the wooden benches." Here, following Quaker custom, she rises during silent worship to speak, in this instance reading out something Grandfather Peck has written down for her: that he wanted heaven to be a small town with a bandstand in the park and a great many trees where he would know everybody and none of them would ever "die or move away or age or alter"—very similar to an idea Anne sometimes had of one day meeting all her characters in heaven and getting to catch up with them.

Roland Park and its inhabitants came in for one or two pointed comments. The neighborhood is described as staid and chilly, "with its damp trees and gloomy houses and its reluctant maids floating almost motionlessly up the hill from the bus stop, following their slow flat feet while their heads held back." The Pecks have pretensions: pronouncing it "Baltimore" instead of the more usual "Balmer," gardening in ragged old clothes that came from Brooks Brothers, wearing riding boots from England though none of them has ever sat on a horse.

Roland Park in the 1970s was still almost exactly the way it was in Caleb's time at the turn of the century, Anne remarked about the novel, "huge gloomy houses, great concern over bloodlines and those upstarts who don't wear gloves," although adding that nowadays it was more a question of whether or not you carried one of those Nantucket handbags with the scrimshaw whale on the lid. She thought the insularity of the upper class still apparent there, the doctor making house calls and the men doffing their Panama hats in a courtly manner as if the ladies they met on the sidewalk were in hoopskirts instead of cut-off jeans. It was this "time-machine aspect" of Roland Park, said Anne, that had propelled it into her novels.

§

Anne now had her working day down to a fine art. Morning was a rush to get the girls off to school, helping them with breakfast and last-minute homework before they slammed the front screen door on the way out with their lunches. Before that she would have risen early to do domestic tasks such as putting dinner in the oven to save time later, but after they left at about eight she would simply turn her back on the used cereal bowls and go up to her study. "I've learned over the years that I can't even put the dishes in the dishwasher," she explained. "As I close the door on the kids I go up to my room—like one of Pavlov's dogs. Otherwise I'll get sidetracked." She mostly felt reluctant to enter and had to walk in "as if by accident," with her mind on something else. The room smelled like a carpenter's shop from the wooden bookcases, ordinarily a pleasant smell but in the mornings one which made Anne feel sick. She experienced something like guilt if she did not do some writing daily.

The rest of her day was just as rigidly structured. "I have perfect control of time," said Anne, "and I can organize it." Five minutes for a peanut butter sandwich lunch. Thirty minutes for the highlight of her day, the mail and its delivery of catalogs, from which she ordered all her jeans and size-ten dresses in four or five different colors at once. She knew all the mailmen who worked the neighborhood and their exact schedules.

Anne was now thirty-five, her eyes variously described as a wide gray-blue or gray-green, the long dark hair that hadn't seen a hairdresser since 1958 now permanently swept up into her trademark bun and straight-cut bangs. About 5' 8" tall, she was ultimately to wear mainly calf-length skirts and long-sleeved tops, a way of dressing probably adopted out of respect for Taghi's religion. According to an interviewer's private notes a few years later, Anne was pretty, walked slowly with grace and poise, and was a "relaxed, gracious, intelligent lady" not at all shy when talking one-to-one.

She disliked being referred to as a housewife who writes. "Is John Updike a father of four who writes?" she asked. From 5:30 to 8:00 in the morning—sometimes even earlier—she was Mrs.

Modarressi, wife and mother. Monday through Thursday, from 8:05 to 3:30 when school got out, she was Anne Tyler, writer, and her small number of friends knew not to call during that time. When the girls returned she was back as their mother, baking cookies and refereeing arguments. The children were her "anchors to reality," said Anne; the only reason she knew anything about popular culture was that the children dragged it in. She would take Bethany the dog for a run, read *Peanuts* in the afternoon paper (perhaps, as a dedicated Orioles fan, also checking up on the latest baseball scores) and maybe do something with the girls. In an article she wrote with Mitra for her neighborhood newsletter a few years later, "A Child's Tour of Homeland (or, The 120-Minute Mile)," she described how a short, fifteen-minute walk around the locality turned into a long drawn-out marathon as Mitra stopped to look at everything on the way and gathered interesting objects to take home— discarded Venetian blinds, gerbil cages, sets of wooden window shutters. Meanwhile, the characters Anne was writing about in her study upstairs would "grow paler and paler and finally slink away."

Friday was for errands like groceries and snow tires, Saturdays for the weekly family excursion to the library to get stacks of classical records. And one trip a year for the family's holiday in Bethany Beach in Delaware, an enforced period away from home that Anne did not much relish (especially the scary merging onto freeways during the drive, a dread she shared with her heroine Eudora Welty).

§

In her study, Anne worked sitting cross-legged on a very hard black-and-white checkered daybed surrounded by a sea of notes. She wrote on white paper attached to a clipboard, the paper unlined because following lines felt constricting. Her pen was a Parker ball-point, of which she kept a constant store of two dozen in fear that the company would go out of business and leave her helpless. (Another terror, her greatest, was of going blind and being unable to see how the words looked on the page, which mattered greatly to her—followed by the fear of getting arthritis and being unable to physically write.) While gathering her thoughts Anne would sometimes doodle in the margins of her paper, and even draw sketches of her characters when they were giving trouble because it helped in understanding them.

The study was what she called a "stern white cubicle," the only room she could work in. Two large windows looked out onto tree-lined Tunbridge Road; the bookcases were full of old almanacs, a collection of *Time Life* history books decade by decade back to 1870 (perhaps the source of the meticulous detail in *Searching for Caleb*) and several photography books "just to sink into...To fill up on when I feel empty." There were also dictionaries of slang expressions, lined up by year, to give her historical characters an authentic voice. It drove her crazy to see anachronisms when reading novels, Anne was to complain.

It happens in movies too—a waitress will put down some food and say, "enjoy," and it's supposed to be happening in the 1950s where she would not be saying "enjoy."

The wall opposite the daybed was covered with family photographs, including the sepia photograph of her great-grandfather playing the cello that had inspired the image in *Caleb*; and a handwritten copy of Richard Wilbur's 1969 poem *Walking to Sleep*, its lines "Step off assuredly into the blank of your mind / Something will come to you" acting to inspire her writing—and the poem itself perhaps speaking to Anne's chronic, inherited insomnia that kept her awake from two to four every morning scribbling notes. (She had been able to sleep through the night from sheer fatigue when her children were babies, but had been far less productive. She needed the insomnia time for "thinking" and "hearing" her characters.) Another poem was also to join the gallery: John Updike's *Marching Through A Novel*, with its words "Each morning my characters / greet me with misty faces / willing, though chilled, to muster / for another day's progress."

Anne hated to travel away from the room or even to rearrange the furniture or start writing in the mornings at an unaccustomed time. Her habits and surroundings were all "magic spells" to get her going; over the years she had learned just to go to her room and "plug away." She knew that if she waited until the day she was inspired and felt like writing, she would never do it at all. If she did not succeed in getting anything down on paper, she still had to sit there with the paper in front of her, knowing that taking one day off often extended itself into taking another, and then another. When she did write, she had learned that even if not quite finished at the end of her working day, it was better to leave something "sort of hot" to come back to the next morning. It was an iron discipline. Reynolds Price was to comment that Anne "could maintain her lifestyle in a tornado."

The initial month of a new novel was not much fun. The first half hour of every morning would be spent just clicking the point of a pen in and out until her thoughts snagged on something, some long ago passerby or intricate family situation. Sometimes a picture would pop into her mind and she'd ask herself questions about it: putting all the answers together made a novel. Another avenue was to go through a couple of boxes of notes written on unlined index cards, a habit of hers since high school: ideas and snatches of talk that had been left to ripen, sometimes for years ("and I mean years"), as she rejected the same card over and over again until she felt she could make something of it:

They are things that at one time or another I thought I would like to explore, maybe a conversation I've overheard on a bus that I wondered where it was going or what did it really mean. At every fifth card or so a little click will go in my mind and I think boy, that would be fun and I start to expand on it and then I set the card aside.

At the end she might have around ten cards, a clutch of such disparate items that the problem was how to get them all into one framework. It could take a month before Anne was able to work it out. Once a novel was underway, further cards on her characters would be scattered about the house as inspiration came and eventually filed away in their turn.

Character was what interested her, Anne said. In fact character was everything: "I never did see why I have to throw in plot too." An idea for a novel always started with character, whereas plot had to be worked for, although sometimes Anne found that an automatic pilot solved plot problems while she was asleep. Characters arrived far more easily. Little flashes of their voices would come to her almost on a subconscious level; someone would just take over and start talking, and she then worked it in where she could. But it had to be written down as it came: if she stopped to go and make a cup of coffee it would start to slip away (although eventually, on realizing that ideas were limitless, Anne began to opt for the coffee). What was more tedious for her were the mechanics of moving characters from one room to the next.

The real joy of writing was how people, her people, could surprise. They "wander around my study until the novel is done," and that was one reason she was now becoming more careful not to write about anyone she didn't truly like. If she found somebody creeping in that she was not really fond of, she usually cut them out: it took her two or three years to write a novel and she certainly didn't want to spend all that time living with someone unlikable. And while her good characters had serious flaws, Anne observed, and quite base motives, they were never evil. Also, she never wrote about people she knew, which to Anne would be no fun. It would be just as boring to write about herself: even if she led an exciting life, why live it again on paper? She still did not believe that one chance was all she got, still wanted to live other lives (and to get readers to see what it would be like too). Writing was her method of making other chances, and she was lucky to do it on paper, Anne joked, otherwise she would probably be schizophrenic and six times divorced. "I would decide that I want to run off and join the circus and I would go. I hate to travel, but writing a novel is like taking a long trip. This way I can stay peacefully at home."

Her characters did not always obey her, sometimes refusing to perform in an event she had planned for them: a wedding, a departure, a happy ending. She used to arrive at the point but find that the sentences came out stilted or the dialogue sounded wrong, as had occurred in *Celestial Navigation*. After trying it again from different angles she would give up and allow the plot to go their way. Then it would all fall into place.

There were some central preoccupations that kept popping up in her books, Anne acknowledged. She was very interested in day-to-day endurance, and the space around people, particularly in the family. Depicting families was convenient for studying how individuals adapt and endure when forced to stay together, how they last and go on loving and adjust to the "absurdities of their confinement." For Anne, the real heroes in her books were firstly the ones who managed such endurance, and secondly the ones who somehow were able to grant others privacy and yet still show warmth. She also wanted to see how people could maneuver and grow within the small space that was the average life. She acknowledged, too, her obsession with time.

Anne was not exactly driven to write, more to get things down before she forgot them. Work for her came in two parts, the first part the story, with her characters talking and surprising her but with their author still not knowing what it was about or what it meant. The second part came when she read it through, and suddenly it seemed as if someone else was telling *her* the tale. Then she would go back and insert references to what it meant. She used to tell Taghi to burn any manuscript if she died before she got to part two. "It isn't mine until I see what my subconscious is up to." No one was shown any part of a book until it was completely finished.

Anne never expected, and claimed not to want, huge commercial success. In 1976, her best year to date, she made just $35,000 (paltry in comparison to the millions that were to come). She did not want the "intrusion" of fame, although very much hoping that somebody out there was reading the books. Earlier, she had put her limited popularity down to some people just not liking her work, rather than any failure to write about fashionable topics; she thought she was the kind of writer only read by those interested in getting inside other people's lives.

She did not see herself as building up to "the great book." It seemed to her that what she was doing with her books was populating a town:

Pretty soon it's going to be just full of lots of people I've made up...Populating the town is what's most important, but it does matter to me that I be considered a serious writer. Not necessarily important, but serious. A serious book is one that removes me to another life as I am reading it. It has to have layers and layers and layers, like life does. It has to be an extremely believable lie.

Akin to her idea of heaven, Anne would sometimes imagine retiring to the peaceful little town where everyone she had invented was living on Main Street. It would be an enjoyable retirement: after all, she said, they were people she had loved.

§

Anne's last work of the decade was *Earthly Possessions*, published in May 1977 but first appearing in condensed form in *Redbook* magazine the preceding February. Charlotte Emory, a 35-year-old mother of two living a quiet life in the invented town of Clarion, Maryland, is taken hostage at gunpoint during a bank robbery. Her captor is the inept Jake, a young drifter who takes Charlotte with him on the run as a bargaining chip in case he gets caught. Baltimore is the first stop on their getaway by bus (the driver shouting "Balmer!" as they arrive at the terminal). Charlotte, who was actually in the process of withdrawing her savings to run away herself, seems happy to go along for the ride. She muses about her life and her marriage as she builds up some sort of relationship with both Jake and his teenaged pregnant girlfriend Mindy, whom they rescue from a home for unwed mothers. Jake and Charlotte each find their own fate, with Charlotte finally understanding that there is no need for travel because she has been on a journey all her life.

Anne wrote the novel in the first person, a format that occasionally seemed to her the only path for a particular work and therefore hardly needing a conscious decision. But she would notice a feeling of disappointment on realizing that the work was going to have to be that way: first-person books felt less rewarding to her as a reader, something she thought possibly to do with her suspicion that a character who talked about himself for the length of a whole novel must be a little self-centered.

101

Writing the novel was Anne's usual process of discovery, story first and meaning second:

The story of Earthly Possessions was written before I realized what the pattern was—that a relationship as bizarre as a bank robber and hostage could become a bickering familiar relationship. Anything done gradually enough becomes ordinary.

She based the robber Jake, who likes taking part in demolition derbies, on a *Baltimore Sun* piece about a young Maryland derby driver; another article about storefront churches in cities probably provided the inspiration for Charlotte's preacher husband Saul.

The resolution that is ultimately achieved for all of the characters is not necessarily what they wanted, but was to a point that was satisfactory to Anne: as with all her books, she ended it when she felt she knew forever what their future lives would be like. "You know what Charlotte is doing now," she commented. "I build a house for them and then I move on to the next house." She had liked all the characters in the book, a surprise to her mother, who asked Anne how she could *like* the criminal Jake. Anne replied that what she liked was a sense of character, however spiky or difficult the person may be.

Time and the family were again explored and, more fully on this occasion, one of Anne's personal dislikes: interfering ministers. The work featured yet another negative portrait of a clergyman, following on from Meg's dull husband in *Searching for Caleb* and Elizabeth's rigidly religious father in *The Clock Winder*. Charlotte's husband Saul—a man of whom Charlotte's mother had initially been wary but eventually liked "a lot more than she'd ever liked me," according to Charlotte— unexpectedly turns preacher, to the considerable dismay of his wife. (Mostly a non-believer, she laughs at a free offer on the radio of a pamphlet entitled "What if Christ Had Never Come?" She could think of a lot they would have missed if Christ had never come: the Spanish Inquisition, for one thing, and for another, losing her husband to bible college.) Saul's beliefs lead him to avoid sex on Sundays and Charlotte spends the hour of his sermon in church thinking of ways to get him into bed when they got home, sometimes winning, sometimes not. But she makes no attempt to dissuade Saul from his chosen path. "I hate the whole idea," she tells him, "and I would try to make you quit if I were sure that I had any right to change people...Preachers never ask themselves that question, that's what's wrong with them." Neither does Charlotte make any attempt to dissuade her daughter from turning to religion at the age of seven, the exact age when Charlotte herself and Anne, too, had gone firmly in the opposite direction. "I thought of seven as the age when people come into their full identity," Charlotte says, similar to Anne's own remark that she had never been as intelligent or thoughtful as she was at seven.

Anne denied any specific reason behind her creation of a string of unappealing ministers, or even that they were in any way unpleasant. She was very fond of Saul, she maintained, and did not think of him as a horrible character at all. It was not that she had anything against ministers, "but that I'm particularly concerned with how much right anyone has to change someone, and ministers are people who feel they have that right." Equally, she had nothing against religion, Anne said, but felt that people should not proclaim that their way was the best way, as some believers did.

There was something of herself in Charlotte, Anne revealed. Both "share a voice—I tend to be ironic, I place great value on stoicism, and most of what I see strikes me as funny." She also shared Charlotte's refugee fantasy, a conviction both had had since that magic age of seven that "a long footmarch" would one day be expected of them.

Many reviewers were enthusiastic, perhaps now more awakened to the talent on their doorstep. Miss Tyler wrote in a cool, wry style, sketching bit-part cameos with spare, deceptively easy prose, said the *Times* in Britain: the narrative was funny and moving in turns. For the *Times Literary Supplement*, though, the novel was over-controlled, and Anne needed to let her imagination run away with her more. Back home the *New York Times*, quoting extensively from the novel, dubbed Anne a "fierce and lyric witness...this guerrilla in diffident prose," and declared **a** taste for Anne Tyler, once acquired, a splendid addiction. A second review from the same paper felt it to be a novel "that—like all of Anne Tyler's—holds us, delights us, and illumines our lives." John Updike in the *New Yorker* again waxed lyrical about Anne's "remarkable talent" and unmistakable strengths—her serene, firm tone, smoothly spun plots, apparently inexhaustible access to the personalities of her imagining, infectious delight in "the smell of beautiful, everyday life" and her lack of any trace of intellectual or political condescension.

However, he also pointed to a "possible weakness" in Anne's writing: the tendency to leave the reader just where she found him. He accused her of coziness (probably the first time, but certainly not the last, this accusation would be leveled). He added that Charlotte also belonged to what was becoming a familiar class of Anne Tyler heroines: women admirably tuned into the details of living yet alarmingly passive in the broad sweep of their lives, riders on "male-generated events, who nevertheless give those events a certain blessing, a certain feasibility." An Anne Tyler "type" was beginning to emerge in the critical consciousness.

Other critics had their own reservations. The *New Republic* did not see the novel as an advance: the wheels were audibly clicking, and inspiration seemed secondhand, the reviewer wrote (although adding that anyone who wrote *Celestial Navigation* and *Searching for Caleb* was allowed a breather). The *Sewanee Review* thought the characters and action interesting enough but with little depth; *Time* magazine agreed that it was not Anne's best book, even if her standard was so high that secondary works were equally compelling.

Yet others saw it as just a runaway housewife novel, a cliché of current feminist fiction. Anne commented that this view of the novel as "another Unhappy Housewife Leaves Home book" was the last thought on her mind. She regarded it more as "the work of somebody entering middle age, beginning to notice how the bags and baggage of the past are weighing her down, and how much she values them." But she made no comment about the other negative opinions. Ideally, a writer shouldn't read reviews, she was to say later, "but of course you do." A bad review was bad for your writing, "a good one is very bad for your writing, because you keep those opinions in mind when you work."

Earthly Possessions sold 10,900 in hardcover and the following year was added to the Popular Library's paperback collection of Anne's works. Her editor Judith, sending Anne the galley proofs, had asked: "Don't you find yourself impressed by that growing list on the Also By...page?" Foreign editions of *Earthly Possessions* were eventually to follow, including French, Finnish, and Korean, and in 1991 the work was adapted for the stage—the flashback structure causing problems—and in 1999 produced as a made-for-cable TV movie (after earlier interest from filmmakers in 1982). Susan Sarandon played Charlotte, Stephen Dorff was an impossibly good-looking Jake, and a very young Elizabeth Moss was the pregnant Mindy. The film was shot not in Maryland but entirely in the New York and New Jersey areas at the request of Susan Sarandon, who often chose filming projects near to home during the school year in order not to disrupt her children's routine. Her performance as a runaway was inevitably compared to her earlier role in *Thelma and Louise*. The plot took a swerve with a sexual relationship developing between Jake and Charlotte, who starts as a repressed housewife and then becomes ever bolder. Hardly surprising, decided the *New York Times*: Charlotte was, after all, an Anne Tyler character, and—in contrast to John Updike's perception that her women were always passive—"Ms. Tyler's heroines have been known to make bold moves of independence when the people around them least expect it."

But this time Anne declared herself "really upset" by the alterations in the plot. The central characters ending up in bed together was contrary to the spirit of the book, she objected, and had been motivated by crass considerations of box-office appeal. Her by then adult daughter Mitra pronounced the movie "horrible."

§

Just before the publication of *Earthly Possessions* in 1977, the American Academy and Institute of Arts and Letters honored Anne with a citation for "literary excellence and promise of important work to come," and a few months later presented her and nine other writers with an award of three thousand dollars each.

As the 1970s drew to an end Anne was thus the recipient of a major literary award and the author of seven acclaimed novels; in the second half of that decade she had produced more novels, short stories, and reviews than at any period in her career to date. Things were going well generally: Taghi had progressed rapidly in his career and had now been appointed Director of the Children's Service of the University of Maryland Institute of Psychiatry and Human Behavior.

But then came a dispiriting setback for Anne: a novel, *Pantaleo*, that had to be abandoned.

I wrote a novel that I ditched. A year's work, out the door...I sent it to my agent, who didn't like it; so I said, don't send it out [to publishers]. Now if I had really liked it myself, nothing would have stopped me. The problem was that it was boring.

Her agent was now Timothy Seldes, who had taken over from Diarmuid Russell at Russell & Volkening. He never edited in any way or suggested changes or different titles but was no yes-man, according to Anne. When he stated flat out that the book should be put away in a drawer, she trusted his judgment and unquestioningly followed his advice.

Turning out a work that failed—*Pantaleo* had been a suspense novel about a mysterious stranger stalking a young man raising his dead girlfriend's child—was unnerving, but Anne plunged back in, continuing to juggle writing and home. She planned to get her next novel started after the children's spring vacation, she wrote in an essay about her life at around this time, "Still Just Writing," but found herself sidetracked with errands such as taking the dog to the vet for worms. Her writing time from

Mondays to Thursdays when the girls were in school was interrupted by sales calls, the washing machine repair man, the tree man, the meter reader, and sundry Jehovah's Witnesses and Mormons. She described how her Fridays were reserved for tasks like scrubbing the bathrooms and picking up bedding for the gerbils, and how every so often she would have to assist those of Taghi's visiting relatives who did not speak English and needed help with shopping, or stop work early for the cat's rabies shot or the girls' dental appointments and gym meets. Sitting on the bleachers in the school gymnasium Anne would tell herself she could use the experience somehow in her work, but couldn't imagine writing a novel about twenty little girls in leotards trying to walk the length of a wooden beam without falling off (although in fact she did use exactly this scene in her next book).

Come summer and Anne knew she would get nothing done before the children went away to camp. She put the new novel away, "closed down my mind," planted some herbs and played cribbage with the girls, hoping that her characters would keep themselves going without her so that when she came back to them in the fall they would not, after all, "have crumbled to nothing as I always fear they will" (yet also contradicting herself to state that she did not *really* fear this, and trusted her characters to be OK). Once the girls were finally at camp, Tezh at a sleep-away camp in Virginia and Mitra at a local day camp, Anne could knuckle down—though learning the hard way not to try and write for longer than she usually did. "I tried it for three days, that's all. By five o'clock on each of them, I was in tears."

Once in her study Anne struggled to recapture a character that she wanted to build a novel around, someone who had just wandered into her mind: a man with a beard and a broad-brimmed leather hat, who now seemed in real danger of fading away. Then she had a phone call that Tezh in Virginia was seriously ill in hospital. Anne and Taghi left Mitra with friends and drove three hours in a torrent of rain. At the hospital they found their daughter frightened and crying with suspected typhoid fever, and another girl they happened to know who was equally frightened and crying in the emergency room with possible appendicitis. They spent the night on chairs alternating between the two, then in the morning loaded Tezh into the car for the ride back to Baltimore. After six wretched days in bed Tezh recovered from what had now been diagnosed as a simple virus, and was returned to Virginia on the evening train. The following day Anne was free to resume her writing but, instead, found herself sitting in her study staring blankly at the wall. It took a week's work to get the man in the hat back, but he finally "perked up."

It was tempting to draw some conclusions about the effect that being a woman/wife/mother had on her writing, Anne went on to observe in her 1980 essay, were it not that her novelist husband Taghi had had to give up his own writing for a while during his medical training. You couldn't be on call in the emergency room for twenty hours and then write a novel in the other four, she wrote. Now that he was a fully qualified, full-time child psychiatrist he had at last gone back to it, snatching odd moments here and there to work at a novel in his native language. (Sometimes one of the girls would interrupt him in English and he would answer in Farsi, staring blankly when they asked "What?") Every morning he got up at five-thirty, did some writing, then put on a suit and tie and drove to the hospital in the dark.

Both of us, in different ways, seem to be hewing our creative time from small, hard chips from our living time.

Anne at least got to take the occasional day off, going to a friend's for lunch or weeding the garden or rearranging her linen closet. After one of these breaks she would feel guilty enough to exaggerate the hardships of her day to Taghi, how she nearly got sideswiped in traffic or had a long wait in line to buy flip-flops for the girls. Anne still fully recognized, as she had done when the girls were babies, that unlike her husband she at least had a choice about doing any work in the first place, or what to work on: she could turn down writing an article if it didn't appeal to her, or refuse to change a short story or hurry a novel—all luxuries not available to Taghi, although she pointed out that his luxury was that nobody expected him to drop everything and take two weeks off work for an ill child. The only person who had no luxuries at all, it seemed to Anne, was the woman writer who was the sole support of her children. If she was in that position, she mused, she would not choose writing. It would have to be manual labor (running a toy repair shop, she thought, or starting an herb farm, or working for one of those companies doing jobs for old ladies). She had spent so long "erecting partitions around the part of me that writes"— learning how to close the door on it when real life intervened, and to close the door on real life when it was time to write—that she was not sure she could fit the two parts back together again.

These partitions in Anne's mind had gone up when the children started school and she went up to her study to spend the day writing. If a child happened to come home early she would feel "a little tug" between the two parts of her, and would be absent-minded and short-tempered. The transition became easier when she learned not to try and mix it up by sneaking off when the girls were at home to finish that one last page. Instantly, as if by magic, they would be pounding on the door, demanding "Band-Aids, tetanus shots and a complete summation of the facts of life." Eventually she was to claim being unable to write if other people were even in the house.

She had once bought a miniature tape recorder to carry around with her to record odd thoughts about her ongoing novel, often occurring while vacuuming, which was when the best insights came to her. One of the girls would be telling her about their day at school and suddenly Anne would whip out the tape recorder, dictate something like "Get Morgan out of that cocktail party; he's not the type to drink," and her daughter would stare at her in confusion. Anne realized she was ignoring the compartments, letting one half of her life intrude upon the other, with both beginning to seem ludicrous and unsynchronized. The tape recorder went back to the store. But she still suffered from a tendency to think about her work at the wrong time, such as at the supermarket, when she would cause offense by failing to recognize friends (who might also call during her working hours only to feel she was absent from the conversation, or would unthinkingly request that she babysit their children all day because she was "just sitting home").

109

Anne could still hardly believe she was being paid for an occupation that consisted of writing down "untruthful stories." She did worry that writing was a finite job and that she would one day run out of things to say; if she used up all her characters, she might have to find real work. In putting her ideas down on the index cards she was clearing out her head, which would one day be empty and spacious, and she could get on with her real life. But for now, her head kept loading up again, and even when she was bereft of ideas there was a sense of something still bottled inside trying to escape.

As the 1980 essay ended Anne recounted how she had been standing in the school yard one day when another mother came up to her. "Have you found work yet?" came the question. "Or are you still just writing?"

No, I tell her.

I'm still just writing.

§

The novel Anne experienced such difficulty in writing was the unusual and often very funny *Morgan's Passing*, published in 1980. Her confidence had been knocked by the failed novel preceding it, and her concentration dented by worries like her daughter's illness while away at camp; that summer there was always something happening—it was one child after the other, Anne later recalled. Her central character in the new work, Morgan, was "so obstreperous and contrary, I feel that every day I stop in the door of my study and roll up my sleeves and then march in and wrestle with him." She wrestled with Morgan for so long, in fact, that she had been uncertain the novel would ever see the light of day. It had given her "a hell of a time," although enjoyable to write, with Morgan becoming very real to her. She finally finished, typing up the fair copy herself as usual and mailing it to her agent. This time her work passed muster and was dispatched to Knopf, her publisher of the last sixteen years, for the attentions of the unflagging Judith Jones.

The central character—the bearded man in a wide-brimmed leather hat (which Anne had seen in a catalog)—was Morgan Gower, a forty-ish hardware store manager with a wealthy wife and seven daughters who live in a tall brick Colonial house in rarified north Baltimore. Morgan is a fantasist who tries out myriad imagined lives with the assistance of a wardrobe of disguises: sailor and soldier outfits, a riverboat-gambler costume, sombreros, pith helmets, a bowler hat. Pretending to be a doctor one day, he delivers the baby of young Emily and Leon Meredith on the back seat of his car, and they become friends. Over time, Morgan grows ever more obsessed with golden-haired Emily, finally falling hopelessly in love with her when he sees a series of luminous, magical photographs she has taken of members of his family. Everyone's lives are disrupted, and for Anne at least the novel ends sadly, although she was surprised when very few people realized it.

Morgan's fantasies enable him to maintain some distance from life, as though it is just a rehearsal and he will get second and even third chances, the best out of three. This fantasizing about living other lives was something that Anne, of course, felt intensely drawn to. The novel dealt with a situation she had been intrigued by most of her life, "one which is probably not unrelated to being a writer: the inveterate imposter, who is unable to stop himself from stepping into other people's worlds." Writers go in and out of other lives all the time, she remarked, but she had wondered what would happen if an imposter got into another life and could not get out again. The inspiration for the plot had come from an article she clipped from the *Baltimore Sun* about a local man who was discovered to be impersonating a doctor, and who had previously pretended to be a clergyman (as does Morgan in the novel). The man in question had even appeared on TV talk shows, with people calling in to say he was not who he said he was. An article about puppeteering had also provided the inspiration for the Merediths, who make their living giving puppet shows.

Anne's publisher was optimistic that this would be the book to bring Anne into the mainstream. Hopes were high, and the paperback rights were sold in advance of publication for a larger sum than usual. But *Morgan's Passing* sold only a little better than previous works—a disappointing 15,000 hardbacks.

Anne had feared that some readers might not like Morgan:

My big worry in doing the book was that people would be morally offended by him. He's not a full-fledged con man, though. He's not out to do harm. He's sort of amoral—but basically a kind man.

She saw him more as simply eccentric: people had always seemed "funny and strange" to her, she had declared in the "Still Just Writing" essay. She could not shake off a sort of mist of irony hanging over whatever she saw. Perhaps this was what she was trying to put across in her writing, Anne mused: perhaps she believed she was the only person holding this view. She thought life itself very funny, sometimes in pathetic ways: her humor came from the "appalling realization" that even the largest and most tragic events had their quirky little funny details underneath. The funny things in life were sad, and the sad things were funny. But Anne was always hurt when accused of writing only about bizarre or eccentric people. It was not a matter of choice—it seemed to her that even the most ordinary person, in real life, would turn out to have something unusual at their center. She liked to think that she might meet up with one of her quirky characters for real at the very next street corner, and to Anne the odd thing was, she had sometimes done exactly that.

But she had still felt mostly happy with *Morgan's Passing*, wondering if this might be the first work where she managed not to read reviews. "I always say I won't, but I wind up reading them anyway," she said again.

Anne's fears about Morgan were partially realized, although not because of any lack of morals on his part—more that the very odd, chain-smoking Morgan was seen by some to be wearying as a character. For author Eva Hoffman in the *Saturday Review* it was a story "about weirdness, and weirdness, as a novelistic subject, is simply not enough." The *Wall Street Journal* simply grew tired of him, and for the *New York Times Book Review* Anne was too fond of her strange character to subject him to a proper scrutiny. Morgan was the problem with the book, wrote the *New York Review of Books*, but Anne Tyler seemed to "adore" him. For John Updike, Morgan was "fey," and the novel forcedly buoyant and manic—leading him to suspect that Anne was suffering from fatigue.

Others found the main character downright lovable, however, and many reviews were glowing. *Morgan's Passing* was the first of Anne's novels to be honored with awards, winning both the Janet Heidinger Kafka Prize for fiction by an American woman and the inaugural Towson State University Prize for Literature, a $1000 award given to a young Maryland writer for the best work of the year. (Anne suggested that, instead of a public ceremony at nearby Towson for the presentation of the award, she could come and speak informally to the university's writing students, which she then did on several occasions over the next few years.) The novel was also nominated for both the National Book Critics Circle Fiction Award and a National Book Award.

"Pure magic, a contemporary fairy tale that overflows with affection, mystery and laughter," said the *Washington Star*, while the *New York Times* dubbed Anne "witty, civilized, curious," with radar ears and a pen dipped in acid. In Britain the *Times Literary Supplement* found the novel funny and meditative, and Anne so successful at describing the extraordinary and the unexpected because, paradoxically, she was so good at evoking the commonplace. She had such an eye for the oddness of ordinary life and about what people assume to be normal, the review perceptively commented, that the extraordinary no longer appeared so: the novel's "normal" characters seemed progressively more eccentric. Miss Tyler's art was to "reveal the strangeness of the ordinary and the banal." An enchanting modern fairy tale set in Baltimore, wrote an approving *Times*, "full of cockeyed humor." The work was later translated into at least Swedish and French.

Charm City as the setting at first seems just as cheerless as Anne had previously depicted it. Out-of-town Emily finds the city narrow and confining: gloomy row houses with boarded-up windows, alleys choked with discarded tires and bottles and bedsprings, useless-looking, hopeless men slumped on their stoops and a woman on hers in nightgown and vinyl jacket, nursing a Rolling Rock beer.

But, as in *The Clock Winder*, a note of fondness still manages to poke through:

It was a warm, sunny morning. The city looked freshly washed, white gold-lit buildings rising through a haze in the distance, women in spring dresses sweeping their stoops, green ivy flooding through the windows of an abandoned row house.

(Morgan's Passing, 1980)

Anne also brought in her own Homeland neighborhood as the venue for one of Emily and Leon's puppet shows—a house stiff and icy, with satin striped chairs and pale rugs that never seem to have been walked on. A woman carries one of the Nantucket bags Anne had been so scathing about, a basket-shaped purse "that was sure to have a whale carved on its lid."

Other echoes of Anne's own life, past and present, are again scattered throughout the novel. Emily's daughter does gymnastics with other little girls in leotards; she goes away to camp in Virginia. Emily reads Tolstoy at college (politely refraining from contradicting Leon's father when he insists Tolstoy was Lenin's right-hand man). She comes from old Quaker stock and is comfortable with long silences; when leaving home for college she announces to her mother that she will no longer be attending Meeting—she is getting out and going to *join*, get to be part of some big group, "not going to be different ever again."

Clearly Anne's early experiences in life were continuing to resonate. When Emily attends a Quaker funeral service, her boredom and lack of connection are likely reflective of Anne's own. A hush falls, the quiet in which Emily had grown up: not a total silence, "but a tocking, breathing quiet, with the occasional sound of cloth rubbing cloth, little stirrings, throats cleared, people rustling coughdrop packets or fumbling through their purses." Emily, never religious, expects nothing from it, and in her mind tries to name all the States in the Union.

§

That year Anne went to visit her heroine Eudora Welty at her home in Jackson, Mississippi, where the venerated author had resided her entire life. White-haired Eudora, now in her early seventies, still lived in the solid, high-ceilinged house built by her father in 1925, wrote Anne in a profile for the *New York Times Book Review* (the piece later bound and produced in a limited edition of one hundred copies, not for sale). But now Eudora lived there alone, the last of a family of five and, despite her success as a writer, struggling to keep the house up. A porch needed new screening but the price was so high Eudora had simply closed it off.

 On a picture rail hung a painting of Eudora as a young woman: blonde, with large, luminous eyes. The older Eudora was troubled by arthritis and walked with some care, but for Anne her eyes were as luminous as ever, radiating kindness and gently amused attention. When she laughed, Anne could see how she must have looked all those years ago —shy and delighted. She seemed to Anne to be that rare kind of person who took an active joy in small, present moments, and in particular was pleased by words and "snatches of dialogue overheard," just as Anne herself was. The visit was marked by the similarities between them, already present or still to come. They talked of their shared fear of merging into freeway traffic, which Eudora compared to constantly putting off the moment of entering a jump-rope game; like Anne, she was a baseball fan, at least in girlhood. And, as Anne was to admit about her own early novels, Eudora regretted some of her youthful works because she had not yet learned to rewrite. Very unlike the soon-to-be-reclusive Anne, however, she enjoyed going out on speaking engagements, and was frequently invited because "I'm so well behaved, I'm always on time and I don't get drunk or hole up in a motel with my lover."

Anne was entranced by the way the older woman hunted for just the right word to describe something, and took such pleasure in an overheard country phrase. She recounted Eudora's writing methods: waiting for things to "brood," usually situations from her own life that then became alchemized into something entirely different—not dissimilar to Anne's approach, as she was eventually to admit—and how fiercely their shared literary agent Diarmuid Russell had wanted to represent the young author in her earliest days. Eudora told her visitor how, when she arrived to lead a writing workshop at Duke in the 1950s, Reynolds Price had met her train at three in the morning wearing a pure white suit; she talked eloquently of the wonders of her traveling days, making it difficult for Anne to remember that she was supposed to be taking notes.

Writing was quite simply Eudora's life's work, Anne observed. That October, reviewing a new collection of Eudora's stories for the *Washington Star*, she wrote:

Eudora Welty is one of our purest, finest, gentlest voices…

Recognition...and Retreat

Anne's most significant and successful decade now lay before her. First, though, her family was to be directly affected by international events. On 4 November 1979, fifty-two American diplomats and citizens were taken hostage at the US Embassy in Tehran. The majority were held until 20 January 1981, a total of 444 days.

The Shah of Iran had fled the country earlier that year after increasing turmoil and revolt against his autocratic, Western-backed rule and torture of political dissidents. President Carter's reluctant admission of the Shah into the US for cancer treatment later in 1979 was one of the drivers for the hostage-taking, with Iranians seeing American support of the deposed Shah as complicity in his former atrocities. The Shah was soon to leave American soil, but the hostages remained in captivity as complicated negotiations and a failed rescue attempt then played out.

It was a difficult time for the Modarressi family. There had been rumors of something wrong in Taghi's home country during the visit soon after their marriage in 1963 for Anne to meet his family (described by Taghi as "religious, but not obsessive"). Much later, in February 1979, she wrote in a *New York Times* review of two Iranian novels that even back then there had been reports circulating among her husband's writer friends of people who had simply disappeared. As time went on, the news she and Taghi heard from Tehran grew ever more worrying. People vanished in the dead of night or were marched away, returning with terrible unexplained scars or not returning at all. It became accepted that no one should speak openly, even in front of the closest servant, in fear of who they might be working for. Letters from Anne's mother-in-law, rambling accounts of household matters, arrived opened and clumsily, stickily resealed.

For some reason, it was the clumsiness that was most annoying—the fact that the secret police hadn't even bothered to cover their tracks. I certainly hope they enjoyed her knitting patterns.

When Anne watched television reports from Iran during the tumultuous period prior to the hostage-taking, she would wonder if anyone could possibly continue to hold her own romantic image of "Persia" as a land of minarets and indolent veiled women. The minarets were there, but nearly obscured by army tanks. The veiled women she saw in the reportage—one emerging, with both fists raised, from four years of torture in a political prison—were anything but indolent, she remarked. But no matter how long Anne watched as events unfolded, she was never to feel quite certain that she adequately understood the confusing political situation.

Then the hostage crisis broke and coverage swamped all the TV channels. CBS Evening News anchor Walter Cronkite would end each show with a tally of how many days the captives had been held, and anti-Iranian protesters in Washington, DC brandished signs reading "Deport all Iranians" and "Get the hell out of my country." Some Iranian American students hid their Iranian identity to avoid getting beaten up, even at university. A young immigrant suffered protests at her high school: "... every morning another student would write F*** Iran on all the chairs surrounding mine."

The situation was "very uncomfortable for us," Anne commented at the time. But it was hardest on their daughters. One day 12-year-old Mitra told her mother that she had heard whispering behind her at school: "Pass it on. There's a rumor Mitra Modarressi is Iranian." Mitra had turned round to say "It's the truth!" and then returned home in confusion. "Yes, I am Iranian. But no, I'm not—I'm American." Fortunately the girls' closest friends made nothing of it. Anne was irate about the situation, then discovered that Taghi did not share her feelings:

I just feel angry about the hostage business. My husband doesn't feel <u>that</u> angry about it all. He's seen so many of his friends tortured and killed by the Shah's people. It's the first time I've really noticed that we're not from the same country.

It was not the only instance of prejudice the family had encountered. On moving to Baltimore in 1967 they rented a home in a stuffy neighborhood where old ladies lived in six-bedroomed houses, and a neighbor with a drinking problem would open his window and shout "Iranians go home!" In retrospect Anne claimed to find it more funny than upsetting, just "pretty mild" racism.

Taghi's professional life was not seriously affected by the crisis, as far as is known, although friends of his had felt it best to claim they were Turkish rather than Iranian. He continued to be greatly respected and by 1982, a year after the crisis had ended, the University of Maryland Medical School was planning to establish a child study center in Baltimore with Taghi as director. The proposed center should be in the heart of the community to make it easily accessible for mothers with their babies, Taghi told a *Baltimore Sun* journalist. It would be a "teaching device for effective parenthood, as well as a place to study." Society had a big stake in child mental health, he declared. When a baby started off with failure at its beginnings, problems could be expected later on, in school or in relations with others. As an adult, such a child could be a candidate for mental institutions or prison. Intervention needed to start early on, he stressed, when there was a greater chance of success.

But despite Taghi Modarressi's abiding interest and success in his chosen field, despite his happy family life in America, he must have been profoundly shaken by events in his homeland. He had taken American citizenship in 1977 but remained deeply proud of his Iranian heritage. Not long after the crisis he was to produce his first novel in many years (later translated into English, with Anne's help). Set in Iran and dealing with the effects of the Shah's oppression on an ordinary family, it was titled *The Book of Absent People*.

§

As the hostage crisis took its course, Anne was absorbed in perhaps her darkest novel yet, *Dinner at the Homesick Restaurant*. For many years it was to remain her favorite work, the "book of my heart." All her ideas and preoccupations about people and

119

family seemed to come out in it, she commented, although she had not deliberately set out with that aim. The novel came closest to what she had wanted of it from the start, conveying something she felt "very, very deeply" about families, about how they work and how they don't. It was a hard book to write, in fact later acknowledged by Anne as the hardest but also her best. It was "depressing me considerably," and "very gloomy," she commented in a letter in 1981. She had "scraped off so many surfaces of her skin" to get to it that for a while after it was finished she experienced a sort of pain. This was some of the reason the work had such value for her, because she knew what had gone into it. After that, though believing that she had subsequently written more polished books, Anne felt she had said the main thing she wanted to say. "The rest is just gravy."

However, she was at pains to make one thing very clear: while it was "sort of the book of my life" in terms of her beliefs and feelings, it was not *her* life. Nobody in any of her books was real, she still maintained, including the angry, bitter mother in the novel who favors one child over another and whose violent explosions terrify her young family. "My mother was *not* Pearl Tull," Anne stated firmly (perhaps in response to suggestions that she might be).

Dinner at the Homesick Restaurant is the story of single mother Pearl and her three children, all living in a Baltimore row house —bad boy Cody, dreamy young Ezra, and their brittle little sister Jenny. Born in Raleigh of a good family, Pearl has been abandoned by her husband Beck and must now work as a checkout clerk at a grocery store to support them all, feeling tense and unhappy and making the children miserable with her eruptions. When he grows up, Ezra starts the Homesick Restaurant, where he cooks what he thinks people might be homesick for: tacos or North Carolina barbecue, gizzard soup "hot and garlicky" and made with love, or anything else Ezra feels would do them good, such as okra stew instead of the ham they actually ordered. He continually invites his family for meals in his restaurant on St Paul St that are never completed, always interrupted by someone walking off in a huff. When Ezra becomes engaged to one of his employees, the boyish Ruth (who is staying at the boarding house from *Celestial Navigation*, the first time Anne had recycled from one book to another), Cody's deep jealousy of his younger brother impels him to pursue Ruth precisely because she belongs to Ezra.

2nd draft

I. SOMETHING YOU SHOULD KNOW

While Pearl Tull was dying, a funny thought occurred to her. It twitched her lips and rustled her breath, and she felt her son lean forward from where he kept watch by her bed. "Get . . ." she told him. "You should have got . . ."

You should have got an extra mother, was what she meant to say, the way we started extra children after the first child fell so ill. Cody, that was, the oldest boy. Not Ezra have beside her bed but Cody the troublemaker — a difficult baby, born late in her life. They had decided on no more. Then he developed croup. This was in 1931, when croup was something serious. She'd been frantic. Over his crib she had draped a flannel sheet, and she sat out their skillets, saucepans, buckets full of water that she'd heated on the stove. She lifted the flannel sheet to catch the steam. The baby's breathing was clotted and rough, like something pulled through tightly packed gravel. Toward morning, his skin was blazing and his hair was plastered stiffly to his temples. Fingers still he slept. Pearl's head sagged in the rocking chair and she slept too, fingers still gripping the ivory metal crib rail. Back was away on business — came home when the war was over, Cody toddling around again with nothing more than a runny nose and a loose, unalarming cough that Back didn't even notice. . . .

Pearl told him, he asked surprised, though, cleared . . .

. . . she said, for it had struck her during the croup. If Cody died, what would she have left? Then little rented house, fixed up so carefully and pathetically, the nursery with its Mother Goose theme, and of course, but he was so busy with the Tanner Corporation, away from home more often than not, and even when home always fretting over business — who was on the rise and who was on the studs, who had spread damaging rumors behind his back, what service he kind of being let go now that times were so hard.

"I don't know why I thought our little boy would suffice," said Pearl. But it wasn't as simple as she had supposed. The second child was Ezra, so sweet and clumsy it could break your heart. She was more endangered than ever. It would have been best to stop at Cody. You never learn, though. After Ezra came Jenny, the girl — such fun to dress, to fix her hair, so different. Pearl felt she couldn't give Jenny up. Still, she thought, girls were a kind of luxury. what she had now was not one loss to fear but three spare children, like spare tires, either. spare children, a time with each pain.

it had seemed a good idea once upon a time. "Ezra," she said, or extra little stockings they used to package free with each pair. "You should have arranged for a second-string mother, Ezra," she failed to form the words, for she heard him sit back again without comment and turn a page of his magazine. "How short-sighted of you." But evidently Or she meant to say.

She had not seen Ezra since the spring of '75. four and a half years ago, when she first started losing her vision. She'd had a little trouble with blurring. She went

Surprisingly, Anne was ambiguous about whether the work was a novel at all. To begin with, she did see it as a series of separate stories that were sufficiently interrelated to eventually "sneak up" on being an actual novel—but then, seemingly, changed her mind. The decision to issue the work as a novel met with her resistance. Editor Judith informed Robert Gottlieb, editor-in-chief and president at Knopf, that Anne had labeled the manuscript "Stories" and was strongly insisting it was not a novel and should not be called one. Robert just as strongly felt it *was*, and suggested not labeling it at all, but to let critics and readers make up their own minds. After its huge success he was to remark that *Dinner at the Homesick Restaurant* would never have done so well had it appeared as Anne had wanted.

Some of the work did appear as standalone stories, however, as with previous works. Anne first offered one or more of them to the modest Palaemon Press, a North Carolina publishing company specializing in Southern writers that had long been angling for some of Anne's writing, but she left the final decision to her agent Timothy Seldes. For a long period the little press simply never heard from him, despite Anne writing a letter prodding Timothy to get in touch. In the end two chapters were published separately in magazines—one in the *Boston Globe Sunday Magazine* and one in an abridged form in *Harper's*, at Timothy's request carefully billed as an excerpt and not as a story.

Anne later talked at length about the impetus for *Dinner at the Homesick Restaurant*, published in 1982, and some of the ideas and experiences that lay behind it.

It had been triggered by a dream about her daughters. She was listening to what she called a "sermonette" on her clock radio after being woken up by it, as usual, when Taghi rose very early in the morning for writing and work. Then a hymn was played, *In the Sweet Bye and Bye,* with its line "We shall meet on that beautiful shore." As Anne went back to sleep the hymn filtered in through a dream of meeting their daughters on the beach on the first day of their summer vacation, with Tezh and Mitra little girls in tutu bathing suits rather than the teenagers they now were. She and Taghi were young again too. When she woke she thought she had just seen a vision of paradise—to be back there, to have that time again, would be "so heavenly." This vision she gave as a dream to Pearl.

Pearl's diaries in the book were inspired by the diaries of Anne's own Great-Aunt Sadie, written in 1903 and 1908. Except for the heartbreakingly brief description of her fiancé's death from typhoid, Sadie had written only about domestic details, which were nevertheless fascinating to Anne when she read them in the 1970s. She thought Pearl "in one of her softer moods" might even have resembled a photograph she had of Sadie. Cody's bout of croup as a child was also based on a very early, "startlingly clear" memory of her own croup aged about two and a half, when she spent two nights alone in hospital in an ivory-painted metal crib, crying every moment of the stay. She "gave" the same crib to Cody.

She knew Pearl was a "terrible, terrible mother," for which there was no excuse, but because she recognized the many different sides there are to people she also wanted readers to understand that Pearl didn't mean to be cruel, and to feel partly sorry for her. She deliberately made Pearl an abandoned wife because of her huge interest in people who endure, who evince that "everyday strength" she felt women more often than men are called upon to exercise. She wanted to investigate how they managed to "keep on keeping on" when things were less than perfect. In fact, the novel was meant to embody Anne's conviction that she had joked around about families long enough, to say "let me tell you now what I really believe about them." A quintessential scene for her in *Dinner at the Homesick Restaurant* is when, after a brutal episode in which a rampaging Pearl physically attacks her children, the family is then shown playing Monopoly together as if nothing has happened. This is how families worked, Anne believed: "You can't walk away, you have to say well, we're going to go on coping," and families were the purest example of people cast together who cannot get out of it and, therefore, eventually have to show their true colors. Pearl herself in the book insists that "with your family, if with no one else, you have to keep on trying." If this had been merely a group of friends, Anne observed, they would long ago have split up and she wouldn't have had a novel to write.

Anne also wanted to convey that pain and wounds, and family traits like dissatisfaction, envy, and jealousy, could certainly persist through generations but could also be healed. She pointed out that when Pearl's daughter Jenny is briefly abusive herself as a young mother, it is, significantly, Pearl who comes to the rescue by taking care of Jenny's child (reading her Anne's old favorite, *The Little House*, over and over again). Patterns could be broken, and by the very people who have made them. "That's an important thing I want to say about families, any time I write."

Anne additionally revealed that in *Dinner at the Homesick Restaurant* there was, unbeknownst to anyone but her, "some military thing or reference to war or fighting" in every single chapter, because she felt the family was at war so often. The little brown airplane droning overhead in the very last line of the novel was a military plane, for example. The airplane also referred to something that had occurred to her once when thinking back to a quarrel in her own family when she was a child; she remembered how, immediately after the dispute was resolved, her father had tossed a ball back and forth with Anne and her brothers outside. She saw the little white ball rising in the sky and falling back down and it seemed like such a carefree, happy image after the memory of the family fight, and in a way this too was reflected in the image of the little airplane.

Pearl and Jenny's frustrations as mothers were something Anne could sympathize with. She was a very happy wife and mother but often had fantasies about running away from home, planning what to pack, which sweater to take:

It was all done perfectly happily, I can't explain it...I think it's because the minute you have a baby you know you're in it for the long haul. It's one of the reasons I love to write about families, you are stuck, now how are you going to do this? How are you going to manage all these years?

She thought everyone must have had an urge to up and leave at some point, packing no more than a toothbrush. She had been fascinated all her life by the tension between "the wish to fly and the resolve to stay earthbound."

Anne's favorite character in the book was Ezra, the sort of person she had often come across who just accepted things as they came, who didn't bear grudges and had no edges—a type actually somewhat irritating to her (and frequently a middle child, she had noted). But she "just loved him," even though he made her a little angry for not standing up to Cody. He was too meek and passive, but for Anne there had been no choice—that was who he was. Cody himself she made a time and motion expert precisely because of her great interest in time, and she gave him a moving speech in the novel about its significance.

Cody and I feel the same about time...Time is about the only way I can give my books any plot, since I'm not very action oriented.

The Baltimore setting, in Anne's words that "rich, gritty, textured place," was by now automatic. She felt almost as if her characters were in a tapestry and the tapestry was Baltimore. It was the most Baltimorean of her novels, she commented around this time, because when she wrote it she had lived there the longest and more of the atmosphere had soaked in. The city was wonderful territory for a writer: so many different things to poke around in. If she tried to picture the characters anywhere else she saw a blank, so it had to be her home city, as it now was after fifteen years' residence. In the novel, Anne's deepening affection can be sensed more than ever: she describes how on hot summer nights whole families perch on their white stoops with a beer cooler, an oscillating fan, and the baby in a mesh crib while they watch a TV placed on a car hood at the curb, so that people passing between have to excuse themselves as if walking through a living room. Specific streets and the surrounding region are mentioned by name: Calvert Street, Ritchie Highway, Garrett County (although at the same time she made up many of the street names to stop readers writing to say there were no traffic lights on that street like she said). Pearl, like Anne, is a fervent Orioles fan. But Anne also had her eyes open to the realities of life in the city, now suffering ever-increasing violence and drug problems. For Cody on a walk, the back of his neck takes on "that special alertness" required on the streets of Baltimore.

As for the lovingly described food at the restaurant—and even the awful food dished up by Pearl—Anne explained why so much of the important action in her novels occurred at meals and celebrations. She was drawn to scenes involving food because people's attitudes toward food revealed so much about them:

Are they feeders, or withholders? Enjoyers, or self-deniers? What exactly is on their plates—or in the saucepans they're eating directly from as they're hunching over the stove? It's all a kind of shortcut to tell my readers whom they're dealing with.

In fact she was wary of anyone who did not enjoy food, Anne was to declare. When she was a child her family had always eaten their meals together, and as an adult she had been constantly amazed how often in real life someone said, describing how some crisis began, "Well, we were just sitting around the supper table," and knew it could not all be coincidence. This was where events took place.

For the final dinner at the restaurant at the end of the novel she created worksheets for the table seating: a list of fourteen names, eight of them children with a note as to their ages and whose child each was—Cody's, or Jenny's from an earlier marriage, or Jenny's husband Joe's from *his* earlier marriage, or Jenny and Joe's together. As part of her preparatory work Anne also drew up a typical menu for the restaurant:

> *A. Curried Eggplant Soup*
> *B. Minted Leg of Lamb*
> > *Mushroom Kasha*
> > *Tossed Salad*
> > *Wine*
> *C. Chocolate Mousse*
> > *Dessert Wine*
> *D. Coffee*

§

Writer and critic John Updike spotted that each chapter was "rounded like a short story." He wrote in his highly favorable review that Anne had created real people with real psychologies that made their next moves "excitingly unpredictable." He saw in this latest of Anne's works the previously lacking "darkening" that would give solidity to the beautifully sketched shapes of her earlier books: "Now, in her ninth novel, she has arrived, I think, at a new level of power."

Other critics shared his rapture, particularly at the *New York Times Book Review.* The novel edged deep into truth that was simultaneously (and interdependently) psychological, moral and formal—"deeper than many living novelists of serious reputation have penetrated, deeper than Miss Tyler herself has gone before. It is a border crossing." The author of the review, which for the first time was impressively located on page one of the magazine, was the influential critic Benjamin DeMott, professor of Humanities at prestigious Amherst College. He also waxed lyrical about the structure, the plot, the suspense, the hilarity, the all-round superb entertainment: "We're speaking, obviously, about an extremely beautiful book." The *Boston Globe* thought *Dinner at the Homesick Restaurant* "a book that should join those few that every literate person should read...You surface from this marvelous novel as if from the bends, lungs nearly bursting, tears rattling on the page." For *Newsweek* it was "extraordinarily good." Abroad, Australia's *Canberra Times* found the novel "excellent" and for the *Times* in Britain it was a "most rewarding and compassionate" work that made the reader see in family life the endurance between the cracks: Anne was "gripping and wise, sardonic and affectionate."

(Photo credit: Helen Marcus)

One budding writer in Britain, the later author of *About a Boy* Nick Hornby, was especially struck by Anne's work. Reading her for the first time was a very important moment in his creative career, a recognition of a great writer who wrote "simply and with humor and with soul" about domestic life. He had never realized that a novel could be that warm and wise and engaging, he commented, because he had never read the literary greats in college. "I had always wanted to write but I thought, well I can't do *that* and I don't want to do *that* so maybe I am not a writer. But when I read her I felt that I understood every creative impulse she had. I am quite obsessed with her." Up until reading Anne, Nick had been an unsuccessful scriptwriter with no ambitions to write prose, but then he suddenly saw how it might be done and what kind of novel he wanted to write. He credited her with inspiring him to start writing, even conceiving an ambition to be the male Anne Tyler. He went on to become a highly popular, bestselling author.

Anne's hero Eudora Welty said of the novel: "If I could have written the last line of *Dinner at the Homesick Restaurant*, I'd be happy for the rest of my life."

But there were dissenting voices amidst the acclaim. *Esquire* found the novel "grindingly forced and unfelt," with a rickety plot structure, and the *Village Voice* labeled Anne a case of arrested development because her novels, including *Dinner at the Homesick Restaurant*, contained no sex. Her prose was "sexually anesthetized" and instead there was "an endless child-parent interchange prolonged into listless adulthood." Anne Tyler was unable to depict the normally active years of adulthood, the paper complained, leaving her characters living those years in "fantasy-ridden sedation." The novel was only successful in communicating the depression behind the whimsy, and Anne Tyler's readers loved her because her writing skill invested the infantilism of American family life with "a tender glamor" that allowed the middle-brow middle class to love itself. Novelist Adam Mars-Jones in Britain's *Times Literary Supplement* likewise noted that sexuality was allocated an unfashionably small part to play, and also detected "a certain forced poignancy" in some of the chapter endings because of the way each had been constructed as a self-contained short story and therefore demanded its own emotional release. Anne Tyler was deemed a remarkable writer, nevertheless, who was incapable of writing unconvincingly.

Despite such reservations, nominations for fiction prizes came thick and fast: the novel was a finalist for the National Book Critics Circle Award, the American Book Award (now the National Book Award), the PEN/Faulkner Award and—a first for Anne—for a Pulitzer Prize, but losing out to Alice Walker's *The Color Purple*. In the end, however, the book won no prizes at all, to Anne's disappointment: as her favorite, she was always to wish *Dinner at the Homesick Restaurant* had been the one to gain a prize rather than the others. But it remains one of her most popular books, eventually translated into twenty-two languages and featured on radio (to Anne's delight, at Thanksgiving, "a time when so many people dread coming together with their families"). The year after it was published she was proud to be elected to the American Academy and Institute of Arts and Letters (now just the American Academy of Arts and Letters), the nation's honor society of leading architects, artists, composers, and writers.

It became the first of Anne's novels to be a bestseller: with initial sales of 71,000 hardbacks it finally fulfilled her publisher's dream of what they called a "breakout book," one that would win her a larger audience and greater recognition. The paperback version a year later was heralded with the kind of fanfare usually reserved for popular blockbusters: billed as the publisher's lead title for March 1983, it was advertised in newspapers, trade journals and on posters and displayed in prime selling space in major bookstores. At the same time Anne's previous eight novels were reissued in paperback at the rate of one a month, starting with *Morgan's Passing*. Anne told reporters that she loved the thought of more people reading her books, and was glad students would be able to get copies at relatively low prices, but was having trouble conceiving of readers in large numbers. She could imagine one person reading and reacting, and could make the enormous leap to imagining 10,000, but just couldn't envision anything beyond.

The first paperback print run for *Dinner at the Homesick Restaurant* was, in fact, half a million copies, with Knopf aiming "to bring Anne Tyler the huge mass-market readership she so richly deserves." Requests for foreign editions had arrived in advance and quickly snowballed after publication: contracts were closed not only with Britain and other English-speaking markets but also Sweden, Germany, Portugal, Norway, Finland, Italy, France and French-speaking Canada, Turkey, Israel, Bulgaria, Czechoslovakia, the Soviet Union, Yugoslavia, South Korea, and the Netherlands (where the translator requested a change of title because it didn't quite work in Dutch). Interest was not universal, however: in Denmark, at least to begin with, the book hardly sold because reviewers ignored it; in Japan, publishers turned it down flat.

The novel's huge success also sparked requests from abroad for foreign editions of earlier works: an Israeli and a Bulgarian edition of *Morgan's Passing*, a French magazine serialization of the same, a Swedish version of *Celestial Navigation*, a Dutch version of *Searching for Caleb*, new British editions of *If Morning Ever Comes* and *The Tin Can Tree*. There was renewed interest in Anne's older stories too: the British *Good Housekeeping* made an offer for "Your Place is Empty" and in 1983 another British magazine, *Woman*, published her story "Laps" under a different title. A French publisher asked for several stories for an upcoming collection of American writing.

Dinner at the Homesick Restaurant went into its fifth hardback printing only one month after publication, in March 1982, when existing prints already numbered 47,500. Knopf sold the large-type rights for the highest advance they had ever received for a large-type work. The orders kept arriving: it was all very exciting, Judith wrote to Anne. Money was flowing "in gratifyingly large amounts," agent Timothy Seldes informed his doubtless happy client in August.

Anne had achieved her first real commercial success.

The year the novel came out the movie rights were sold to the Broadway producers McCann and Nugent, who were eager to make it their first film in the wake of a series of stage hits. But the plan fell apart, and although the company eventually renewed the option, nothing further transpired. A few years later came interest from actress and producer Joanne Woodward (not mirrored by her actor husband Paul Newman) and gossip columns also mentioned attention from Diane Keaton, but again nothing came of it. A script for the novel had been written by Hume Cronyn and Susan Cooper, and *Baltimore Magazine* reported that Anne was happy that it was true to the book, although she claimed to be unable to read screenplays: "It's all such a foreign language to me—it doesn't really seem like it has much to do with me." Again the project petered out. Yet another wave of interest crested in 1997, with entertainment magazine *Variety* reporting that the option had been picked up by TriStar Pictures after a bidding war with two other parties—but the movie of *Dinner at the Homesick Restaurant* remains unmade.

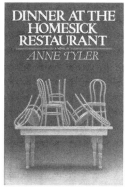

Many years later, in 2014, Christie's auctioned a first edition of *Dinner at the Homesick Restaurant* still in the original dust jacket designed by the celebrated illustrator Fred Marcellino. The auction was part of a project called "First Editions, Second Thoughts" run by PEN America, the writers' organization, in aid of free expression for artists worldwide. The many writers and artists whose works were being auctioned were asked to annotate their works for the event, and on the front pages of hers Anne wrote:

Still the book closest to my heart, not counting whatever I'm currently working on. A.T.

I had the title before I had a novel to go with it. And I had the restaurant idea before I had the title. Anne Tyler.

Other annotations were scattered throughout the copy: Anne's memories of being in hospital with croup as a child, and, next to the section about Pearl and the children playing Monopoly after their terrible scene, the comment that she considered this passage "the most important one in the book" because it illustrated how families had no choice but to keep on grating along together. She and Cody felt the same about time, Anne also wrote further along. At the end of Chapter 8, which is written from the point of view of Cody's son, she scribbled along the top and side of the page that she could write forever about how people's stories completely transform themselves depending on different viewpoints—and how every version is as sincerely believed as the previous one. She stapled in photocopies relating to her Great-Aunt Sadie, whose diaries had provided the inspiration for Pearl's. She also admitted to an important second thought about a key point in the plot, Pearl's abandonment by her husband Beck: "If I were writing this book now, I think I would have had Beck leave Pearl for another woman. It seems slightly unrealistic that such a garrulous man would simply strike off on his own the way he did. He'd have met some woman who flattered him, and he would decide he was in love with her, at least briefly."

In the auction the book went for $22,000.

When much older Anne was to observe that, when she looked back at *Dinner at the Homesick Restaurant*, she could see that she used to be a far better writer—an uncomfortable thought:

That's not a good feeling at all.

§

Her unexpected new wealth now impelled Anne to make provision for her daughters. In November 1982 she signed a trust providing for their private education, college tuition, related travel, and general welfare; on reaching twenty-five, both could request their share of the capital if they so wished. On Anne's death, royalties from her works would be collected for the trust, which also allocated limited funds in support of Taghi's aging mother Razieh Modarressi. A few years later Anne further assigned each of the girls a 6.25% interest in *The Accidental Tourist*, intending to transfer the same amounts again a year later.

With her worldwide reputation Anne was now becoming increasingly in demand. As the decade advanced a stream of requests started to arrive for new fiction, nonfiction, book reviews and blurbs; she was asked to judge literary contests and literary fellowship applications, nominate writers for prizes, write introductions, provide evaluations on writers seeking university tenure, attend literary conferences, lecture or be a Visiting Professor at universities, and even to contribute to a recipe book for a good cause. She was invited out to lunch with publishers, both native and foreign, and asked to appear on television, speak at annual dinners, donate signed copies of her books for charity, and even be photographed for *Sports Illustrated*. Many of these requests she was of course unable to meet, or more likely was unwilling to do so. She would have been left little time for her writing—let alone all the signing in triplicate and copious filling out of a constant stream of contracts and foreign tax exemption forms now arriving from her agent.

But she did agree to some entreaties, such as the plea for a recipe, and the request for an evaluation of the work of writer Lamar Herrin for tenure at Cornell University (he got it). She also agreed to contribute front matter to a number of other works. Starting in 1983, for example, she was invited to introduce and help select at least four anthologies of short stories (where she wrote that she was a firm believer in the short story and its special place as an art form all its own, not as a truncated, substitute sort of novel). Anne also provided the introduction to *In Black and White*, an evocative 1985 collection of photographs taken by Eudora Welty during the Depression. Many of Eudora's subjects had been black and living in difficult circumstances; Anne observed in her introduction that the most important factor in the pictures was Eudora's "affectionate and unjudging regard" for those she photographed, the same regard she had shown for her fictional characters that made them feel safe in her hands.

Anne always clearly stated her preference for fiction, both writing and reading it, but she dabbled at least a little on the other side (if once declining a request from Times Books to write a biography of Jane Austen, spelled "Austin" in their letter). In 1977 her "Trouble in the Boys' Club," an article about the corrupt Maryland mayor Marvin Mandel, had appeared in *New Republic* magazine; in the November 1985 issue of *Art and Antiques* magazine she published a three-and-a-half-page article on Dr. Claribel and Miss Etta Cone, two wealthy Baltimore sisters who in the early twentieth century amassed a surprisingly modern art collection that is now the pride of the Baltimore Museum of Art. Her piece painted lively character portraits of the two ladies and pointed to the startling, even laughable nature of the art to many at the time—colorful, splashy paintings by Matisse, Picasso, Gauguin, Renoir, and Cézanne that now glowed with what Anne called a "quiet, warm exuberance" in the chilly spaces of the museum. She wrote of conjectures that Miss Etta had conceived a passion for their friend Gertrude Stein, the famous writer who introduced them to some of the artists in person and spurred them to their many acquisitions. Anne told the magazine that she had had a wonderful time getting to know the two sisters.

The following year she also wrote a moving profile of her former Duke University teacher Reynolds Price for *Vanity Fair* magazine. Two years earlier the ebullient Reynolds, now a celebrated novelist, had been diagnosed with cancer of the spinal cord. The tumor was arrested with surgery followed by radiation and steroid therapy, but Reynolds was no longer able to walk and used a wheelchair. In due course he returned to writing, and when Anne went to visit him at his home near Durham she found him as high-spirited as ever, showing off his new biceps from working the chair. He had even returned to teaching, the "serious hobby" that he said kept him in touch with the next generation. As Reynolds zipped around, Anne wrote in "Reynolds Price: Duke of Writers," she could still see the scarlet lining of the long black cloak swirling out behind him that she had misremembered from her youth.

§

Anne no doubt enjoyed the sales and often stunning reviews of her novels but, as usual, she did not enjoy the publication phase. Every time the actual writing was over she would wish anew that she was not a writer, saying that she hated the stage after finishing a book—the "bad part" when she had to deal with galley proofs, publicity, and biographical sketches.

She was protected and cushioned by her very understanding agent Timothy but could not avoid the editing process with Judith at Knopf, which forced her to see what she had previously overlooked and made her hackles go up. She hated turning in a novel and having to face what she called "this day of reckoning." Judith would suggest alterations that sometimes included a change of title that might not have come so easily in the first place, leaving Anne to spend ages thinking up a new one. (*Celestial Navigation* was one that came to her before she had a book for it: at the time she was simply in love with the phrase and had even given it as a name to a cat.) Then, when the work finally saw the light of day, with perhaps one narrow volume the result of all that time and effort, on the very first page Anne would see something she wanted to cross out. "By that time you hate it because it's too long ago, and you're too embarrassed about the whole thing. I think that's much harder than writing."

Publication itself, making the book available to readers (as much as a year later in most cases), Anne saw as almost an invasion of privacy:

> *Publishing a book is just about the worst thing that can happen to a writer...It's like losing your soul, in a way. It's something very private that you have made and one day it comes out, and people read it, and talk about it in front of you. And ask questions.*

In acknowledging that her work would actually be read by other people, Anne was obliged to accept that "daydreams I've been weaving are no longer my private property." She was to learn that it was best not to think about readers while writing, just to try and sink into the world she was describing. But at the very end, of course, she had to think about them. She would read her final draft pretending she was someone else, to make sure that what she had written made sense from outside:

> *At that point, I seem to picture my readers as brand-new to me. They have the neuter, faceless quality of people in dreams. It comes as a shock later when a real-life reader writes to me and turns out to be a specific human being.*

It was hard enough just having to end the book and to find that she intensely missed her characters: it was as if she had a "bunch of imaginary playmates and you get all excited about them, then all of a sudden you have to expose them to the cold, cruel world and have people judge them." When she sent the latest book to New York to be read by her agent she used to picture her characters taking a train to the city and feel that her heart was broken—they were limited or shy people, brave to be going up there on their own, and some of them unable to fend for themselves. She could only hope they would make it. But then, after they had been accepted for publication and were out by themselves in a book, Anne gave them no further thought. Sometimes she would even need to re-read a novel to find out what she had written about someone.

All the same, Anne would look forward to ending a work:

For weeks before I finish a novel I swear I'm going to celebrate the minute I've mailed it off—throw a party, take to strong drink. But when I come back from the post office the house seems so quiet, and I can't believe how white and bleak my study is.

She would then have to endure the disruptive effect of publication, the constant ringing of the phone, followed by the inability to get anything new off the ground. When she went to her room to write, it didn't happen. "I go there every day no matter what. For three weeks nothing. Not a word. Then two days went by, and I got a quarter of a page." There would be false starts: beginning with one book in January and ending up with a different one in December, or stories that trailed away and died just after the second paragraph, others that looked wonderful on Friday afternoon and terrible on Monday morning. Anne, forty when *Dinner at the Homesick Restaurant* was published, was all too aware that there were limits to what she should attempt.

What Anne did like about a career in writing were the appreciative comments from readers, people sending her letters to say they had been up all night reading her book and had forgotten to feed the cat (although she stated modestly that such letters were rare). Then she would feel that she and the readers, in their respective solitudes, had somehow managed to touch without intruding upon each other. "We've spent some time on neutral territory, sharing a life that belongs to neither of us. That I do care about."

Retreat

But the worst aspect of a writing career for Anne, ultimately, was publicity. For the first time she was really dealing with fame.

I used to think I'd like to be famous but that was based on a misapprehension: I pictured fame as my entering other people's lives, not their entering mine. Besides, I've never been able to autograph a book without feeling like an imposter.

In her earlier years as a novelist Anne had been fairly open—willing to be interviewed in her house, to write about herself, and to be out in public. She had happily spoken to a reporter in Montreal and agreed to a book-signing in a department store after the publication of her first novel; welcomed journalist Clifford Ridley into her home in Baltimore as she was writing *Celestial Navigation*; taken part in the panel discussion at Duke in spring 1974; and produced a very personal article about her writing for the *Washington Post* in 1976, followed by the equally intimate essay "Still Just Writing" a few years later. She had been interviewed at home once more in 1977 (this time early in the morning, during her sacred wife-and-mother time), again around a year later by British author Paul Binding—afterward driving him to the bus station in Baltimore—and yet again in 1980, on which occasion she admitted to the journalist that the last time she was in New York was fourteen years earlier, when she had been forced to return home with morning sickness from pregnancy.

But the feeling that she was wasting energy better spent on writing, and that talking about writing affected her ability to do it, was gradually encroaching. Following the publication of *Earthly Possessions* Anne had gone to Iowa City for a particularly heavy engagement: a reading, a party, a special workshop for fiction students and a discussion of the novel at an undergraduate seminar. She even agreed to be interviewed in the car on the way to the airport afterward. During the interview—despite the packed eighteen hours she had just put in—Anne articulated her growing unease about such engagements:

I feel that I've become increasingly closed down, self-protective...There are things I just refuse to do. I wouldn't go out and give some sort of talk. Not only because I'm nervous in public but because I feel that kind of a thing is a drain.

She would not even go to a PTA meeting—they could get along without her, Anne maintained. She was in any case naturally solitary. Far from seeking to lose the sense of distance bestowed by her unusual childhood, Anne had come to cherish it, and neither she nor her brothers could stand to be in a crowd of people for very long. The only real trouble that writing had ever brought her, Anne voiced at about this time, was the occasional sense of being invaded by the outside world. And, as the exterior world began to feel less dependable, the interior became more of a refuge: in her own words, "I keep buttressing my inside world, where people go on meaning well and surprising other people with little touches of grace."

There was a visit to nearby Loyola College in Baltimore in January 1982 for two hours of a writing class followed by a lunch, and at the end of the year Anne also consented to another discussion panel arranged by Reynolds Price back at Duke, to which she was now regularly donating manuscripts and signed editions of her work (no doubt at their eager request). But, after years of effort from Reynolds to get her back on campus, she reportedly only agreed because Eudora Welty was also participating. A week before the event in December, a reporter called Anne at home and asked for an interview. "I'm allergic to that sort of thing," she responded cheerfully. "I did learn long ago not to talk at all. It doesn't seem to have anything to do with writing." She had talked too much in an interview about one novel-in-progress [*Pantaleo*] that then turned out to be unpublishable, she explained. Talking about writing made her "nervous" and "superstitious," even with other writers. (With her one writer friend around this time, a children's author, Anne claimed mostly to discuss what was on sale at the supermarket. She felt "so vulnerable" about her work.) Informed that there was going to be a press conference as part of the upcoming program at Duke, Anne joked that she hadn't heard about it and that if she hadn't heard about it, she wouldn't have to turn up, right?

The night before her appearance Anne attended a dinner hosted by the president of the university and was introduced to David Guy, a young novelist also on the panel; he found her "beautiful, brilliant, and entirely gracious." She had taken the trouble to read David's first book *Football Dreams* and immediately complimented him on it, quipping that she had been expecting someone a little beefier. The following day David noted that, while Anne remained gracious throughout the proceedings, she also seemed "testy." Before the press conference in the morning she and Eudora disappeared to the restroom for a remarkably long time. On emerging, Anne drily asked Reynolds, "Did you think we'd taken a powder?" Wearing a tweed jacket and wool skirt, and flanked by Eudora in a plain gray dress, she took her place and deftly fielded questions from a dozen journalists. Both authors talked admiringly of each other's work and about their writing methods, although Anne deflected some questioning with the statement that if she talked about a process then for a while she would be unable to use it.

The panel later on was in a large auditorium holding around four hundred people. It was mid afternoon on a weekday, but the place was packed. As Anne, Eudora, Reynolds and David waited in a small anteroom, the noise from inside was horrifying, like a mob. David looked at Anne, who had gone white.

"Why did I ever want to be a writer?" he asked her.

"So you wouldn't have to do things like this," she replied.

As they all walked into the auditorium the crowd spontaneously burst into loud applause. But the panel did not exactly go as planned: there had clearly been some kind of change in Anne since her seemingly free-and-easy participation on the previous panel at Duke back in 1974. Now she gave almost monosyllabic replies and to David she seemed in some fundamental way to resent—or at least resist—the whole situation. Anne was extraordinarily intelligent and articulate, he observed, but on this occasion she was "right on the edge of bristly, as if she wanted to say, to every question, what right do you have to ask me that?"

Even Reynolds could not get Anne to hold forth. Fortunately, Eudora loved to talk, and was an acute and entertaining speaker who wound up dominating the proceedings and making it a success.

In the evening Anne was due to give a reading from her own work, although revealing at lunch that she had never been to a reading herself. "I've never wanted to. I don't understand why people go to readings." When she was reading a book to herself she brought so much to that experience, she said elsewhere, and did not necessarily interpret it the same way as the author. David could see that she didn't want to be gawked at but this time, for him at least, her performance proved excellent: he thought her a good reader with a strong stage presence, and could not understand why she disliked doing it.

However, there were differing opinions: the mike had failed to work properly, and Anne later received a letter from someone in the audience complaining it was the worst reading they had ever been to. That did it, Anne remarked to a friend. For the next thirty years, she refused all public appearances and interviews and became famous as a recluse.

She used an unlisted number with her editor Judith, who was always very firm with anyone who wanted to get in touch with Anne, agreeing only to forward any letters. In 1983, when Anne was elected to the American Academy and Institute of Arts and Letters, Judith knew without being told that she would not turn up in person at the ceremony to sit on a platform in front of an audience. The same held true when *Dinner at the Homesick Restaurant* earned Anne her nomination for the PEN/Faulkner award: Judith just assumed she would not attend the event. Anne's agent Timothy Seldes informed Penguin Books in Canada, who were anxious for Anne to come and promote her work, that she was a very private person who had not done and never would do a book tour. Anne was also strictly incognito on a week's visit to Britain in spring 1984, when she and Taghi and the girls stayed at the Strand Palace hotel in London—although she did have lunch with the directors of her British literary agency A.M. Heath (who wrote to Timothy to say what a delightful person Anne was, "totally unspoilt by her success"). Even when Duke University offered her an honorary degree a few years later Anne turned it down, despite promises that she would not have to say a word at the ceremony.

Later she would instruct her mother to destroy all the letters she had written home as a young woman. (Phyllis was very loath to do so, and instead apparently passed what she described as the "wonderful" letters to academic Elizabeth Evans—whether with or without Anne's permission is not known.) Phyllis said she was "shamefully proud" of Anne, and regretful that her daughter was so reticent. She and Lloyd once had the happy experience of waking up on October 25 and hearing on National Public Radio that it was Anne Tyler's birthday.

Anne had decided on her priorities, and saying no, more and more, made her happier and happier. She was learning to be what she termed "narrow" as regards what she was willing to do. Often her books came out of her own confinement, she maintained.

Why do people imagine that writers, having chosen the most private of professions, should be any good at performing in public, or should have the slightest desire to tell their secrets to interviewers from ladies' magazines? I feel I am only holding myself together by being extremely firm and decisive about what I will do and what I will not do. I will write my books and raise the children. Anything else just fritters me away.

Invited to visit the White House by President Bush, Anne turned down the offer.

§

Anne's next novel, arguably her most famous, was *The Accidental Tourist*, published in 1985 with illustrator Fred Marcellino's iconic winged armchair on the cover.

The novel had taken a while to gestate: she had poured out so much in her last book, said Anne, that she had had trouble "refueling." It eventually got off the ground but, as usual, she was superstitious about discussing any book-in-progress, even with Taghi, and refused to talk about it—though mentioning in a letter that the new novel was "going ROTTENLY." The draft ended up going through so many changes that, looking back, Anne found it hard to think what she had had in mind when she started.

The central character, Macon Leary, writes guidebooks for American businessmen who hate to travel and want to know where they can buy Kentucky Fried Chicken in Stockholm. Macon's 12-year-old son Ethan has been murdered in a hold-up in a burger restaurant, and he and his wife Sarah have been left alone in their home in an older part of Baltimore (probably Roland Park). When she moves out, uncomforted by her husband, the grieving but self-contained Macon slowly descends into obsessive behavior. After breaking a leg falling over a laundry basket that he has strapped to Ethan's old skateboard to make clothes washing more efficient, he goes to recuperate with his eccentric siblings in the old family home. When his son's dog Edward starts biting people Macon engages a dog trainer, the talkative, spiky-heeled Muriel, who lives a precarious existence with her sickly young son Alexander. A relationship slowly develops and Macon starts to feel more alive, although uncertain about his future with Muriel; nevertheless, he moves into their shabby home in a rough area of Baltimore, so unknown to Macon that it is almost a foreign country—friendly neighbors, but also muggers—where he can be an entirely different person. Then Sarah decides to return to the marriage, confronting him with a terrible choice.

Anne may have been having some amusement at her own expense with her choice of profession for the routine-loving Macon. She felt exactly the same about travel as he did, liking to stay in one location and just examine it more and more deeply, rather than skimming across the surface of a whole load of other places:

> *I like routine and rituals and I hate leaving home; I have a sense of digging my heels in. I refuse to drive on freeways. I dread our annual vacation. Yet I'm continually prepared for travel: it is physically impossible for me to buy any necessity without buying a travel-sized version as well. I have a little toilet kit, with soap and a nightgown, forever packed and ready to go. How do you explain that?*

Other of Anne's traits surface in Macon: obsession with correct grammar, dislike of shopping malls (Macon's "notion of hell"), insomnia, love of orderliness and routine—including a specific day for grocery shopping—and a tendency to retreat from the world. Most interesting people were "a bit on the spectrum," Anne believed, admitting that two of her brothers never let their wives fill the dishwasher because they did it all wrong, and that her father used to say the same to her mother. She herself admitted to alphabetizing her spices just like Macon's eccentric sister Rose, who arranges her groceries in the kitchen cupboards according to the letter they begin with.

143

Muriel, conversely, at first felt very foreign to Anne. She had worried that Muriel would put readers off or bore them with her monologues, but did grow fond of her as she came to know her better, and wanted her to be seen in the best light.

Anne deliberately did not depict the moment of Ethan's death. Part of the unusual difficulty in writing the book was because she hated to handle even the thought of a child's dying. Anne was "guiltily aware" that, as in all her books, she tended to avert her eyes from the huge events, especially those that were physically confrontational. She did not know whether this was due to the Quaker in her, or being female, or just general cowardice. It was not something she was proud of, believing it to be a kind of shirking. Similarly, she was not interested in having one of her characters commit murder, which was "a big outside thing, I want something internal going on." Superstitiously, she had also deliberately made Ethan younger than her two daughters, so she would not start thinking as they came up to that age, "Oh no, what have I set in motion?" and could take comfort from the fact that they were already past that danger.

Another problem was the ending, originally intended to be entirely the opposite to the version that finally appeared. Anne wrote the whole final chapter the first way and then realized she could not do it, not only because it spoiled the dramatic line of the plot, but also because it meant abandoning Muriel's son Alexander. She decided instead that, in the end, the relationship between Macon and Muriel definitely had a future:

I see Macon and Muriel in an edgy, incongruous but ultimately workable marriage, Macon forever frustrated by Muriel's behavior and yet more flexible than his old self. Alexander turns out <u>wonderfully</u>. (By that I mean: happy.)

One of Anne's daughters remarked that if Macon had not stayed with Muriel, Alexander would have grown up a nerd. Anne thought Macon would always be "appalled" by Muriel, on some level, but at the same time "heartened and warmed" by her.

Thirty-five years later, Anne re-read *The Accidental Tourist* for the first time in decades, and approved her then approach, if again feeling that she had been a better writer when younger:

I was more detailed, I took more time. It's not as if I'm in a rush now, but I trust the reader more. I don't feel like I have to say that much about the character's inner feelings. But then as I read The Accidental Tourist I thought, Well, it's kind of nice to see all of Macon's inner feelings there.

At the time of publishing, Anne had become a known quantity in the book world and *The Accidental Tourist* had an initial print run of 75,000 copies. Paperback and book club deals made $1.3 million before it was even released, with the paperback edition published in 1986 selling nearly two million copies in five years. The novel was another huge success, the second of Anne's in succession to be a finalist for the Pulitzer Prize (this time losing out to Larry McMurtry's *Lonesome Dove*); it also won the National Book Critics Circle Award for Fiction in 1985, the Ambassador Book Award for Fiction in 1986, and was a Book of the Month Club main selection. Magazines had been surprisingly uninterested in prior serialization, however: Anne's agent sent it round the upscale publications *McCall's*, *Vanity Fair*, *Playboy*, *GQ* and *Redbook* with a $25,000 "floor" for further bids, but received no offers. *Playboy* commented that the "floor" was rather steep.

Critics were rapturous. For the *Times* in Britain, Anne Tyler's "marvelous talent" took Macon from the brink of madness to acceptance with a comic skill that never quite eclipsed the tragedy behind the novel's deceptive simplicity. The *Times Literary Supplement* wrote that Anne had achieved a distinctive comic combination of warmth and astringency that was likely to make her a powerful influence. "Brilliant, funny, sad and sensitive," Nick Hornby would later write of the novel.

"Words fail me: one cannot reasonably expect fiction to be much better than this," enthused the *Washington Post Book World* back home. The novel was "beautiful, incandescent, heartbreaking, exhilarating," wrote the reviewer, and the fiction of Anne Tyler was something both unique and extraordinary in contemporary American literature. Once again, Anne achieved the honor of a page-one review in the *New York Times Book Review*, this time by her Pulitzer competitor Larry McMurtry: "Miss Tyler shows, with a fine clarity, the mingling of misery and contentment in the daily lives of her families, reminds us how alike—and yet distinct—happy and unhappy families can be." The *Los Angeles Times Book Review* did not know if there was a better American writer going, and could not think of another major novelist "who so plainly is still gaining on herself." A page-turner, said John Updike, who with blurred eyes had stopped his night-time reading twenty pages before the end, fallen into a troubled sleep, woken before dawn, then read to the end and only then was able to relax.

Photo credit: (c) Diana Walker

The novel was full of wonderful characters, commented the *Canberra Times* in Australia, not the least of whom was the neurotic Edward (a corgi just like Anne's dog Ernest, and with the same personality). The *Wall Street Journal* agreed: Edward was "the most winning Welsh corgi in American fiction," and for John Updike, Edward was for a good part of the novel the most sympathetic and intelligible of the characters. More than a few critics felt that the irritable Edward, with his lip curling, moaning, and suspicious looks, was expressing the rage and confusion that Macon himself holds down. Anne's portrayal of Baltimore, too, came in for specific comment. As one who had spent most of her life there, wrote critic Barbara Rich in the *Women's Review of Books*, she could "attest to the fidelity with which Anne Tyler captures the essence of the city, its insular neighborhoods and clannish residents." Anne had made

Baltimore her own, said John Updike, echoing the point: her Baltimore, though a city of neighborhoods and ingrained custom, was also a piece of the American Northeast and Western culture.

However, in contrast to the general enthusiasm, John Blades in the *Chicago Tribune* let rip with savage accusations of soap opera, cockeyed humanism and, above all, sugary sweetness, "sedative resolutions" to life's most grievous and perplexing problems. He felt that for all Anne's seductive qualities—"the great charm and coziness of her fictional universe, her compassion for misfits, and, not least, her soothing, almost tranquilizing voice"—there was something annoyingly synthetic about the work itself. However wise and wonderful, her fiction was seriously diluted by the promiscuous use of artificial sweeteners, making Anne "our foremost NutraSweet novelist." A British critic some years later was in agreement, amplifying that John Blades' use of the word "Nutrasweet" was worse than simply saying sugary: Anne's sweetness was not even real and might furtively do harm, fooling us when we think we are being comforted.

John Blades went on to carp that, while Anne had been deservedly praised for recreating Baltimore in crisp and evocative detail, it was a place that did not exist outside her own imagination: it bore no relation to the real world and neither did "those homey, endearing creatures" who inhabited it.

Anne claimed that early on she had been able to stay detached from both good and bad reviews by becoming enmeshed in the next novel, granting that there was an element of self-protection in this. She tried to read reviews as if referring to a completely different person, or would sometimes read them to see if they could tell her what she was writing about, although declaring she had never seen a review that could do so—perhaps a reference to the very different interpretations critics and academics have put upon her novels. (She also claimed to be unable to answer most of the questions set at the end of her books for reading groups.) In the *New York Times*, for instance, critic Michiko Kakutani once wrote that for Anne, the family—and its alternative, a life alone—had come to stand for two particular imperatives in American life: the need for community and safety, and the desire for flight, adventure, and independence. "This is why I don't read reviews," Anne laughed in response. "I'm not thinking at *all* about what it means to be American." She tried to think as little as possible about critical reception, or sales figures, because the only way she could happily write a book was still to pretend that no one else would ever read it—knowing this to be a "cowardly approach."

It is likely that Anne saw or was aware of the *Chicago Tribune* review, frequently quoted for its "Nutrasweet" label. Against similar accusations she later had this to say:

I know the word "sentimental" has been used. I'm aware I'm not confronting things. That might be one of the make-believes in my novels, that people always mean well, no matter what their flaws are, and try to be optimistic.

Ultimately, she was to arrive at a point of no longer being able to read any reviews at all.

§

A few years after publication the novel was made into a movie starring Kathleen Turner as Sarah, William Hurt as Macon, Geena Davis as Muriel, and four Welsh corgis alternately playing the pivotal part of Edward the dog. The rights had sold for a six-figure sum.

In the fall of 1987 Anne found herself driving the movie's director Lawrence Kasdan around Baltimore in her little Toyota, showing him possible places to shoot: the supermarket Macon had gone to, the kind of neighborhoods where Muriel would have lived. She was delighted that the decision had been taken to film her novel in the city (not necessarily a given). "I love the idea that it's being shot here," she announced. "I'm proud of Baltimore, and I like to think that they're using the places that I had in mind when I was writing." A number of exterior scenes were shot in Roland Park, and in other locations around the city such as St Paul's Street and Cold Spring Lane, where a set was built to represent the animal hospital where Muriel works.

Locals were agog at the filming going on around their streets, and in Roland Park locations like Eddie's grocery store. About 500 Baltimoreans were cast as extras. Other scenes were shot abroad, in London and Paris, while most of the interior scenes were shot at Warner Bros studios in Los Angeles.

Anne had nothing to do with the actual making of the movie —having reportedly declined to write the screenplay—but was involved throughout. She was invited to sit in on a read-through of the script, which had been co-authored by director Larry. He was very nervous about having Anne present, he recalled, as was the cast, but all went well and afterward Anne complimented each cast member individually on some aspect of their performance. She also later visited the set to watch some of the filming, enjoying it because it seemed sensitive to what her novel was about (and helping out by taking Larry's son for a long walk to keep him occupied). It was interesting to Anne to see the level of patience and attention to detail that making a movie demanded, and she went to view some of the "dailies"— unedited footage—and even flew out to Los Angeles to see the Leary siblings' house constructed on the Warner sound stage. Ultimately Anne thought the adaptation very true to the book, and was particularly pleased with William Hurt's portrayal of Macon.

Macon's supposed travel guidebook featured in the film, but with a slightly different title from the way it appeared in the novel. Other changes included an enlarged role for Macon's wife Sarah, perhaps because she was played by big star Kathleen Turner, and omitting some of Macon's more peculiar time-saving ideas such as washing his clothes in the shower—

perhaps to downplay his incipient eccentricity and present him as a more conventionally tragic figure.

Reviews of the movie varied. One *Washington Post* reviewer was happy to see it so faithful to the original, and film critic Roger Ebert loved it. William Hurt as Macon achieved the impossible, in his view: playing a character who was depressed, low-key and intensely private through most of the movie, and yet somehow winning sympathy. What director Lawrence Kasdan had achieved was just as tricky: "I've never seen a movie so sad in which there was so much genuine laughter." For Roger Ebert *The Accidental Tourist* was one of the best films of the year.

Richard Schickel of *Time* magazine, on the other hand, dubbed William Hurt's performance of a monosyllabic role monotonous —too hard to tell the difference between William Hurt sad and William Hurt happy. Everything was dim about this "glum and self-important adaptation of Anne Tyler's upper-cute novel." A different *Washington Post* critic thought the adaptation *too* faithful to the novel and therefore unsuccessful as a movie. The *New York Times* was equally unimpressed. One review pointed out that a key revelation of character in Anne Tyler's novels was more apt to occur while someone was driving a car or putting away groceries than during a more conventionally dramatic situation: Anne's writing was beautifully attuned to the minutiae of daily routines, to the seemingly trivial habits that both defined and circumscribed her characters' lives. But in the movie version of *The Accidental Tourist* it was the broad strokes that stood out, said the critic. In the novel Anne depicted Macon's long slow awakening after the tragedy of losing his son "in tiny, artful increments," while in the movie Macon barely seemed to change at all until the lengthy, meandering film was almost over: "Mr. Hurt flinches his way through the story with a pained morose expression that doesn't lift until the film's final moments." Much of Anne's dialogue from the novel had been included but not with the same effect, the review continued, leading to scenes of "crashing obviousness" that could have been better handled. Geena Davis tried hard but was "sandbagged" by her role, coming across as insufferable.

Another review from the same paper felt the movie had no particular reason to exist, bringing virtually nothing—no color, no nuance, not even much liveliness—to bear upon the novel on which it was based, "a novel whose author, Anne Tyler, said all there was to say about her characters on the page."

Despite the criticism, the movie was nominated for two Golden Globes and four Oscars: Best Picture, Best Adapted Screenplay, Best Original Score for John Williams, and Best Supporting Actress for Geena Davis, which she won. It was also voted Best Picture of the Year by the New York Film Critics Circle (a choice protested by *Time* magazine's Richard Schickel).

Baltimoreans, naturally, approved of the movie. The director of the Maryland Film Commission thought it made the city look great and was "really classy." A number of locals were offended that the movie had opened in Washington, DC first, declaring that the national premiere should have been in their city and that without Anne there would have been no film.

Anne was not at the Washington opening, but agreed to attend the movie's Baltimore premiere at the city's Art Deco Senator Theatre in 1989 on condition the event be used to benefit a worthy cause. About 800 tickets were sold (including Anne's own, which she paid for), raising $20,000 for the Juvenile Diabetes Foundation. She told the Foundation she would not turn up at anything "black-tie" and was late arriving at the champagne and dessert reception, accompanied by Taghi and about a dozen friends and family—passing, on the way in, a cement block commemorating the event that she had already signed with Baltimore mayor Kurt Schmoke. Described by local journalists as pale and "demure as a schoolteacher," Anne declined to comment on the film: "I can't, I'm sorry."

Also present at the Baltimore premiere, if none of the big names from the movie, was local legend John Waters, director of that year's hit movie *Hairspray*. John made up for Anne's reticence by chatting freely to the press and signing popcorn boxes. "It's show business," he declared.

On the day of the movie premiere of her wildly successful novel, Anne dropped into Eddie's supermarket as she often did. "She's a nice lady," one of the staff told a reporter; she had shopped at the market for two or three years before they realized who she was.

§

Anne had given Taghi a word processor for his writing with a dual program in English and Farsi; in return, he gave her an antique lap desk that she could use to lean on when sitting cross-legged on the hard couch composing her first drafts. Taghi, now fifty-three, was still rising extremely early in the morning to get some writing done, either at home or in the office, before starting his work as director of the new Center for Infant Study in the Psychiatry Department at the University of Maryland School of Medicine. (On the wall of his office hung a monochrome photograph, begged off his wife, of a black mother and child—one of Eudora Welty's striking images.) He attributed his return to writing to the many Iranians who had arrived in America after the upheaval in their country: listening to his fellow countrymen talking his native language as they tried to bargain in the shopping malls, Taghi had felt his senses stirred. The excitement became almost unbearable. He felt impelled to write what he called his "invented memoir," *The Book of Absent People*, an Iranian family's secrets in the period leading up to the revolution against the Shah.

Anne's agent Timothy acted for Taghi in trying to interest publishers (mentioning in their covering letters that he was Anne's husband). The manuscript was returned a couple of times before eventually a deal was agreed with Doubleday. The book, published in 1986, achieved a review in the *New York Times*: a wonderful novel, was the verdict, "a veritable enchantment." There was no mention of its author being married to Anne Tyler, although there would be in reviews of his next novel three years later. This was *The Pilgrim's Rules of Etiquette*, greeted by the *Washington Post* as a glimpse into a culture that had seemed elusive and threatening, written by a risk-taking novelist blessed with unusual powers of language and observation. Taghi and Anne had become a masterly team, Taghi writing in Farsi and Anne then helping him translate into English.

Taghi never discussed his psychiatric work at home. Anne thought that psychotherapists really did the opposite of what novelists do: psychotherapists gave a specific label to neuroses, while novelists showed how many mingled colors and shades there were. However, Taghi did present his wife with a work that was of particular help to her as a writer: Erving Goffman's *The Presentation of Self in Everyday Life*, which likened the way people present themselves in society to a sort of theatrical performance. Anne found it to be the most valuable book a novelist could possibly read (and the only sociologist or psychologist she would ever read in her life). "We are always trying to decipher gestures, or as writing teachers say, how to show rather than tell." She was intensely interested, in fact riveted, by peculiarities of manner, just loving that a little sideways slip of the eye or a little compression of the lips could reveal so much. She felt other authors could really benefit from knowing about the book:

I have cause to think about Erving Goffman nearly every day of my life, every time I see people do something unconscious that reveals more than they'll ever know about their interiors. Aren't human beings intriguing? I could go on writing about them forever.

Anne was to remain eternally fascinated by what was unspoken in a conversation, what was revealed by mere gesture or by silence, or by talking too much about something completely irrelevant.

The girls, meanwhile, had grown up and left school, both embarking on careers as artists. Tezh graduated from the Rhode Island School of Design in 1988, and Mitra from the same school a year later. Tezh was exhibiting her lonely, eerie depictions of empty interiors from about 1990, and paintings by Mitra had been on show at a Baltimore art center as early as January 1986, part of an art exhibition by alumni of the Friends School. Anne and Taghi were greatly supportive of a life in art for their daughters—Anne occasionally bought original paintings by artists herself—and happy that they had found something they were passionate about. Seeing both her parents do what they really loved had been a big influence, Mitra was to comment.

But, just as her daughters were gaining independence and going out into the world, and she and Taghi had begun to travel abroad a little, Anne found herself needing to become more involved in the lives of her aging parents.

Returning in the early 1970s from their time helping refugees in Gaza, Phyllis and Lloyd had continued their political activism in Raleigh. For many years they participated in a weekly vigil on the steps of the city's State Capitol against planned production of the B-1 bomber, a costly strategic aircraft capable of carrying nuclear weapons. The nationwide campaign eventually succeeded. Phyllis was integral to the founding of Raleigh's Women's Center, which provided a refuge for ex-prisoners, victims of rape and any woman in need of friendship and support. She also worked very hard lobbying against the death penalty and became particularly well known for her battle to save Velma Barfield, a serial killer who was sentenced to death in 1978. Every week for four years Phyllis visited Velma in Raleigh's Central Prison before Velma was executed by lethal injection in 1984, the first woman to be executed after the resumption of capital punishment in 1976 and the first to die in this way. But over time Lloyd and Phyllis' names appeared less and less in the local press, in protest or support. In 1988, after so many decades of helping others, both were presented with awards by a local chapter of the American Civil Liberties Union. It was likely a parting gesture: they were just about to move to Baltimore to be closer to Anne, leaving behind the house in Raleigh where they had lived for nearly thirty-five years and where Anne had grown up. Both were in their seventies, and would always retain their pacifist stance—Lloyd still turning out the occasional strongly worded letter to the press (this time to the *Baltimore Sun*) on subjects such as Iraq's nuclear weapons program.

With her parents now close by, Anne was glad she no longer needed to go down to Raleigh to see them, but probably had a little less time available for writing. However, another work was already on its way. That same year came the comic, occasionally dark *Breathing Lessons*, her eleventh novel and the one finally to win Anne a Pulitzer. She had written it with the thought that it might be interesting to cover twenty-four hours in the life of a marriage, and she could easily imagine why she had chosen the subject—to her mind, there was no better mirror of character. (It was eventually to feel very claustrophobic, working for so long on the events of just a single day.) Anne admitted "donating" to the novel's main character, Maggie, her own anxiety about getting things right in life: Maggie observes that a state-approved course of instruction is required to drive a car, but that driving a car is "nothing, nothing, compared to living day in and day out with a husband and raising up a new human being."

It was another bestseller (despite sometimes being placed in the childbirth sections in bookstores). The initial 220,000 sales in hardback were nearly double those of *The Accidental Tourist*; sales of the paperback topped a million within two years of its release in October 1989. Figures like these had an inevitable knock-on effect. By September 1991 the latest paperback edition of each of Anne's previous works had sold more than ten times its original sales in hardback.

Breathing Lessons takes place within the span of one hot summer's day as the bickering, long-married Ira and Maggie Moran drive from their home in Baltimore to a funeral in Pennsylvania. As the day progresses Maggie ruminates on her worries—their son Jessie's broken marriage to his wife Fiona, and how they never see their granddaughter—and at the same time harks back to her beginnings with Ira and the decades of their own marriage. Meanwhile, the uncommunicative Ira mulls over what he perceives to be a failed and uneventful life. He had planned on a career in medicine, lying in bed when a little boy and pretending to see patients over his drawn-up knees as a desk (just as Anne had done); instead, he had been obliged to take over his father's picture-framing business, and had married a woman who now drives him mad—a meddler and a muddler, too emotional, too talkative, and too slapdash. He loves Maggie, but can't stand the way she refuses to take her own life seriously, seeming to believe that it's a sort of practice life that can be played around with in the hope of second and third chances coming along to get it right.

On the way back from the funeral Maggie persuades Ira to take a detour to see their former daughter-in-law and grandchild; once there, she persuades Fiona to come back to Baltimore with her little girl for a visit, in the hope that Fiona will reconcile with their son. Maggie still thinks change is possible but Ira understands that this is not the case; events then teach her that she must learn to endure, rather than trying to stage-manage other people's lives. For Anne, both the book and its title were about grasping the hard things in life that should be instinctive.

Breathing Lessons won the Pulitzer Prize for Fiction in 1989 (leaving Anne "flabbergasted"), and was also a finalist for the 1988 National Book Award and listed as one of *Time* magazine's best books of 1988. With this ultimate stamp of approval the serious academic studies of her works, previously a trickle, became a flood. And yet, to a number of critics the book was a disappointment. The Pulitzer award is sometimes viewed as more about past literary achievement and the establishment of a respected niche in American letters than the actual qualities of any one book, and it was argued that Anne's success was of this ilk. A scathing piece in the *National Review* suggested she was an unworthy winner, giving an undiscerning audience "all-encompassing, non-judgmental, low-grade soap-opera formats." Anne Tyler paid no attention to evil in the universe, thundered this critic, and if she were a better writer the disruptive heart of darkness might pierce through.

Certainly the *New York Times Book Review* thought the novel a "slightly thinner mixture," lacking the characterful Muriel of the previous novel, and, in an echo of the *National Review* comment, observed that Anne's books in general lacked any hint of the racial friction eating away at the very Baltimore neighborhoods she was devoting her life to depicting. Her people were "eerily virtuous, Quakerishly tolerant of all strangers, all races." Sex, too, was touched upon too lightly, so that compared with Anne's graphic realism in other matters, her total portrait of motivation was tilted out of balance. The humor in *Breathing Lessons* was "unfunny slapstick," an effort to corral extra readers. The *New York Review of Books* also saw the work as less substantial, and as demonstrating the "whimsicality and even cuteness" that it believed sometimes affected Anne. In Australia, the *Canberra Times* dismissed the novel as essentially a boring account of human failings and stupidity. Insular and provincial with little concern for the outside world, sniffed their critic Michael Denholm, wondering on the basis of this book why Anne Tyler was so popular in the US. "In its concentration on the personal, this novel reflects only too well the myopia of Middle America."

Anne was particularly upset by one review in her home country—David Klinghoffer in the *National Review* claiming that her distaste and condescension [for her lower-class characters] were palpable:

I'm very distressed to hear that someone thinks I'm mocking my characters. Why would I bother writing about people I look down on?

But critical comments were in the minority. Most reviewers enjoyed the comedy and loved Maggie, recognizing her essential innocence and humanity despite the damaging interference in other people's lives. *Newsweek* deemed Anne to be moving from strength to strength; the *Washington Post Book World* thought she had surpassed herself. Another *New York Times* review saw the Morans' outing as "a metaphor both for their 28-year marital odyssey, and for the halting, circuitous journey all of us make through life—away from and back to our family roots, out of innocence into sorrow, wisdom and loss." In Britain the *Times Literary Supplement* felt *Breathing Lessons* fully confirmed Anne's reputation as one of the most skilled and sensitive contemporary writers, and understood Maggie as a "sloppy, aging, American version of Jane Austen's Emma." The sheer power of the novel was immensely comforting, decreed the *Times*, while for the *Observer* the work was "enchantingly peculiar," teetering on the edge of being cute but redeemed by Anne's sense of the sadness of things; she was "remarkable."

A chapter from *Breathing Lessons* was published in the *New Yorker* and the novel was a Book of the Month Club main selection. In 1994 it became a made-for-TV movie with James Garner and Joanne Woodward in the main roles, with Joanne winning a Golden Globe Award and a Screen Actors Guild Award. The work was also adapted as a stage play that ran in Seattle in 2003; in 2021, it was translated and published in Iran.

The morning after winning the Pulitzer, Anne reportedly dismissed an inquisitive reporter with the polite statement that she could not be interrupted because she was in the middle of a sentence, although declaring at least that she was "very pleased." She sent a proxy to pick up the Pulitzer.

By the time I won it I'd been on a number of prize-judging panels, so I knew if you win a prize it just means you're the one that everyone agrees they don't hate. There's so much horse trading, I can't take it terribly seriously.

She did love getting a literary prize, she admitted many years later, but added that in the long run it was not as meaningful as she might have thought it would be. Prizes were not the real reward: being in the middle of a writing day was. After a slow morning she would look at what she had already written, spot something not working and pick up a pen to change a word, and then another, and then all of a sudden three hours would have gone by. That was the part that made her "so happy."

§

By 1988, the year *Breathing Lessons* was published, Anne was as much a Baltimore character as director John Waters. As a marketing ploy a Roland Park deli owner wrote her an open letter in the press, suggesting she come by for a lunch that would be served so quickly she would be back at work in thirty minutes. The following year a local community college academic arranged a two-day Anne Tyler symposium at a

Baltimore hotel, offering about 200 scholars and devotees a multitude of academic papers on her work and throwing in a literary tour of Baltimore (to include Roland Park).

Washington Post book critic Jonathan Yardley, a reviewer and fan of Anne's novels who coincidentally lived in Roland Park himself, felt that the titles of the papers presented at the symposium were obscure and pedantic, and that it was premature to subject Anne at this stage of her life to a scrutiny usually offered to the likes of Byron or James Joyce. It was true that a number of titles seemed a little rarefied, including as they did *Welty, Tyler and Traveling Salesmen: The Wandering Hero Unhorsed*; *Something Out of Nothing: Creative Crazies in the Fiction of Anne Tyler*; and *Macon Leary: A Character in Search of his Anima*. Other even more obscure suggestions had arrived from universities all over the US—part of the burgeoning industry in Anne Tyler studies that continues to this day—but had been refused, including an entire paper on the role of Edward the dog in *The Accidental Tourist*.

Anne, predictably, declined to take part in the symposium, although wishing the event well. She allowed the use of a simple self-portrait she had drawn in 1976, which was later used, slightly altered, on the cover of a book gathering together a selection of the papers presented at the symposium.

Some years later, Anne also allowed one hundred commercial copies of the drawing to be printed and sold by the University of Charleston in West Virginia for a good cause. She signed each copy, waiving the suggested fee of $500. Writing to the university she stated that what linked the artist and the writer was "a noticing eye" but that the painter also required a skilled hand. In her own case, she continued,

I learned that I came much closer to my eye's vision when I translated it into words. That is why I don't paint anymore.

§

As 1989 neared its end the *Baltimore Sun* declared Anne Tyler "Marylander of the Year"—clarifying that it was for her contribution to American letters, rather than her welcome services to Baltimore tourism in attracting the many visitors now flocking to check out the locales featuring in her work.

But Anne in her novels had remained never less than realistic about her adopted city: the frequent coldness of upper-class Roland Park, the poverty and dilapidation of the inner city but the warmth of its residents. Even in the 1980s when Baltimore was finally in the ascendant, Anne, or at least her characters, continued to take a clear-eyed view. The action in *Breathing Lessons* mostly takes place away from Baltimore but Anne inserts a flashback to a family visit to Harborplace, the glitzy new waterfront of boutiques and restaurants, surrounded by modern office blocks and hotels, which had now replaced the rotting if historic old warehouses and piers. Harborplace was generally seen as a shining symbol of reversal of decline, a hopeful new start for the troubled city, but Ira Moran is not a fan:

He felt it was un-Baltimorean—in fact, a glorified shopping mall.

Loss

Βy 1989 Anne professed to have entirely given up reading her reviews, perhaps disheartened by what seemed to be a rising tide of criticism.

I don't read reviews at all. (I don't want to know how often I've missed connecting)...

She had also entirely given up publishing short stories. The last few had appeared that decade: "C.C. Mulvaney," sold to the British magazine *Woman's Own* in late 1982; "Teenage Wasteland," about a wayward teenager getting treatment from a trendy psychologist, which was published in a youth magazine in 1983, again in an anthology of short stories in 1985, yet again in a book of stories about psychology in 2002, and once more in 2020 as an ebook; and "A Woman Like a Fieldstone House," the life of a woman told within the framework of the seventeen-year cycle of the cicada. Anne donated this last to be printed in an anthology in aid of a hunger relief charity, and reportedly also gave the charity the $3,500 she earned from the sale of the story to the *Ladies' Home Journal*. One story, "Hidden Dangers," had surprisingly been turned down, even at the height of Anne's fame, by the illustrious *Harper's* and *McCall's*—the latter claiming to be looking for younger characters. It was eventually published in August 1984 in the *Washington Post Sunday Magazine*.

Anne had once thought that short stories were all she ever wanted to write, and had published forty by the late 1970s. "I liked the quick in-and-out of them, the setting up of a situation and then letting it go." Having knuckled down to the task of churning out a few novels after learning from her agent that publishers would only buy short story collections from an established novelist, she later saw a pretty clear "gritted-teeth effect" in her first three, ultimately disclaimed novels. But writing them had been a revelation:

I was under the impression back then that revision killed spontaneity, so I just wrote them lickety-split and sent them off. Then by the fourth novel [The Clock Winder] or so, I started discovering the pleasure of losing myself in a project over months or even years, so that the characters became people in their own right who surprised me with what they took it into their heads to say and do.

In fact Anne once expressed the wish that she could just "dissolve" the first *four* books she had written, thus even including *The Clock Winder;* "I won't even claim any novel written before *Celestial Navigation,*" she maintained. She went so far as to say that she hated them, they were "loosely and sloppily written," and she had been very young when she wrote them. In those early works, Anne realized, she had not been far enough inside her characters and had been merely pushing them around on the page. She had felt no "pressing urge" to write about them, had just wanted to write something. But by the fifth novel she was allowing the characters to lead their own lives. She saw that if she wrote about someone for a long time, looking so closely, she could not help but understand why they did some of the things they did. "I often thought if I could handle things like murder it would be interesting to see, would I end up forgiving the murderer." She had also discovered—and it made novel writing addictive for her—that if she launched some dialogue, starting with a sentence she had made up for someone to say and then holding very still, the characters would start to talk on their own and say things she never expected. She became practically their scribe, writing it all down. It was fascinating to her.

From that point on Anne was hooked on novels, having likewise learned to rewrite "endlessly" because revision was so necessary: the first draft was only a skeleton, a "fleshless, meager, textureless thing." She claimed never to have written a short story since (although in fact at least ten more were published in the years after *The Clock Winder*). She did not view the stories she had produced with any sense of pride. To date, the stories—at least fifty—remain uncollected, with Anne specifically listing thirty-five that she did not want re-published, anthologized or put in any collection "due to inferiority." The list even included the famous "The Saints in Caesar's Household" so praised by Reynolds Price. The early stories published in *Archive* magazine at Duke University made her wince, she declared in 1981: "I have often contemplated sneaking down to Duke in the dead of night and burning the *Archive*'s, um, archives." She did not want to "proliferate" her stories, she told the little Palaemon Press, which was interested in publishing them.

The stories were wide-ranging, but often focused on a single character and presented a single incident or a single day as a microcosm of a whole life. The settings were mainly Southern, and the themes much as in Anne's novels: families, loneliness, how people fail to communicate, and the search for meaning in life. Most were far bleaker than the novels. There were a few among them that Anne felt were better than the others: she liked "Your Place Is Empty" and "Uncle Ahmad" because both touched upon the "Iranian side" of her life. She was also pleased with 1975's "A Knack for Languages"—about a goat farmer's daughter, married to a foreigner, whose life has been affected by a mother with violent mood swings—because it was "uncharacteristically strong." In 1992 she allowed "Your Place is Empty" to be published in a limited edition of one hundred.

Decades later she was still to view most of her stories as below par.

I save the best of myself for novels, and I believe it shows. My stories are never quite good enough. I don't know if I'll ever write any others, but of those I have written, there are only five or so that I allow to be reprinted anywhere, and five doesn't make a collection.

Anne had also tried her hand at poetry, including two pieces in honor of the writers who had so influenced her life, Reynolds Price and Eudora Welty. The lengthily titled "Reynolds Price reads 'The anniversary' to twenty-nine freshman English students from the class of '62" appeared in a tribute work to Reynolds on his fiftieth birthday in 1983, alongside contributions by three other well-known writers including Eudora; it was privately printed for limited distribution by

Palaemon Press, presumably as a joint commission from the contributors. Anne also wrote the free verse poem "To Eudora Welty, for showering us with gold" (in reference to Eudora's story "Shower of Gold") for a similar tribute book to Eudora on her seventy-fifth birthday in 1984. Another poem, "The Ice-Pond Alien," was printed in the *New York Times* in 1990 in response to the paper sending nine famous writers a drawing of a strange figure by a pond, with the challenge to use their imaginations. Anne's short, funny, rhyming poem depicted the figure as an alien from a spaceship who is spotted by a local family. He is looking for an "earthling to take home"—the family, filled with Christmas spirit, "donate little Jerome."

   Book reviewing was also tapering off, with Anne concerned that she was gradually running through her capacity for enthusiasm: "I felt I'd used up the vocabulary for it." With all the book royalties now flowing in, and with her daughters' education complete, there was little need to carry on. The focus hereafter would be on novels alone, although she continued to participate as a judge on the occasional book panel, including one with the difficult job of drawing up a list of the twenty best young American novelists.

   Writing was now firmly Anne's profession, if not exactly one deliberately picked:

   I didn't really choose to write; I more or less fell into it. It's true that it's a solitary occupation, but you would be surprised at how much companionship a group of imaginary characters can offer once you get to know them.

   As the 1990s dawned Anne went on composing her drafts in longhand, still feeling very strongly that she needed to, but having made one concession to modernity with the purchase of a word processor for typing up the final copy. (Replies to fan letters were still by hand in many cases.) Although the girls had by now flown the nest she kept to a fairly firm writing schedule to give her day some shape, if finding that with more hours at her disposal she had become "slightly less rigid." Her twelfth book was underway: *Saint Maybe*, published in 1991, the year Anne turned fifty.

The setting is again Baltimore, this time during the period of the Vietnam war, which is alluded to several times. Anne had wanted an Edward Hopper painting for the cover, but in the end Knopf commissioned illustrator John Collier to produce a Hopper-type design of a house typical of certain parts of Baltimore.

The main character of *Saint Maybe*, Ian Bedloe, believes he has caused the death of his brother Danny; when Danny's wife dies too, he follows the advice of a well-meaning minister of a local sect, the Church of the Second Chance, and drops out of college in order to atone by bringing up Danny's children. As the years pass Ian becomes more and more involved with the church—much to the unease of his non-religious family—but continues to feel the burden of his responsibility for the children, even while loving them, and that God has not forgiven him. When the three children have finally grown up Ian feels that life has passed him by, but as the novel draws to a close he at last gets his own second chance.

His three young charges all grow up to be exactly the kinds of people they had been as children, a trajectory deliberately depicted by Anne, who believed that everyone has a "fairly immutable" self issued before birth. Change was still possible, but she tended to be skeptical about wholesale transformation much beyond childhood. In the same way, she saw Ian's religious conversion as not a personality change but rather a course of action from a character already in this sort of mold. Ian is painted as a young man of great charm, sleepy-eyed and sexy, and Anne includes some frank references to sex, perhaps in response to recent comments about the lack of it in her novels (although in fact she had occasionally been frank enough in earlier works such as *Earthly Possessions*). Nevertheless, Anne still maintained that she would never be in bed with her characters, instead trying to show them respect.

She has some entertainment in the book bringing in characters from previous works. A private detective is again the cadaverous Eli Everjohn from *Searching for Caleb*. The Bedloes get a meal at what appears to be the Homesick Restaurant—not named, but later confirmed as such by Anne—where they are served by owner Ezra, who keeps the place open on the holidays for people without families who have nowhere to go. It was a private joke, said Anne, and she had not been expecting anyone else to notice. (She returned to Ezra because she was still so fond of him: she felt now that he would never marry, and that his nephew Luke would come in and take over the restaurant.) She also has fun—perhaps bordering on caricature —with the Bedloes' neighbors, a bunch of interchangeable accident-prone male students from abroad, always referred to by everyone as "the foreigners," who were all based on some of her Iranian in-laws.

Saint Maybe became a *New York Times* Notable Book of the Year and another Main Selection by the Book of the Month Club. The fifth chapter, "People Who Don't Know the Answers," appeared as a standalone story in the *New Yorker*, which along with the *New York Times* came up with glowing reviews. A "warm and generous novel, a novel that attests once again to Ms. Tyler's enormous gifts as a writer and her innate understanding of the mysteries of kinship and blood," judged one *New York Times* critic, while celebrated author Jay Parini of the *New York Times Book Review* downright adored it. The narrative was not as complex as either *The Accidental Tourist* or *Dinner at The Homesick Restaurant*, nor as whimsical as *Breathing Lessons*, Parini wrote, but in many ways the novel was Anne's most sophisticated work. Family life was celebrated without erasing the pain and boredom that families almost necessarily inflict upon their members, and Ian Bedloe sat near the top of her fine list of heroes. It was a mystery to Parini exactly how she made the reader care so much about Ian, but that, perhaps, was the mystery of art.

More eulogies piled in from abroad. The celebrated British publisher Carmen Callil wrote to Anne that she was "so grateful" to be issuing the work and that Anne's books always left "a sort of ache of pleasure and acceptable pain." For London's *Time Out* the new novel showed Anne Tyler "at the peak of her power—a real slice of middle America, blessed with equal amounts of humor, pathos and compassion that will ensure heartfelt devotion from all her readers" (although the *London Review of Books* saw the novel as told in an "artfully off-hand way" that teased the reader into close engagement while suggesting that Anne herself was only just this side of sarcasm). For the *Canberra Times* in Australia, *Saint Maybe* was characterized by that "deftness, humor and sympathetic understanding that we have come to expect from Tyler." The novel sold well and in 1998 was made into a TV movie starring Blythe Danner, Tom McCarthy and Mary-Louise Parker. (Anne was to say that every so often, when film options on her books were bought up, she would think "Why? Nothing happens in them!")

Anne's treatment of religion in the novel came in for various contradictory comments. In Britain a *Times* critic who had loved Anne's previous two novels was now experiencing qualms, a "moral queasiness." It was still quintessential Tyler—a family living in a battered frame house, an array of stock characters with Ian Bedloe the new version of the vulnerable man hijacked by events who had already featured in *Dinner at The Homesick Restaurant* and *The Accidental Tourist*. But Anne had not allowed Ian the dignity of a faith commensurate with his intelligence and humanity, protested the reviewer, instead having him swept into a "wretched little backstreet sect." For the *Washington Post* Anne never really got inside Ian's faith, while the *Christian Century*, conversely, felt that his religious commitment did inform the novel and that Anne displayed an acuity about "everyday holiness" all the more effective for being understated. Other critics saw the saintly Ian as just "awfully boring."

Anne certainly makes fun of the Church of the Second Chance and its flock, but it is gentle, almost affectionate fun; to avoid giving offense, she had deliberately invented the sect, rather than writing about an actual church. There is seemingly more antagonism in the novel toward another religious grouping, the judgmental and self-righteous Holy House of the Gospel. Ian's church's belief that their faith is best demonstrated through the lives they live, rather than evangelism, is close to the Quaker position (and the church also resembles Quakerism in other aspects). Anne stated that she had no intention of satirizing Ian's religious beliefs, and thought of his faith as literally his Second

167

Chance at a moment when he had given up hope. The portrayal of Ian was in her own words an attempt to inhabit a character the most opposite to her that she could think of: a "concretely religious person."

All I knew at the start was that I wondered what it must feel like to be a born-again Christian, since that is a kind of life very different from mine.

Anne's own position was probably something more akin to the shuffling embarrassment felt by Ian's family whenever he mentions religion. While her Quaker upbringing had left its mark—she was "very comfortable with silence"—Quakerism did not have all the answers. Anti-war like her parents, Anne still could not see that the faith had any adequate response to the obvious challenges that people brought up in relation to religion, such as the existence of evil as personified by Hitler in the Second World War. Her father would say well, if we had done the right thing all along, there would have been no Hitler, but Anne felt this was "kind of the easy answer." Nevertheless, still feeling in her own words like a secular Quaker, she continued throughout her life to espouse some of the bedrock principles of that religion:

I'm not religious but something about the way they live and the feelings they have about equality and so on, makes sense to me.

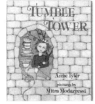
In 1993 Anne and her daughter Mitra collaborated on Anne's first foray into writing for children: *Tumble Tower*, the story of messy Princess Molly, whose untidiness helps to rescue her compulsively clean and tidy family from a flood. Critics liked Anne's "nimble, witty" treatment of an old topic, and there was admiration for Mitra's distinctive watercolor illustrations. For *Publishers Weekly*, the otherworldly, angular faces of her characters and the profusion of details, patterns and objects

hinted at the dreaminess of Modigliani and the "cozy amiability" of *Winnie-the-Pooh* artist Ernest H. Shepard.

Mitra, twenty-six that year, revealed that the messy princess might have been rooted in reality. "I'm a slob," she admitted, unlike her mother. "Mom's the queen of decluttering. She's got it down to a science." The *Tumble Tower* story had come to Anne, whole, one sleepless night. Because she had been convinced for a long time that Mitra's paintings had an enigmatic, storylike quality, she asked her daughter if she would consider illustrating it—feeling "unexpectedly shy" as she watched Mitra reading the manuscript.

Mitra naturally said yes, and quit her job running the children's section at a Borders bookstore in Philadelphia (where her sister Tezh was also living). The success of the book opened a lot of doors for Mitra. Anne admitted it had been a project "to get her started," but also pointed out that while publishers may have been initially interested in the Tyler name, they still bid on the book as illustrated by Mitra, and later bought books produced solely by her daughter. In the catalog and jacket notes Mitra elected not to mention their relationship but some reviewers worked out the connection anyway. A British critic at the *Sunday Times* wrote that Mitra's gentle illustrations "suggest that Tyler's own parenting has instilled a talent for clarity rather than chaos." Anne herself thought Mitra's drawings had "mood and wit," and she particularly liked the little visual jokes such as the doll castle instead of a doll house, and incongruities such as the skateboarding princess and the ermine-clad king mopping the floor.

For her daughter's sake Anne agreed to a joint book-signing at Borders. The whole collaboration experiment was "enormous fun" for her, although one she initially said she was scared to repeat, feeling that the humor and exuberance of Mitra's own storytelling went beyond what she could produce herself. However, Mitra was invariably glad of any help from Anne with her writing and, as her literary and illustrating career progressed—she later became an editorial illustrator for distinguished newspapers like the *Washington Post*—she did not hesitate to ask her mother for advice. "She's really good about stepping back and saying, well, you know best. She tries to give me the faith to do it on my own and get confidence, which is a hard thing to do, but then she's always there if I have questions or want a second opinion, to proofread and do grammar checks." Even now that she and Tezh were old enough not to have to come first with Anne, said Mitra, their mother was still there for them whether she was in the throes of writing or not.

Mitra denied that as children, she and Tezh had had to raise themselves because their mother was forever working. Anne was very organized, she recalled, with a real grip on her schedule, and did a very good job. Anne mostly only wrote when they were out of the house, and "then when we came home, she was there. So it was a really nice arrangement...a good division of time." There was no conflict as far as Mitra was concerned. (Anne, too, thought she had eventually achieved the right balance, particularly with tending to tilt slightly more toward her family than toward work. Tell her one of her daughters was there and she would "joyfully fling" her novel to the winds, she maintained, and believed that this degree of imbalance was a great factor in accounting for her amazingly happy life.)

It had taken the young Mitra a while to understand that Anne was famous. She always knew her mother wrote books, but did not realize that other people knew it too, and it was not until high school that Mitra finally saw that her family was special. Nobody had ever recognized Anne on the street, and because she did so few interviews or public appearances it had not affected the girls' family life in any way.

Mitra confirmed that there were various real-life elements in her mother's work, tiny little incidents and everyday conversations that she could remember really happening: the old boyfriend of hers who saw stars when he chewed tinfoil, and her own remark about how great it would be just to whistle and have your car come up—both used by Anne in her writing, she believed. But the bigger picture in Anne's books, Mitra stressed, the strange, quirky families, was pure fiction.

Neither Anne nor Taghi pushed their children to succeed, she also commented: they were very laid-back. But seeing them both so successful in their chosen fields did become a kind of pressure she laid on herself to succeed in her turn: "The more successful your parents are, [the] harder to match up."

There was to be a further mother-and-daughter effort in 2004, this time between Anne and Tezh for a touring exhibition originating in Baltimore. The show, "Conversations," asked contributors to offer works in collaboration with other artists, and Tezh produced a haunting painting of an ambiguous interior that she framed with a pencil-written fragment of a story by Anne, written to reflect the mysteriousness of her daughter's image.

Tezh had by then become a much exhibited painter of lonely, empty interiors and outside scenes of abandoned cars and barns. In a statement for a gallery showing her work, Tezh wrote that she wanted to create imaginary rooms with a history, a feeling that people had lived there and that the light coming in had a mystery to it; her paintings were small because she wanted viewers to feel they were looking into the room through a tiny doorway. What she would love most was for people to forget they were looking at a painting and to think that they were sitting in the room themselves. She cared about the realities of space and light, about creating a space the viewer could actually move through. Her paintings were given evocative, eerie titles like "We Hardly Go Outside" and "(They Should Have) Let Me In"—perhaps indicative of an inherited way with words.

In 2005 came a second collaboration between Anne and Mitra, the children's book *Timothy Tugbottom Says No!*, about a little boy who doesn't like change but eventually—when his clothes grow too small for him—learns to embrace it. As Mitra's career as an illustrator proceeded, Anne was to be struck by the parallel between painting a character and writing a character:

I hadn't realized that artists, no less than novelists, need to reflect for a long time on the style and manner and inner nature of a person before they feel ready to pick up their tools and start in.

Anne loved her talented daughters as adults, but mourned the loss of the children they had once been: if she looked back on them as little people, they had "basically died." It made her very sad to think about it. She was so happy to have them as grown-ups, she said, but they were "other people, totally other people."

§

(Photo credit: National Portrait Gallery, Smithsonian Institution, gift of Diana Walker)

In 1994, British author Nick Hornby and Irish author Roddy Doyle jointly nominated Anne Tyler as the greatest living novelist writing in English. Nick had remained obsessed with Anne's writing, although initially unable to meet her in person because of her habitual seclusion. When he published his first novel, the bestselling *High Fidelity*, Anne sent him what he described as a long and beautiful letter about it, which he promptly arranged to have framed as maybe the "single greatest moment" of his early career. "*High Fidelity* was one of the few books in my life that surprised me," Anne said elsewhere. "It was so original and seemingly uncalculated." Nick thought it interesting that Anne absolutely could not see what her writing had to do with his work, which he saw as the "beauty of influence." He realized that a novel about an Englishman obsessed with rock and roll did not very obviously have anything to do with Anne's writing, but for him it was about tone and spirit, not language and subject matter. For Nick, Anne Tyler was simply "the best line-and-length novelist in the world" (a British cricketing term meaning she hit the mark consistently and skillfully). They did eventually meet. Baseball fan Anne was grateful that soccer-obsessed Nick did not try to convert her to fandom of England's famous Arsenal team—he knew there was no hope, she said.

Charm City, meanwhile, had continued its rebirth with the construction downtown of the spectacular, retro-styled Oriole Park baseball stadium, once cited as the single most important piece of athletic architecture ever erected in America. But in Anne's next work, *Ladder of Years*, published in 1995 with the book cover painted by Tezh, the new stadium receives a less than positive mention:

She looked ahead and saw the Baltimore skyline—smokestacks, a spaghetti of ramps and overpasses, monster storage tanks...gray-windowed factories and corrugated-metal warehouses. Everything seemed so industrial—even the new ballpark, with its geometric strutwork and its skeletons of lights.

(Ladder of Years, 1995)

Roland Park naturally also features, this time as the home of forty-year-old Delia Grinstead, who shops at Eddie's market store and is wary of those "drawling, gravelly, Roland Park matron voices." (Another character remarks that everybody in Roland Park has a last name for a first name.) A doctor's wife who feels increasingly irrelevant to her nearly grown family, Delia has begun to suspect that her husband Sam married her for the wrong reasons. After a spat with Sam at the beach during the family's annual vacation, Delia on a whim hitches a ride to a completely unknown town, still wearing only her skirted swimsuit, Sam's beach robe and a pair of espadrilles. Here she starts a new life, initially as the severe secretary Miss Grinstead with a room in a shabby boarding house, then slowly making more and more friends until she becomes a popular and well-known person in the little town. In intermittent contact with her family but seemingly happier where she is, Delia eventually decides to go back just for her daughter's wedding, leaving behind the likable father, son and cat she is now housekeeper to. Enmeshed in a new life but still in thrall to her past, Delia finds herself taking up the reins in her former home and suddenly facing a difficult choice.

Anne carried out her usual meticulous planning for the work, sketching a layout of the shop, schools, and homes in Delia's new town, tracking down a log of the weather during the last week of September 1993 for a particular scene, and copying out the recipe for a Chinese dish made by Delia.

Critical response was positive, but muted. For the *Sunday Times* in Britain, the novel "ruefully contemplates the unhaltable passage of time" while scintillating with *joie de vivre*. In Australia the *Canberra Times* found it "utterly charming," and Anne as a writer "the complete professional." For the *New York Times*, "so measured and delicate is each observation, so complex is the structure and so astute and open the language, that the reader can relax, feel secure in the narrative and experience the work as something real and natural—even inevitable." Anne Tyler's most conventional novel so far, wrote Joyce Carol Oates in another review—its concerns familial, the quiet, touching drama of a mother's need to acknowledge that her children no longer require her as they once had, just as her husband no longer loves her as he once did. A poignant work, she judged, but overall a bleak vision somewhat at odds with the affable tone of Anne's prose. The novel was chosen by *Time* magazine as one of the ten best books of 1995, and in 1996 was shortlisted for the Orange Prize for Fiction (now the Women's Prize for Fiction).

A reviewer in Canada's *Globe and Mail* was to argue that *Ladder of Years* was Anne's most memorable novel, the one about "every married-with-children woman's occasional secret fantasy." Not only was it entertaining, engrossing and moving, wrote the critic, it also proved to be, years after its publication, a common reference point among women—mentioned during long walks when the conversation turned to the delicate topic of marital contentment. The story of Delia's impulsive escape and adoption of a whole new life is certainly strangely compelling, gripping the reader with its practical details. Arriving in the unknown town Delia uses the family's vacation cash to buy underwear and a single dress to replace her swimsuit, rents her sparsely furnished room, and finds herself a job as secretary to Bay Borough's only lawyer (a man fascinated, like Anne, by mail-order catalogs). Trying on the dress in a shop she suddenly becomes "The Secretary" and begins walking differently, to the accompaniment of a commentary in her head describing "the secretary, Miss X, speeding back to her office." She falls into a routine of working, eating, sleeping, and reading serious novels instead of her usual escapist romances. She is almost blissfully alone, unencumbered and in command of her own time.

Anne was amazed by how many letters she received from readers saying they had always wanted to do exactly this, some of them men. (In years to come she would see that the disappearing acts in her novels would no longer work as a device. The existence of cell phones utterly changed plot possibilities, she recognized. If you moved to a new place, everybody still knew how to call you.)

The main impetus for writing *Ladder of Years* was, in fact, Anne's own longstanding fixation with the idea of running away:

I surely can't be the only person in the world who has thought, every now and then, "Wouldn't it be nice just to walk straight out of my life? To go off and be someone else?" I've considered how I would cover my tracks: the changes I'd make in my hairstyle and clothes, the bus ticket I would buy with cold cash, the false name I would adopt when I settled in some little town where nobody knew me.

She had continued to ponder how she would earn her living. With writing her only trade, would she carry it on in this new life? There was something so particular, so individual, about a writing style that her own might be a dead giveaway. Would she really be able, no matter how hard she tried, to write like someone else? In short, was it truly possible to begin a new life, or would she just end up living the old life at a different

175

address? It was thoughts like these that had set in motion the story of Delia Grinstead.

However, it was no midlife crisis story. A heroine simply reacting to the sight of a few wrinkles in the mirror would have been of little interest to her, Anne declared: it was more about the death of Delia's father. Anne was fascinated by the way in which we can appear to absorb some hard fact, more or less adapt to it, carry on as before—and then find ourselves ambushed by it when least expected. She believed Delia's state of mind to stem from her grief for her father, whom she still mourns without realizing quite how deeply. This leads her to take a "time trip," words Anne gives to a character in the book. Delia's journey was nothing but an attempt to travel back through the life she had already lived, she explained, but this time doing it right: symbolically speaking, Delia in her relationships in the strange town acquires new sisters, a new son, a new husband, and a new father, and tries to make a better job of it the second time around (as in the movie *Groundhog Day*, described but not named in the book).

Delia is her father's favorite out of three sisters but Anne denied any *King Lear* connection—she had chosen the name "Delia" before it occurred to her it might be short for Cordelia, the youngest and most beloved of Lear's three daughters in the Shakespeare play. She was very fond of Delia, and wanted readers to be fond of her too; one of the qualities she hoped they would find endearing was her graceful and intuitive touch with both cats and children. (Like Anne, Delia as a young mother is "so afraid of dying while her children were small.") In fact the hardest part for Anne in writing the character had been the difficulty justifying, to herself and to her readers, a mother walking out on her family, and she had been very concerned that Delia did not abandon children who were still young. "That would have been so harmful to them that I'd have had trouble liking her." As ever, Anne knew she would be living with Delia for a couple of years, so being able to like her was important. She had therefore tried to render it less appalling by making the children almost grown, and to make clear that Delia's disappearance was a decision of the moment—more of an event that ran away with her, another preoccupation of Anne's—but it was still difficult.

A further problem in the writing was how to let Delia turn her back on the family she becomes housekeeper to, the sympathetic high-school principal Joel and his sweet, needy little boy Noah. As she drew near the end of the novel, Noah and Joel became "almost a moral burden" for her. But she ended up believing that Joel's estranged wife Ellie would return to them: "In my mind, it's a done deal: Ellie comes by the house, she and Joel get to talking, she stays on after she has settled Noah in bed...So I can leave them with a clear conscience."

Other, lesser figures in *Ladder of Years* had arrived in Anne's mind fully formed, as minor personae tended to do with her, often as the result of some long-ago, superficial encounter. The physical model for the novel's passing character Rosemary Bly-Brice was a young woman she had glimpsed in a grocery store many years before who was very conscious of her asymmetrical, angular, high-fashion haircut, holding her head constantly to one side as if to accentuate it. Anne didn't know why she remembered things like that, but was happy that she did because they often came in handy. Other characters were closer to Anne herself. Educator Joel is obsessed with the correct use of English and Anne admitted that every example of poor or vulgar speech Joel objects to, she did too (although agreeing with Delia that some of the most vivid language evolves from everyday usage).

She had been certain from the start how the story would end and this time was proved right. The plot had started with an index card on which she had written, years before, something like, "Woman leaves her family only to find in the end that she's just been trying to figure out how to say goodbye when they leave *her*." It turned out to be slightly more complicated, but all along Anne had had the book's last line in her mind. She was surprised by the number of readers over the years who wrote to say that they wished Delia had not returned home to Sam, and asking why Anne had sent her back. Her answer was that it was because she believed Sam to be a good man and even a good husband, and that he definitely loved Delia, as evidenced by the letter he writes her (or, more importantly, what he crosses out in it). He might be reserved and cautious and closed off, but to Anne this seemed sad and endearing rather than a sin, so naturally Delia should go back to him. She had never doubted that Delia would return, because her marriage was not the problem. She thought the state of their marriage rather hopeful, if anything: the fact that this mingling of two sexes and two entirely different personalities worked, and that in general husbands and wives did, for the most part, muddle along more or less happily together, amazed and delighted Anne. She saw marriage as a very useful subject for a writer. "Marriage works in novels the way an earthquake works in disaster movies: it throws people together at close quarters and allows their true characters to emerge."

Delia's real problem to Anne was the passage of time, the losses she has experienced over the years and the further losses that she senses will be coming:

Delia is a woman whose family is leaving her (children growing up, husband aging and obviously not far away from dying), and her trip to Bay Borough is, as the last line says, her way of figuring out how to say goodbye.

For Anne, the book was about how the experience she goes through allows Delia to come to terms with her life as it already is. At the end of the book, Delia is wiser, said Anne. "I think that's one of the most valuable changes anybody can hope for."

§

How to say goodbye was now Anne's own reality. Taghi, in his early sixties, was seriously ill. About a year before the publication of *Ladder of Years* he had been diagnosed with both leukemia and lymphoma.

His illness became progressively worse but Taghi continued working for as long as he was able, only retiring from his beloved Center for Infant Study in 1996. After that he devoted himself to writing, completing his latest novel and embarking on the arduous task of translating it from Farsi into English—as before, with Anne's help. He jokingly called producing a book in another language "writing with an accent" (and wrote an interesting essay with that title). Far from being a handicap, translation became a voice for him, giving his work an atmosphere that immediately showed his characters were not American-born. Creating the internal world of a character, Taghi remarked, was not unlike the way psychiatrists go about constructing the inner life of an infant. Both author and psychiatrist had to answer the same question: who is this character waiting to emerge?

As treatment went on, with chemotherapy, a bone marrow transplant, many blood transfusions, and intermittent hospitalizations, Taghi eventually began wearing a cap and using a cane. But for a long time he remained the man he had always been: intellectual, funny, and creative, loving books and films and art and music, especially Bach and Mozart. Before he became ill his attitude to death had been very serious, he commented around this time: he thought he would be frightened and depressed, without the stamina to confront the end. In the event, the emotional effect of imminent death for Taghi was "a sense of loss," not fear. He sensed how small he was in the face of it all. At the same time, awareness of death heightened his response to the world around him, somehow liberating him and making him feel more alive. "It's so funny to say—but I'm enjoying life," he remarked. "Since I have been ill, I really feel I'm tapping some resources in me that I didn't know I had." He was very grateful for the good life he had enjoyed.

But although Taghi was comforted by his own reflections, death was not something he talked about with either Anne or his daughters, seemingly refusing to acknowledge to them that the end was drawing near.

He was sick for about three years. The hardest thing was that he wouldn't admit that he would die, or could die. It was odd for a psychiatrist. He was a very honest man, but I wish we could have had one conversation about it. It's as if I went through his death alone. I guess I could have taken him by the shoulders, but I couldn't say anything. It wouldn't have done any good.

There were periods of hope, as when Taghi's hair grew back after a bout of chemotherapy, and Anne was glad to be asked to cut it—having griped in years gone by when she was expected to serve as barber—before going out for a meal together without his cap. But there were also periods of deepening worry. There were other concerns too, as when an imminent three-month visit by Taghi's nephew threatened the loss of Anne's freedom to write and to wander around the empty house thinking about her work.

In the evenings Anne would read aloud to him. Taghi's English was now excellent, but reading books in English always seemed like work. Toward the end of his life Anne read him *Anna Karenina*, which previously he had known only in his native language.

At the end he was crying, because of what happened in Anna's life. That was very moving.

As time went on Anne noticed that Taghi no longer wanted to listen to music. Before, he would always have the great classics playing in the house whenever he was home, especially his favorite, Bach's "Sheep May Safely Graze." Now, even when she offered to put something on for him, he would say not to bother; then, said Anne, "I think I faced the fact that he was going to die."

She received a letter of support from her old friend Reynolds, who had visited Anne's family a few times over the years and developed a joking relationship with Taghi—both possessing the same irrepressible high spirits. He ended his letter with Emily Dickinson's moving poem about endurance, "There Is Strength In Proving That It Can Be Borne."

Mitra, now in her early thirties and living in San Francisco, came home to help her mother during the last six weeks of Taghi's illness but remained in complete denial until nearly the very end. "He was such a positive person, he said he could beat it and we believed him." She knew this attitude had probably helped prolong his life.

Taghi did not finish translating his book, managing only a few pages. On April 23 1997, aged only sixty-five, he died at home with Anne and his daughters around him as he had wanted. No services were held; the family requested memorial donations to the groundbreaking Center for Infant Study that Taghi had been so passionate about (today known as the Taghi Modarressi Center). He was celebrated in obituaries as a pioneer in the exploration of infant psychology but also as an accomplished writer of fiction and, of course, as the husband of Anne Tyler. His private library was donated in his memory to Duke University.

Taghi had been instrumental in educating a whole generation of mental health specialists to treat children and families in distress; previously, therapists had believed it impossible to treat very young children because they were too difficult to work with. Taghi, conversely, had always felt that children were trying to tell him a story. "Babies *can* talk!" he would say excitedly. "The language of babies is feelings. And babies are able to create or reflect feelings around them. By action, by a smile, by posture, by a gesture—they communicate." He had once invited Anne's friend Eudora Welty to a convention of child psychiatrists for a discussion of infant creativity, where she read out a story and answered the psychiatrists' eager questions about the art of writing. (Eudora had been unable to resist the invitation because she wanted to see Anne.)

Babies were just as liable to suffer from depression as adults, Taghi had believed, and the symptoms were similar: insomnia, poor appetite, weight loss, and inability to relate to others. Infants as young as two months old could have the condition, and he had found that one of the most prevalent causes of the disorder among infants was depression and child abuse suffered by the mother—if a mother was depressed, her child would sense it and suffer the same. And by treating the mother, the baby could often be cured. As part of treatment, Taghi also advocated frequent physical contact between parent and offspring, and consistent behavior by the parent.

181

As well as performing this vital work with families, Taghi had risen many times as early as three or four in the morning to write his novels on the sun porch before setting off for a day's work at the clinic. A review of his novel *The Pilgrim's Rules of Etiquette* declared that he had done for his native country what Gabriel García Márquez had done for Colombia.

The translation into English of his last work, *The Virgin of Solitude*, was completed by family friend Nasrin Rahimieh and then published in both languages. Anne assisted and, as they worked, they sometimes found themselves dissolving into surprising giggles; for Nasrin, these were moments that resonated with memories of Taghi and his own endearing laughter.

§

Anne's grief was terrible. She knew the deaths of parents were extremely sad, but it was what was supposed to happen, not the death of a husband.

For a while I thought, "How do people stand this? How will I go through the rest of my life?" It was a great comfort to know that people had lost people before me. I looked around to see little old ladies walking little lapdogs, thinking, "They've lived through this and they're cheerful, and it's going to be all right."

She imposed a rule on herself that she had to have one human contact every day, because she knew that otherwise she would never leave the house. She did this for a long time, although finding that she was mostly fine when on her own at home, but almost "unbearably lonely" when out. Then came the point of thinking, "Does visiting the dentist count?" and realizing that perhaps the rule no longer needed to be followed. As the first few months passed after Taghi's death, the finality of "never" began to sink in, the full realization that she would never, ever see him again. It was almost impossible to comprehend, and these days were harder than the days just after he had died.

Anne did not believe in an afterlife. Part of her occasionally enjoyed inventing heavens and thinking she could see Taghi again, but she did not really feel it. "I believe you see the car coming at you and nothing. That's the end." Though people said things like they would meet again, or they knew this was not the end, neither she nor Taghi had believed this. She had been desperately afraid of dying when a young mother, then growing less so as the girls became adults and she saw they would manage perfectly well without her. Death was a part of life, the old cliché, said Anne, a thing "that gives life its texture and depth and poignancy...the fact that we all die."

Somehow life continued, but Anne's trials were not yet over. Her beloved cat Lucy died of kidney cancer not long after Taghi's death, and Anne herself was diagnosed with breast cancer. She eventually underwent a double mastectomy, and, having seen Taghi in the throes of chemotherapy, was glad to find that surgery would be the only treatment. (She was even able to joke to friends that she had never been the Marilyn Monroe type.) Recovery was inevitably a time of ups and downs, with reconstruction beginning in April 1997—likened by Anne to going through a second puberty—and a period of rest necessary in February 1998 when suffering an infection.

As if this were not enough, at around the same time her daughter Tezh was operated on for a benign brain tumor. Tezh's health had been a concern a few years previously, when Anne had rushed to San Francisco after her daughter contracted pneumonia and possible Legionnaire's disease, dangerously aggravated by Tezh's failure to seek medical help. ("This is a 27-year-old," Anne wrote in a letter. "I am beginning to wonder if they <u>ever</u> grow up.") Tezh's tumor was never thought to be malignant, Anne was to state, but was "scary enough, even so." The operation was successful, and Anne recovered fully from her own surgery. As an intensely private person, she said very little about either of these ordeals, except for one very moving incident. On the morning of Anne's operation a friend came to drive her to the hospital and the girls, who were both at home to be with her, got into the back while Anne sat at the front. The radio came on when the key turned in the ignition, and immediately the car was flooded with the beautiful sound of Taghi's beloved "Sheep May Safely Graze." The girls became extremely still, and so did Anne, not turning around to look at her daughters. "We just listened to that piece of music with all our hearts," she said. It seemed as though Taghi were talking to them, almost as if he were saying he knew what was happening and was with them.

There was at last good news as the traumatic decade came to an end. In 1998 Mitra married Greg Amundson, a fellow artist, and in 2000 gave birth to a son whom they called Taghi. Anne was of course delighted, but full of grief that her own Taghi was not there to see him.

I'm sad for him more so now. He didn't see his daughters married or his grandchildren.

Enduring

During the months that Taghi was dying, and for some time afterward, "writing was the farthest thing from my mind," Anne said. She couldn't imagine ever writing again, she commented in a letter shortly after his death. In fact she couldn't even read—a first for her. She had finished the rough draft of her fourteenth novel, *A Patchwork Planet*, just before the worst of Taghi's illness.

The book was finished well before my mastectomies and Tezh's brain tumor. And I always take a long "refilling" break between novels anyhow, so it seemed natural to wait until Tezh was able to go back to her own life before I began thinking about work again.

The summer after Taghi's death she began the rewriting, grateful to have this job to do rather than attempting something from scratch, which she did not think she would have been able to achieve. Rewriting had always seemed to her almost a kind of handiwork, like knitting or crocheting. It did not give her energy, exactly, but she felt very soothed and sustained by it, and later when Anne thought back to the book's main character, Barnaby, she experienced the sort of "humble gratitude" felt toward a passing stranger who stops to help in an hour of need.

A Patchwork Planet was published in 1998, dedicated "in loving memory" to Taghi. The title came from a patchwork quilt in the novel depicting Planet Earth, made by an elderly lady whose eyesight is failing, her work "makeshift and haphazard, clumsily cobbled together...and likely to fall into pieces at any moment." Unsurprisingly, Baltimore is again the backdrop; a number of scenes take place in the city's Penn Station, with its airy pillared halls, varnished old wooden benches and double doors opening onto steps leading down to the platforms.

Barnaby, thirty, is the likable, dropout son of the wealthy Gaitlin clan in Roland Park. His parents have never forgiven him for petty crimes he committed in the neighborhood as a teenage delinquent, and his wife has divorced him and wants him to stop visiting their daughter. Rather than join the family company Barnaby works for Rent-a-Back, a little business that does odd jobs like clearing attics for elderly or unwell clients (Anne admitting that its inspiration had been "pure wishful thinking"—it was a service she herself would have loved to use). The Gaitlins have a family legend about an angel who suddenly arrives with a vital message, and when Barnaby meets blonde, schoolmarmish Sophia he wonders if she is *his* angel, come to reform his directionless existence. A romance develops and for a while it does seem that the imperturbable Sophia is turning Barnaby's life around, but when Sophia's aunt accuses him of stealing money it is not Sophia who believes in his innocence, but his customers and workmates—especially tiny, acerbic, kindred spirit Martine.

Anne had experienced difficulty at first in getting the troubled Barnaby to "open up" to her; he seemed to be as thorny and difficult with her as he was with his family, and she had a sort of sparring, tussling relationship with the character until she grew more familiar with him. She intended readers to understand that he has not just one but many angels—the network of people he lives among, who see him for the good man he is and wish him well and do what they can to ease his life. Sophia had been a challenge in a different way, because Anne had less sympathy with her than with the other characters and therefore more trouble presenting her fairly. Barnaby's snobbish mother had been more enjoyable to work on, interested as Anne was in the fact that class was very much a factor in America, even though it was not supposed to be: she liked studying the small clues that indicate a particular class level. The novel's wide array of elderly characters came about because of her obsession with time, Anne also explained—what it did to people, how it could constitute a plot all on its own. But she denied ever thinking of her work in terms of themes, like old age. She was just trying to tell a story, she always insisted, not expand some idea.

Any large questions of life that emerge in my novels are accidental —not a reason for writing the novel in the first place but either (1) questions that absorb my characters, quite apart from me, or (2) on occasion, questions that may be thematic to my own life at the moment, even if I'm not entirely aware of them. Answers, if they come, come from the characters' experiences, not from mine, and I often find myself viewing those answers with a sort of distant, bemused surprise.

One *New York Times* critic liked the way Anne always put her characters to work, instead of totally ignoring the world of employment: their frequently humble or eccentric occupations, "carefully observed and threaded with humor," were tightly connected to the rest of their lives, providing both tedium and consolation as well as a lighted stage for the unfolding of their stories. But another of the paper's reviewers, the Pulitzer Prize-winning, sometimes fiercely critical Michiko Kakutani, objected to the novel's overdose of cuteness. Anne Tyler's novels, with their "eccentric heroes, their homespun details, their improbable, often heart-warming plots" had repeatedly flirted with cuteness, wrote this critic, but had been saved from sentimentality by her gifts as a writer, her shrewd understanding of familial dynamics and her rich emotional wisdom. For Kakutani, none of these redemptive qualities was now on display: *A Patchwork Planet* was strangely perfunctory and contrived, a novel that felt "hokey, mechanical...and yes, too cute." *Los Angeles Times* critic Richard Eder felt there was much in the novel that was recognizable from "previous Tyler"—a gently whimsical, depressive central character with an array of quirks, a move out of the trap in a wrong direction that eventually points to a right one, an amiably eccentric family ruled by its family story. Here again was Anne's "limpid, comically ambling style and above all, her integrity: a mercy and respect for even her most ludicrous characters." However, for Eder the book never did more than simmer, its characters unconvincing and Barnaby as the first-person narrator too low-spirited to light up the story. He also pointed out that readers of *The Accidental Tourist* and *Saint Maybe* might just recall the "attraction of thin and peppery young women for Tyler's cloudy and faintly loony heroes."

187

Reception was far better in other countries. Following Barnaby Gaitlin on his quest for his angel and his place on this planet will be an amusing and enlightening odyssey, observed Professor of English Nora Foster Stovel in Canada. British critics were even keener. A "delight from beginning to end," wrote the *Observer*. If the novel were a painting it could be called *Portrait of America*, approved the *Times*, with Anne writing it like a great landscape artist—though, like Richard Eder, reflecting that Tyler aficionados might recognize a certain feisty little figure with barrettes in her hair at the corner of the frame. For the *Guardian* the novel was charming, touching and humane; for *Cosmopolitan*, tender, moving and very, very funny. Probably Anne Tyler's finest novel yet, according to the *Literary Review*. The award-winning author Sebastian Faulkes wrote that at the end of the book the reader may, like him, have the sense of having been played with by a masterly author, but without protest: "Does a piano complain when Alfred Brendel has performed on it?"

Perhaps Anne did not worry too much about the lackluster reviews on her home turf. She had embarked on a new relationship.

Mark Furstenberg, born and bred in Baltimore, was a former *Washington Post* journalist who had also worked for President Kennedy, written scripts for ABC news, and even headed a company manufacturing copper tubes. In 1988, on turning fifty, he decided he didn't like what he was doing—he wanted to have his own experiences, not write about other people's in the *Post*. He decided to take his lifelong love of food and make it into his profession. To find out what to focus on, single parent Mark enlisted the help of his two teenage sons in distributing a questionnaire door to door around his Washington, DC neighborhood, asking people what they felt was missing in the way of local food. The emphatic answer was bread: "Why is there no good bread in Washington? We want bread!" Mark promptly apprenticed at bakeries around the country to learn the business and in 1990 he opened Marvelous Market, credited as the first European-style artisan bakery in Washington. The bread was so good that customers waited in line down the street and had to be limited to buying just two loaves each. He sold up in 1993 and four years later opened The Breadline, a restaurant only one block from the White House that served traditional food and won him a James Beard Foundation nomination for best Mid-Atlantic chef and ratings as a top restaurant in America. Mark met Anne when a friend ordered her a consignment of his bread for Christmas and persuaded Mark to deliver it in person. "One thing led to another," he said.

It was a turning point for Anne, now fifty-seven and still grieving for Taghi eighteen months after his death. Her parents were pleased about the new relationship, knowing how much she missed Taghi. She started to have fun, doing things like writing hundreds of the offbeat messages inserted into the fortune cookies at Mark's restaurant—coming up with funny, disconcerting lines such as "A tall man with a dark pony tail is telling people he's your brother." She invested in a condominium in Washington where she could stay for short periods to be closer to Mark and, from a highly focused, almost homebound writer who had hated even to venture forth for the family's annual beach holiday, she started going away on weekends and traveling abroad, accompanying Mark to Florence and Venice and possibly elsewhere. (As far as is known she did not go as far afield as Australia, a country that interested her. When still a librarian she had worked with an Australian colleague and something about the way the woman described the air, "the way it felt on her skin...made me long to go there.")

Mark, though very outgoing himself, fully understood Anne's disinclination for celebrity. She was intimate with her intimates and behaved like a stranger to strangers, he was to comment after they had been together a few years. She believed that what she had to say went into her work, he explained, and she did not understand why readers of her novels wanted to know about her private life. It made no sense to her.

With Mark's help, Anne recovered enough from the dark time of death and illness to continue working on her fifteenth novel.

I plotted Back When We Were Grownups just after emerging from a year in which there had been several losses and serious illnesses in my family. I wanted my next novel to be full of joy and celebration, which is how I ended up with a main character who earned her living throwing parties.

But the novel had its somber side. Anne conceded that a sense of loss showed through the book anyway, which to her was proof that the subconscious always tends to triumph in the end. She was aware that readers and critics had frequently commented on the way death featured in her books, even before she had suffered any personal losses herself. But for Anne death was something that happened all the time and she had not seen it as anything unusual to include in a novel. She had never thought that much about death when younger, except as an adolescent when she began to feel how interesting it was, and touching, that everyone knew they would die and yet somehow managed to carry on (although what the alternative was she didn't know). "Why would you get married when there's a fifty/fifty chance that you will have to lose that person, if that person doesn't lose you. Why would you do that? And yet we all do." There was something sort of brave about human beings, Anne remarked; she supposed they just decided they had to put up with it.

The central character of *Back When We Were Grownups*, Rebecca Davitch, does indeed throw parties for a living but, at fifty-three (Anne's heroines were slowly getting older, more or less keeping pace with her own age), she's also a widow who greatly loved her larger-than-life husband Joe. The novel includes an extended passage about grief, and although an author is not necessarily speaking through her characters, nevertheless this was the first time that Anne had dealt with the subject more than briefly or in an episodic way, as with Macon and his dead son in *The Accidental Tourist*. Her character Rebecca uses words and phrases similar to Anne's own when describing what Taghi's loss meant to her; other phrases conceivably reflect her own experience also. Rebecca, like Anne, sees how people never consider "how every engagement on earth would have to end up," and recalls her deep grief immediately after the death of her husband: how stunned she had been through the funeral, how she had pored over his photographs and the notes on his calendar, how she found any excuse to mention his name. She was thrilled suddenly to recollect a minor habit of his, like talking to himself in the mirror while shaving. The worst days were when Rebecca had time to think, asking herself, as Anne had done, what she was going to do with all the years ahead of her. Men she accepted dates with were perfectly nice but filled her with despair because they weren't Joe. "He used to exist, was all. And now did not," says Rebecca. She aches to think what Joe is missing—the landmarks in his daughters' lives and how he would have loved having grandchildren.

Back When We Were Grownups—the title one of Anne's few "organic, natural-born titles" that was always simply there—is also the story of a woman who thinks she has become an imposter in her own life. As a timid, earnest young woman Rebecca ditches her staid fiancé Will to marry single parent Joe, and after his early death is then left to bring up her daughter and stepdaughters in an ornate but crumbling Baltimore row house. Here she carries on the Davitch family business of renting out space for parties (often catered by a stepdaughter's startling culinary creations, such as snails in phyllo pastry). It feels to Rebecca as if she has somehow mislaid her earlier, true self to become the forcedly cheerful, party-loving person she seemingly now is: the linchpin of a large and boisterous extended family of stepchildren, stepgrandchildren, an aged uncle-in-law and her close confidant Zeb, Joe's humorous younger brother. Wanting to rediscover her real self she contacts her former sweetheart and the relationship to some degree resumes, but as the novel ends there is just a hint that Rebecca's happiness may reside a little closer to home.

Anne still felt that the point at which a novel was finished was where she said, "My character has arrived, and I can picture him or her more or less settled there forever." By the end of the book she viewed Rebecca as having come to terms with her life and certain to marry again: "The Davitches will be taken aback at first, but they'll warm to the idea wholeheartedly as soon as they've adjusted."

Her favorite character in the novel was Peter, the awkward young stepson of one of Rebecca's stepdaughters. "I'm very fond of Peter. I like his curiosity and his active mind; I think he's going to grow up to be a very interesting young man." She was sorry for Will, Rebecca's former fiancé, feeling "downright guilty" writing the scene where Rebecca rejects Will for the second time, but she knew that to have stayed with Will would have been even more painful. "Sometimes, you just have to make that choice." Once again she inserted a cross-reference to a previous novel—a catering company from *Ladder of Years*—and also a prequel to a novel still to come, a crowd at an airport carrying balloons and flowers to welcome an adopted baby from abroad.

Canada's *Globe and Mail* decided that the novel was well constructed, well paced and ringing with resonance—but not flawless. The overpopulated opening chapter was difficult to follow, practically every member of the Davitch family was saddled with a nickname, and an "appalling bit of off-handed racism" allowed for a Caucasian baby girl to be forever after addressed as Min Foo because she had dark hair, olive-toned skin and, in Anne's words in the novel, "eyes no wider than slits."

In the US the serious literary and cultural commentary magazine *The Atlantic* was not a fan. Starting with objections to John Updike's observation that Anne Tyler was "wickedly good"—always now pasted onto the flaps and covers of her novels, it was acidly pointed out—the respected journalist Katharine Whittemore slashed her way through some of Anne's previous writing before concluding that *Back When We Were Grownups* did not deliver. Its lightness was not unpleasing, its story not unaffecting, but "Tyler's darker books insinuate themselves more deeply into one's heart. And since *Saint Maybe* we've had three 'light' novels in a row. One craves the old heft." (Whittemore did admit to greatly loving some of Anne's more serious works: "She has written one masterpiece, *Dinner at the Homesick Restaurant* (1982), which I love unreservedly.") The stringent Michiko Kakutani of the *New York Times* was again unimpressed, accusing Anne's fiction of always hovering "perilously close to the line between heartfelt emotion and cloying sentimentality," and this novel in particular of veering dangerously into cuteness, but at least being rescued in its latter half by the author's sure sense of family dynamics and domestic ritual.

Other American critics were happier. "It's a delightful gift to a heroine who attempted a new beginning for her life: an entirely open ending," approved the *New Yorker*. Stunning, said the *Baltimore Sun*—Anne Tyler had a talent for spinning out characters who go on living long after their stories end. Her characters endear themselves to the reader with their candor and their wit and their simple decency, observed *Washington Post Book World*: "The charm of an Anne Tyler novel lies in the clarity of her prose and the wisdom of her observations."

But it was now the turn of the other side of the Atlantic to be weary of Anne Tyler. It was the strength of her work and what made it so popular—her writing about the family—that was also its absolute flaw, suggested Britain's *Times Literary Supplement*: there had to be a limit to the amount of true-to-life family drama that anyone could take, either in fiction or reality, and there had to come a point when even Tyler's most devoted readers would begin to feel that there was more to life than she offered. A seductive read, wrote one *Times* critic, but not a life-affirming book—more a harsh, clear portrait of the cooling and hardening of the middle-aged heart. Anne's "zany characterizations" were lazy, said another the paper's reviewers, its plotting too unlikely: how does the Davitch party business stay afloat? How can Rebecca's stepdaughter earn a living cooking such disgusting food? The flimsiness of this fairy tale's construction cast doubt on the people who inhabited it, and none more so than Rebecca. Not quite one of her best, decided the *Observer*: a certain folksiness (as forewarned by the title), a forcing of sentiment; Anne Tyler was coming close to cramping her own style.

Anne rarely commented publicly about her reviews, good or bad (perhaps finally managing not to read them). But when in the novel Rebecca attempts self-improvement with subscriptions to the *New Yorker*, the *New York Times* and the *New York Review of Books*—all of them frequent and not always positive reviewers of Anne's work—but then gives up on them, there may be a touch of Anne's own astringency coming through in her character's dismissive comment about book reviews:

Her New York Times collected in stacks and gradually turned yellow, untouched...She passed her New York Reviews on to Troy without giving them a glance; she told him she thought there was something perverted about book reviews that were longer than the books they were reviewing.

(Back When We Were Grownups, 2001)

Back When We Were Grownups was adapted for a CBS Hallmark Hall of Fame production that aired in 2004. Starring Blythe Danner, Peter Fonda, Jack Palance and Faye Dunaway, it garnered Blythe, as Rebecca, both a Primetime Emmy nomination for Outstanding Lead Actress in a miniseries or movie and a Golden Globe nomination for best actress in a mini-series or television film. Anne had no involvement in the production.

§

Some time in 2003 Anne's relationship with Mark Furstenberg came to an end, having lasted some five years. Reticent as always about her private life, Anne kept mostly quiet about the break-up.

I don't feel like adjusting any more. I've just had it. Now I make it very clear—if some guy asks me for a coffee, I say, "Is your wife coming?"

It seemed obvious to her that there was a stage in life when you could make allowances for people, where you could adapt and change, but also a stage where you felt beyond adjusting. She had given it a chance, said Anne. She was happy to rely instead on her group of women friends. Women had become more interesting to her after she had children and now her closest friends were women: "I don't know what I'd do without them."

She also had other concerns to occupy her. Her mother Phyllis, now in her eighties, had succumbed to dementia, leaving Anne much saddened. The forthright Phyllis—scary and unpredictable to Anne as a child—had become very quiet and meek, making Anne almost wish that she was railing against the disease instead. Her parents were living in nearby Cockeysville at the Broadmead retirement community (founded by Quakers), where initially Phyllis had been a lively addition and one of the founding members of a writers' group started there in 1995. In retirement she had been happier "than I knew how to be fifty years earlier." But now, when Anne visited, Phyllis would say things like "Have you seen my mother? She was supposed to come pick me up." Anne learned finally to say, oh I saw her down the hall, she'll be here in a few minutes—the only response that would not be upsetting.

Anne was now embarked on *The Amateur Marriage*, the story of a couple who are simply unable to get along. An unhappy union was a subject that intrigued her because it provided another good opportunity to observe different types of characters "grating against each other."

The Amateur Marriage grew out of the reflection that of all the opportunities to show differences in character, surely an unhappy marriage must be the richest...I didn't want a good-person-bad-person marriage, but a marriage in which solely the two styles of character provide the friction.

The couple, so wrong for each other, are brought together purely by chance, something Anne enjoyed bringing into her work. She loved to think about how "one little overheard word, one pebble in a shoe, can change the universe," and when an opportunity arose to use chance as a device, Anne always felt as if she were gleefully rubbing her hands together in anticipation.

This time the book was set in the past, beginning in 1941 just after the Japanese attack on Pearl Harbor that brought the US into the Second World War, and then spanning six decades. "I'm finding it an unexpected pleasure," Anne said, "to live in another time for a while." She had worried that it would make her unhappy to write about such an unhappy subject, but she hadn't counted on the "sheer pleasure of the time trip" all the way back to the 1940s, the decade of her birth and childhood. It felt like stepping inside an old photograph, with Anne wishing she was there herself among the men all wearing hats and the women looking so innocent. She almost felt she *was* there as she wrote the first chapter, and gradually, as the characters became animated, she could imagine she really was in the middle of them all, "that the picture wasn't black-and-white anymore, but living color." The music, the clothes, the street scenes, and above all the general innocence and optimism were so appealing, she had hated to leave the period behind when the time came to move on to the next decade. "Oh, drat, on to the bland years," Anne thought when she reached the 1950s.

There was a practical reason for beginning the story so long ago: it needed to be far enough back to show the whole history of the marriage. At first it had felt forced, a matter of cold research—what items would be sold in a drugstore back then? What cars would be driving past? What perfume did the women wear?—and Anne confessed to relying heavily on a daughter to look things up for her online. She had assumed that she could quiz her parents and their friends, but found that people tended to forget the kind of trivia needed by novelists, such as whether blackout curtains were closed every single night or only when the air-raid siren sounded. Nobody could remember, and in the end the answer came from a friend slightly older than Anne who had been eight or so during the war. Other research was more far-ranging: for a section of the book set in the 1960s, Anne went in person to walk around the former hippie enclave of Haight-Ashbury in San Francisco.

The work also has a different setting, at least to start with: a Polish, Catholic, working-class area in Baltimore, making Anne wistful as she conjured up the neighbors coming and going, gossiping, commiserating, and comparing each other's potluck dishes.

So far my people have been mostly "white-bread" types. I thought I'd like to add a group with a richer ethnic heritage.

In the novel the local residents are agog when a romance develops between their own handsome Michael Anton and the wonderfully pretty Pauline, who comes from a Protestant neighborhood nearby. They marry—despite Pauline's doubts almost at the very foot of the altar about how different they are and how much they fight—and eventually have a family of three. They abandon downtown for the suburbs, where Michael starts an upmarket grocery store not unlike the expensive, old-fashioned Eddie's so long patronized by Anne in Roland Park. But Pauline was right: they *are* too different, she emotional, impulsive, a bit glittery-eyed, and Michael cautious, judgmental, and set in his ways. While other couples learn to rub along, they simply cannot get the hang of each other: theirs is an amateur marriage. (Anne suspected that marriage was like parenthood—everybody was a new hand at it at some point. All marriages *were* amateur, she declared, a thought she wanted to occur to readers of the book. She could not even begin to count the friends who felt that had they known what they were getting into when they married, they would never have dared to do it.)

She loved being inside Pauline's head for a while, following every passing whim as it took hold of her—another example of vicarious living made possible by novel-writing, she observed, admitting that she herself was circumspect to a fault. Pauline ended up as her favorite, to Anne's surprise and relief; she had continued to fear the creation of a good person/bad person marriage, which to her would not be half as interesting as a marriage of two good people who go wrong when together. For a while it had seemed she was weighing the scales toward Michael, but by the end of the book it was Pauline she missed the most. The two had married for all the wrong reasons, but to Anne they had still brought so much to each other and different choices of mate might not have given their lives the same depth. Anne still believed in marriage, at least for childbearing couples. Children needed two parents, she maintained (remembering thinking as a young mother that three would be even better.) And she liked to see two gray-haired people holding hands and tottering along side by side: it always gave her a pang.

She again slipped in a few cross-references to previous novels, now a seemingly regular feature of her work: detective Eli Everjohn pops up once more, as does a certain restaurant on St Paul Street that serves an excellent gizzard soup with garlic.

The Amateur Marriage came out in 2004—to cries that Anne Tyler was repeating herself, if with a more somber tinge. Implacable critic Michiko Kakutani in the *New York Times* highlighted its similarity to *Breathing Lessons*: the husbands both proprietors of small businesses inherited from their families, the wives both ditsy and given to over-sharing; both couples inclined to ponder the roads not taken, both having to contend with a wayward child and an unexpected grandchild. But *The Amateur Marriage* was "an altogether darker, less comic production than its predecessor: the melancholy melody that threads through many Tyler novels is more pronounced in these pages; a sense of loss and mortality more insistent." At least the cloying cuteness curdling some of her recent fiction was largely absent here, wrote Kakutani, and while the novel might leave the longtime Tyler fan with the sense that the author was simply pacing out territory long ago annexed and mapped out, it was so psychologically detailed that the story as a whole stood as one of her more convincing efforts: "an ode to the complexities of familial love, the centripetal and centrifugal forces that keep families together and send their members flying apart, the supremely ordinary pleasures and frustrations of middle-class American life."

Books in Canada agreed that the novel was a darker work than usual from Anne, missing the "eccentric optimism" that had shaped the pages of earlier efforts, while Canada's *Globe and Mail* felt Anne had told Pauline and Michael's story with something approaching majesty, simultaneously revealing the exquisite, damning details of their lives while reserving judgment on their behavior; she exposed, with compassion and wit, the mystery at the heart of any marriage. In New Zealand the novel was viewed by some as emotionally bereft: the marriage might span sixty years but for all that it felt too slender, too subdued a story to sustain such ambitious scope, wrote the *New Zealand Herald*. For the *Sydney Morning Herald* in Australia the novel failed to encourage empathy with the characters, while Anne's carefully structured reflection of contemporary culture came at the expense of true insight into the machinations of a family "that one neither understands nor truly desires to." In Britain the *Times Literary Supplement* echoed the perception that Anne was becoming repetitious: another foray into familiar Tyler territory, carped the reviewer, where women are emotional and generous and unreliable, men capable and pedantic and distant. Britain's *Guardian* concurred: "Anne Tyler is a great writer and in a great rut." By the standards of her best work the new novel was perfunctory and mining a worked-out vein, they complained. In comparison with vinegary writers like *Portnoy's Complaint* author Philip Roth, Anne Tyler was "offering milk and cookies, milk and cookies not quite fresh"—a comment that was to become frequently quoted.

Anne did not deny that the comparison with Philip Roth was merited, agreeing that next to him she *did* dispense milk and cookies. She had noticed, as a woman writer, that an event like war was considered a more real literary subject than just a wedding, which made her want to say "Oh, I'm so sorry I haven't been to war." But, she argued, there was more edge under some of her soft language than people realized:

I don't think I'm like one of those little old ladies where everything is so sweet that there's no traction there...It is probably that I just want to be with nice people, which sounds very milk and cookies, I know.

Anne's great fan Nick Hornby, however, really enjoyed *The Amateur Marriage*, praising her elegance and warmth and how she could switch tone in a novel in a way many British writers did not manage to do. Sometimes it was hard for him to believe that her books were going to be as dark as they were, because they were written in such a warm and friendly style: she made good jokes, said Nick, *and* she made you cry and realize how just being alive was quite a journey. He had been a little worried that Anne was slightly off form in the last few novels, and saw *The Amateur Marriage* as a partial return.

Reviewers in the US saw only classic Anne Tyler. The *Chicago Tribune* found the novel a "rich and satisfying addition to the author's distinguished body of work," noting how Anne opened each section in a new decade with every detail of the setting faithfully supplied: the furniture of the era, the clothes, hair styles, language, political and cultural changes. Her writing was "beautifully accurate, more often than not with a glinting vein of humor," enthused the *New York Times Book Review*. For the *Miami Herald*, Anne was "wise and observant," for *USA Today*, she was once again displaying the qualities of "wisdom, insightful writing and compassion" that had made her the most admired serious yet popular writer then at work. "One is never embarrassed to be seen reading a Tyler novel."

The novel's most positive reception was perhaps that from celebrated author Joyce Carol Oates, who felt that when a realistic novel worked its magic, "you won't simply have read about the experiences of fictitious characters, you will have seemed to have lived them." The experience of reading such fiction when it was carefully composed could be breathtaking, she wrote, "like being given the magical power of reliving passages of our own lives, indecipherable at the time of being lived."

§

In January 2006, after three years of worsening Alzheimer's disease, Anne's mother Phyllis died peacefully of heart failure at the age of eighty-eight. She and Lloyd would have celebrated their 66th wedding anniversary that coming March.

She was remembered in the Raleigh press as one of the city's most passionate activists, dedicated, along with her husband, to improving the human lot. Phyllis Tyler had been a regular on picket lines throughout North Carolina and in Washington, DC, the obituary stated, highlighting also her involvement in the founding of the Raleigh Women's Center and the couple's work with an interracial church group to develop a low-income housing development. The Tylers' two-year assignment in Gaza managing preschools for Palestinian refugee children was not forgotten.

Phyllis was celebrated too for her long-running newspaper column *Beautiful Lofty People*, with mention of an article she wrote about a singing trash man because she wanted to shine the spotlight on unsung heroes. The column appeared for over a decade (toward the end getting "a little more political" than the owner liked, according to the obituary).

Anne's old art teacher in high school, Alice Ehrlich, believed that Phyllis had written some books but then abandoned them, and that she might have written more and been more secure in herself were it not for Anne and her success. Alice knew of the highly detailed scrapbook Phyllis had kept about Anne's first years, and felt that she had been obsessed with her daughter more than any of the other children and that it may well have been oppressive to Anne. Phyllis used to come in to the school practically every afternoon, Alice recalled, to see what Anne had done. In Alice's view she was "disturbed," prone to thinking everything was her fault and that she must be doing something wrong.

There were other views of Phyllis relayed in the press. She was a "very quiet, unassuming person, but a woman of strong convictions," a close friend was quoted as saying. "I think of Phyllis as being a gentle person, strictly committed to non-violence." The friend also recalled Phyllis' penchant for wearing large straw hats at protest marches to keep the sun off her face. "There'd be thousands of people there, and the photographers would always head for Phyllis to take her picture. She just stood out in the crowd."

Anne sent some memories of her mother as a contribution to the obituary in the press:

My mother liked to say that my youngest brother learned to walk on a picket line...Because both of my parents had always been so involved on behalf of peace and civil rights, I guess I grew up taking that part of our lives for granted. I have many memories of my mother sitting over coffee in our dining room with someone—a friend, an acquaintance or even a stranger—and listening with sympathy and full attention to his or her troubles and dreams. She was always intensely interested in other people's stories, as I am sure anyone must realize who read her columns.

Although clearly not always a happy relationship, with Anne describing her mother as angry, envious, and unpredictable, nevertheless she could also see the good in her mother—Phyllis' determination that her children should love books, the way she read to them all from the earliest days, her own storytelling skills. She had encouraged Anne's childhood writing, and always shown great sympathy for others. Phyllis and Lloyd had raised her "very kindly," Anne felt, despite the unexpected bouts of anger her mother had been prone to. Anne even conceded that in some ways she *had* been close to her mother, as she was the "book person" who had brought to life that side of her children. But Alice Ehrlich was probably right to say that Phyllis' obsessive interest might have been oppressive. "I have spent an enormous amount of my life defending my privacy from, of all people, my mother..." Anne once observed. Years later, when she first came across the word bipolar, the term used to describe the mental disorder causing excessive mood swings and depression, she guessed this was probably what they had been dealing with. "It was just hard to understand, at the time."

Phyllis had confided to a friend that some of her daughter's books had been a "great sadness" to her, something she never told Anne. (Presumably these included *Dinner at the Homesick Restaurant*, with its portrayal of an abusive mother—even though Anne had strongly denied this was meant to be Phyllis—and perhaps those novels depicting marriages between reasonable, stable men and slightly unhinged women.) She used to think that her one accomplishment in life was being a good parent, "but quite plainly I was not."

Anne's relationship with her father—a kindly, easygoing, and "very peaceful" man, in Anne's view—had been easier, but now she was to lose ninety-two-year-old Lloyd as well. His passing, only fourteen months after his wife, was marked with the same tally in the press of all that he and Phyllis had achieved together. Like his wife, Lloyd had dedicated his entire life to pacifism, non-violence, and the campaign for integration: he was an activist until the day he died, said Anne. At the retirement complex, he had been bewildered to hear from members of a men's group that the central experience of their lives had been military service.

As before, Anne supplied an emailed contribution to the obituary:

He died very peacefully as he was sitting over a newspaper after supper, and for that we are grateful, although we will miss him more than I can put into words...My father worked harder than anyone I've ever known to leave the world a better place than he found it. He was tireless, and fearless, but always so matter-of-fact about it. Even in the face of all that's going wrong with the world today, he maintained his optimism. I don't expect to see his like again.

Years later, as she herself aged, Anne was to get unexpected images, suddenly seeing things like her father's high leather workshoes as she was tying her own footwear. It was a great comfort to her. "I thought, ah, there are daddy's shoes."

Within the space of a few short years Anne had lost her beloved husband, both parents, and also the brother nearest to her in age: Israel (Ty), a physicist, had died in 2002. With the girls leading their own lives many miles distant and her two remaining brothers also widely scattered—each now a respected scientist in his field, Seth a zoologist and Jonathan a biologist—she must have felt very much alone.

Her next work was to reflect, more closely than any other of her novels, the most crucial of Anne's past experiences: her encounter with another culture, and, more significantly, illness and loss.

Coming to Terms

Two families in Baltimore each adopt a Korean baby: the noisy, all-American Donaldsons, and the quieter, olive-skinned, Iranian-born Yazdans. The families become friends after meeting by chance at the airport as they wait to welcome the new arrivals, and through this chance encounter their histories—in the shape of widowed grandmother Maryam on the Iranian side, widowed grandfather Dave on the American side—eventually intertwine.

Building the plot of her seventeenth novel, *Digging to America*, Anne had meditated on the way some people seemed by nature "so exuberant and outgoing and celebratory, larger than life almost," and, having always been fascinated by inborn, dyed-in-the-wool character traits, she came up with the idea of adoption by two families with polar opposite styles. She found it fun setting up that first scene as a microcosm of the two families' future interactions. The storyline also allowed her to write much of what she knew about the Iranian immigrant experience in America—although it was really the idea of adoption that had first stirred her interest.

> *Digging to America began with my thinking about the subject of adoption. (It interested me because it's so dramatic and so sudden, compared with childbirth.) That one of the families should be Iranian was a last-minute whim, just to make the writing more fun.*

She couldn't imagine what the book would have been about if she hadn't made one of the families Iranian, and she was "very grateful" to her subconscious for coming up with the notion. Scenes in the book were much colored by memories of her Iranian in-laws' conversations—their fascination with the issue of American versus non-American, their fondness for a good story and vivid, mesmerizing narrative style, their voices lowered at dramatic moments and other people's inflections mimicked to a T.

But while she had reflected her adopted family's intrinsic way with words, everything else in the novel was manufactured, Anne stated firmly. Nothing in her books came from real life, she still maintained, conceding at most that her personal experiences could occasionally give rise to "flights of 'what if?' thoughts." She insisted that she always relied on imagination rather than her memory, which tended to be "disconcertingly focused" in a not very helpful way. She might have only the vaguest, blurriest recollection of someone, but his cushioned-looking, bitten-down fingernails would stay with her forever.

Despite claiming that nothing came from actuality, in fact Anne not only threw in two real-life incidents but in one case inserted her own family as anonymous bystanders. When the Donaldsons and the Yazdans are waiting for their babies at the airport (similar to the scene that had already featured in *Back When We Were Grownups*), other people there to greet their loved ones include "an older woman with a younger one who might have been her daughter." Anne later owned up that the older woman was herself and the other was Mitra; both had actually witnessed one of these baby arrivals while at the airport in the summer of 1997 to meet Mitra's (very tall) husband-to-be Greg Amundson, who was arriving for the family's annual beach holiday. On turning up he was then ignored in favor of the fascinating tableau unfolding before them. Seeing the baby's new parents reach out to take him was one of the "most moving moments imaginable," Anne remembered. The image of the family waiting for their child stayed on her mind for several years, she said, "germinating in the dark the way seeds for novels often do." Mitra's reaction to the event was faithfully reproduced in the novel, when the first off is a tall young man:

He spotted the mother and daughter and went over to them and bent to kiss the daughter, but only on the cheek because she was too busy peering past him, just briefly returning his hug while she kept her eyes on the new arrivals.

(Digging to America, 2006)

Then the first of the babies is brought in.

"Ah!" everyone breathed—even the outsiders, even the mother and the grown daughter. (Although the daughter's young man still appeared confused.)

(Digging to America, 2006)

There is another glimpse in the novel of the daughter and the young man some years later with their own two children—a boy and a girl, just like Greg and Mitra's.

The second incident culled from real life went back to when Taghi became an American citizen. Anne and the girls had suggested throwing a party but Taghi, suffering mixed feelings, had asked why he should celebrate losing his nationality and becoming something else. Instead, as a joke, Anne and the girls had a T-shirt printed with the word "Foreigner" on the front, only to discover that Foreigner was the name of a rock group. Anne has exactly the same thing happen to grandmother Maryam. (This was probably not the first time Anne had placed her own family in her work: two young women at Baltimore's train station in *A Patchwork Planet* may well have been Tezh and Mitra.)

Families and immigration: two of her favorite topics, Anne once joked. She called it "fun" to write about being Iranian in America but at the same time she pulls no punches about the difficulties encountered by immigrants, gleaned from the experiences relayed to her by Taghi and his family and friends and no doubt from her own knowledge of Farsi as she listened to them all talking. "Taghi was always baffled by the fact that Americans seemed basically ignorant about the rest of the world," she recalled. "Nobody knew where Iran was or what it was." This incomprehension on the part of their adopted country, plus the constant trouble with language, the confusion of dealing with unspoken social rules, and the sense of being always an outsider are all laid out in *Digging to America*—as is the hostility directed toward Iranians during the 1980s hostage crisis. (As balance, perhaps, Anne also included a passage on how hard it was to be an American—always lumped together, having to sail in the same big ship "even if it's behaving like some...grade-school bully.")

When Sami Yazdan and his wife adopt their little girl from abroad, Sami's aristocratic, aloof, immigrant mother Maryam, who lives on the "wrong side" of Roland Park—equally nice but the houses just a bit smaller and closer together—becomes the baby's besotted new grandparent, slowly getting to know the Donaldsons in the process. Much of the action, and observation about immigrant experience, is from her point of view, granting the reader not only the fascinating intricacies of family life, social divisions and political shades in Iran but also all of these things in America from an immigrant perspective. Anne had long understood that her Iranian connection added "immeasurable richness and depth" to her life, yet it was not until she wrote *Digging to America* that she recognized the degree to which she had internalized everything, how readily she could imagine the world as seen through Iranian eyes. For forty-four years, she said, ever since she married Taghi, his very large and complicated family had been giving her a close look at what it meant to be foreign—to view America from the outside, to attempt to "dig" one's way inside:

What surprised me in the writing of this book, though, is that my offhand decision to include Iranian characters (the result of many fond memories of my late husband's gigantic family in Tehran) gradually turned it into a story about a different kind of digging: the immigrant's attempt to break through the crust of a foreign culture.

It was an "Immigration Tango," she observed: the pull toward assimilation at war with the fear of losing one's true self. She did not in the end think a single one of the characters would ever reach the point where he or she would say, "I've succeeded; I'm in. I can sit back and breathe easy now." She hoped her work would remind readers that most Iranians were ordinary, private people just as Americans were, "just as hopeful as we are for peace and for the chance to muddle through their family lives undisturbed." However, much as she would have loved her book to foster international understanding, that had not been her aim in writing it. For Anne, the book was about finding a place in the world, although she had not known this when she began it, seeing it as more about the randomness of families.

The strong autobiographical element in the novel also encompassed cancer, death, and grief. Grandfather Dave on the American side loses his wife from cancer during the novel itself: the reader witnesses an ever frailer Connie as she undergoes chemotherapy and loses her hair. Later, Connie's daughter is also diagnosed with cancer and must suffer the same treatment. Anne hints that she may not survive. Fortunately, Anne's own well-being had remained robust after her mastectomies. "I'm in excellent health, and have been cancer-free for the past eight years," she emailed in response to a reporter's inquiry in early 2006.

After Connie's death, when Maryam becomes more than a friend to Dave, she talks about her dead husband's cancer and how he had changed: watching him go "down, down, down" during his illness was harder than it would have been to lose him when in perfect health, she tells Dave. She cannot mourn the man she once knew, but has only the more recent versions to remember: sick, then sicker, the one who was so cross and hated her for disturbing him with pills and food and fluids, and finally "the faraway, sleepy one who in fact was not there at all." After death came grief, with the thoughts and feelings that Anne herself had expressed reflected in those of Maryam and Dave. Maryam, whose husband, like Anne's, was nearly a decade older, sorrows that he cannot share grandparenthood with her. Dave on first being made a widower is incapable of interest in other women: "the effort of adjusting to a new person was beyond him." When he and Maryam become a couple, Maryam with this new relationship is conscious that everything has an end, that the day would come when he would no longer be there, and that they were "letting themselves in for more than any young couple could possibly envision."

Anne was somewhat in agreement with Maryam's statement that the real culture clash was the one between the two sexes, as she was finding herself more and more struck by the differences between men and women: "All marriages are mixed marriages." She came to feel closest to Maryam, even though like the

Donaldsons she found her a little intimidating; as she got to know the elegant Iranian better, she began to like her "enormously."

I was more and more drawn to Maryam as I was writing about her. I like her dignity. And while she does become more open and flexible by the end of the book, she remains quite firmly herself—not unsocial so much as reserved. I admired that.

Maryam likes to entertain and, commenting about the many party scenes in the novel, Anne explained that her fondness for such scenes was partly utilitarian, as a way of getting something to "percolate" among the characters, and partly wishful thinking —but not at all related to any personal predilection. "In real life I avoid all parties altogether, but on paper I can mingle with the best of them."

Digging to America came out in 2006, with the first chapter published in the *New York Times*. One of the paper's critics detected the autobiographical threads in the novel, suggesting also that Anne had begun to shift her focus and was wrestling with the question of how an individual moves forward: she seemed to be "in search of the road ahead." The paper's regular reviewer Michiko Kakutani surfaced with her usual complaint, an accusation that the arrival of the babies at the airport was "all-too-cute," making the reader worry that this was going to be one of Anne's more cloying performances, like the "mawkish" *A Patchwork Planet*. But she swiftly conceded that while the novel was about families, it was also about what it meant to be an American. Anne had delineated Maryam's efforts to come to terms with her new life in America with sympathy and wit, Kakutani finally decided, with the novel examining the promises and perils of the American Dream and the knotty, layered relationship between native-born Americans and those newer to the country.

The Atlantic, too, saw a swerve away from "the saccharine" at the start of the novel to success on several levels: as a satire of millennial parenting, a tribute to autumn romances, and, most important, an exploration of "our risible (though poignant) attempts to welcome otherness into our midst." There was praise also for Anne's understanding of Maryam's self-imposed isolation, a recognition that it came from an author who had been raised in Quaker communities and was eleven before she used a telephone. The *Times* in Britain, on the other hand, rather liked the opening scene, seeing in it an example of Anne's talent for pushing the reader into empathy for her characters: "This is her method, her quiet virtuosity." The *Daily Telegraph* praised the work as a "comedy that is not so much brilliant as luminous —its observant sharpness sweetened by a generous understanding of human fallibility." Deliciously funny and sharply observed, said the *Guardian*; for the *Daily Mail*, Anne was simply spinning gold. In Canada, the *Globe and Mail* commented that Anne's writing, as always, made for wholesome, comforting fare, spiced with urbane wit and a knack for nailing the small truths behind fine details—even if detecting a sentimentality in which the volatile politics between the United States and Iran were carefully skirted.

Digging to America was a *New York Times* Bestseller and a *New York Times* Notable Book; in 2007 it was shortlisted for Britain's prestigious Orange Prize for Fiction (now the Women's Prize for Fiction). It was later translated into Farsi by Goli Emami and issued in Iran.

§

Two years later Anne, now sixty-seven, took a significant decision: to sell her home of thirty-eight years and move to a smaller place not far away. The large old stone house in the Homeland neighborhood, with its five bedrooms and three bathrooms, was feeling too big.

It went on the market for $599,900. Few of the dozens of prospective buyers at the first open-house event were aware of the identity of its owner: Anne, ever protective of her privacy, rarely mentioned Homeland in her novels and was universally assumed to live in nearby Roland Park, so much a feature of her work. The old property on Tunbridge Road remained much as it had been when the Modarressis first bought it back in the 1960s —Anne had wanted to let the house just be what it was, recalled the listing agent, a friend of the family. It was still furnished and decorated in minimal fashion, a few Persian rugs against a color scheme of deep-water blues and slate greens, one of the bathrooms a simple black and white, another done in blue and cream stripes.

Anne's new abode was a modern low-level brick house with large, light-filled windows and a small backyard, far more convenient to run, although she told the agent she missed her old open fire and the pleasure of serving a glass of wine to friends in front of the flames. But she had looked for years for the right sort of place and was happy to be downsizing to this discreet upscale development. Roland Park was still close by, with its winding, tree-shaded streets and beautiful old houses, and Anne could still take her favorite walk on a road bordered by a stream and a strip of woods. "See, this is where I just think I'm in heaven. I never did like to really rough it...here I can walk in woods on a sidewalk." Her new location was quiet and there were trees and birds and she liked her neighbors. "I have a nice life here."

Much was sold or given away as part of the move, including a great many of her books, which little by little Anne then found she couldn't do without and ended up mostly replacing. Her grandparents' rocking chairs went into the guest room. Much of the furniture in the rest of the house was contemporary Shaker style, with plenty of polished wood. Anne still disliked clutter and her new home was soon arranged as neatly as the last, right down to the alphabetically arranged spices in the kitchen cupboards, which included some exotic flavorings left over from her Iranian cookery lessons with Taghi. Her new fridge door was non-magnetic, ideal to Anne because it avoided untidiness, even if it meant there was nowhere for her grocery list. "I am secretly very organized," she admitted, adding that a lot of her family were the same; she just found it very comforting to have things in order. People laughed at her for her alphabetized spices but how else would you find what you wanted, she asked. She did have a sneaking admiration for those who were less ordered, however: in her view, they tended not to be worriers.

Once again she had an upstairs writing room, with bright sunlight pouring through a dormer window onto her desk and computer and box of index cards full of ideas and observations. Pinned above the desk were the various photos and verses to inspire her writing—the now faded old copy of Richard Wilbur's poem "Walking to Sleep," with its lines "Step off assuredly into the blank of your mind / Something will come to you," and John Updike's poem about characters with misty faces willing to muster for another day's progress. Amongst the photos was a postcard of Eudora Welty and a picture of Elvis Presley standing next to a beaming childhood friend of Anne's (whom Anne remembered remarking, "Nobody knows, as I'm sitting there smiling, that I'm thinking, why am I here? I hate Elvis Presley!").

After all the years of writing, Anne's methods had remained much the same as in her early days. Feeling "all cleaned out" of ideas after finishing one novel, she would spend about a year of "refilling" before the next one. This was sometimes pre-empted by a new character popping into her mind as she was still on the previous effort—which she recognized as a protective device against the panicky sense of having nothing more to work on—and she would have to tell the character to shut up and wait his turn. The decision to start a new one was just that, a decision, since she never felt suddenly inspired. She would tell herself it was time to stop lolling about and think something up:

> Then for a month or so I'll jot down desperate possibilities. "Maybe I could write about a man who does such-and-such. Or wait: I think I already did that. Well, then maybe about that woman I saw in the grocery the other day. What was she up to, exactly? What might her story have been?"

Eventually, one of these possibilities would start flowering, and she would manufacture what was to start with an extremely "trumped-up, artificial plot," still claiming to be very poor at it. "Let's be honest: I basically have no plots. When I'm starting to plan a new book, I always think, oh, Lord, I suppose they think I'm going to have a plot here." However, for a storyline, Anne often decided to have unexpected events disrupt a protagonist's careful routine: she liked the idea of confronting a cautious person with the chaos of normal life, and then watching to see what he or she did about it.

She would still write maybe one long paragraph describing the events of the forthcoming novel, then a page or two breaking the events into chapters, and then her usual profusion of notes delving into characters—family background, history, details of appearance—much more than would ever appear in the book. She would search her memory for telltale traits or gestures that she might have randomly noticed in someone, like the delightfully scatterbrained woman wearing a giant bagel-sized bracelet who was unable to write something down because the bracelet was so thick her fingers couldn't reach the pad of paper her wrist was resting on. "I loved that; I thought it said reams about her." Nothing fascinated Anne more than trying to figure somebody out and suddenly being able to say oh, yes, that's what's operating there (although she also revealed that only a few kinds of people actually interested her).

This deep delving into personality, Anne believed, was what lifted a book out of that early calculated, artificial stage. She needed to know what the character's childhood was like, how he felt about food and clothes and social occasions, his enthusiasms, his anxieties—any detail that occurred to her, she would note down. It helped her understand how the character would react within a given situation.

I really, really know my characters. Ask me anything: What's their favorite color? Do they like their mothers? I have the answers. This is a huge help with the plotlessness problem. If you know your characters, eventually some semblance of a plot will amble along out of somewhere.

She was trying to make it as "visceral" a description as she could, without going on and on and on: she used to hate the type of book they were forced to read in school that began with three pages of scenery description. She wanted there to be a little detail here and there that would make readers feel they could see the person, and were walking alongside him.

Once her characters were in place, Anne was generally ready to begin. Her writing day had grown shorter as she aged, although producing about the same number of pages. At most she would work three or four hours daily, sometimes less. Her one ironclad rule was still always to try. "I have to walk into my writing room and pick up my pen every weekday morning. If I waited till I felt like writing, I'd never write at all." Trusting to routine saw her through. She did sometimes worry that after so many books she might start "phoning it in" (a phrase she loved — in other words, make as little effort as possible), but if that did happen Anne hoped she would have enough sense to quit. The reverse of this feeling was her usual anxiety that whatever she was writing was not going well and that nothing would come of it. Tezh and Mitra told her she said this every time.

She still wanted her writing voice to be unidentifiable, a "clear pane of glass that my characters can shine through on their own." As she wrote, her characters would, as always, begin to surprise her. Slogging through some dialogue early on, all of a sudden Anne would be made to laugh by something a character said. "Where did that come from? I'm not funny!" Then, as so often, another might flatly refuse the plot contrivance she had designed for him and a scene would slow to a crawl and stop, whatever way she tried it. Finally she would give up and drop the contrivance and the scene would fall into place; an unguessed-at motive would emerge and Anne would understand where they were headed. It continued to be as if someone else was telling her the story. She could hear voices, but not in a supernatural way. "I think it's just that when characters are given enough texture and backbone, then lo and behold, they stand on their own."

The central character of her next novel, *Noah's Compass*, is sixty-year-old Liam, a detached sort of man living alone after two failed marriages that produced three daughters. On being made redundant from his lackluster job teaching in a second-rate school, Liam gets a smaller apartment in a modern block to economize. The morning after moving in he wakes up in hospital, with no memory of the intruder who apparently attacked him in his sleep. In an effort to recall what happened Liam scrapes acquaintance with a young woman who works as a "rememberer," assisting a forgetful old businessman with appointments and meetings; she seems to Liam to be someone who might help bring back the blank in his own memory. As he gradually falls for the rumpled, bespectacled Eunice he reflects on his painful past and starts to realign relations with his daughters. Life appears to be opening up—at least until Liam discovers that Eunice has been keeping a secret.

Asked about *Noah's Compass* as she was just starting it, Anne replied that she wanted to write about a man who feels he has nothing more to expect from life, although not sure that the book would go in this direction. But it did turn into precisely that book, she later recognized, something that did not always happen. This time a plot had been delivered ready-made. Anne had been lying in bed one night half-asleep when the house gave an unfamiliar creak, and, frightened, she consoled herself with the thought that if a burglar came upstairs and conked her over the head at least she wouldn't know anything about it. This thought led to another and then another, and in the morning she had the seeds of the novel.

As usual, she had no difficulty writing from the male point of view. With her dearly loved father, brothers, and grandfathers, Anne still never thought of male characters as being all that foreign to her. The biggest stretch she had to make was reminding herself that men need to shave in the morning. About Eunice, Anne commented that she would like to BE a "hired rememberer" rather than hire one, as a way of living another life. She made Eunice, like herself, fearful of merging onto major highways because of the feeling of pressure from those waiting behind her.

But the novel had been "no fun" to write, Anne reported, and hard work from the very beginning, making her wonder if it was because it was a bad book and her subconscious knew it, or it was a good book and they were never easy to write—or whether she was just getting too old for the whole thing. She eventually arrived at the real reason, that it was reminding her a little too much of her own situation:

Like my central character, I have passed all the major milestones and have no more to look forward to...My life is most definitely winding down.

Anne had now arrived at the point of conceding that her books could indeed reflect her current stage of life, although continuing to deny—despite the cameo appearances of her own family—that they were ever based on real events. She acknowledged that *Noah's Compass* took shape in her mid-60s, when, like her protagonist Liam, she had begun to wonder how people live after they have done everything except for dying. That her life was winding down was not such a bad thing, she thought: restful, really, and she enjoyed being the age she was. There was nothing she desperately wanted any more, other than for life to go on as happily as it had in the past.

She was satisfied enough with the novel when finished. These days, on completing a book, Anne felt that it usually came close to what she had envisioned for it at the outset. It might not be exactly what she had projected, but it came closer than her earlier books did, which made her "very happy." *Noah's Compass* —her eighteenth novel—was published by Knopf in 2009, hitting bookstores early in 2010.

Liam's close resemblance to other male characters in her novels was immediately seized upon. Over the years, wrote Michiko Kakutani in the *New York Times*, in a "succession of funny-sad-usually-entertaining novels," Anne Tyler had created a male character instantly recognizable as a distinct species: a lost soul or self-proclaimed failure, detached and passive, who realizes that his life is stalled and who sinks into a low-grade depression. To make her point, she then reeled off a list: Macon Leary in *The Accidental Tourist*, who starts padding about the house in a sweatsuit, eating popcorn for breakfast and forgetting to shower and shave; Ian Bedloe in *Saint Maybe*, who drops out of school and lives an abstemious life to atone for his believed sin; Barnaby Gaitlin in *A Patchwork Planet*, the black sheep of a wealthy family who does odd jobs for a living. But Liam's turned out to be a slighter story than any of Anne's best work, judged the relentless Kakutani—tipping over into the sentimentality the author was prone to and devolving into a predictable and highly contrived tale of a midlife crisis. A flimsy and unsatisfying novel, was her verdict, "a novel quite unworthy of this gifted author's talents."

Other critics made the same points, with the additional observation that Anne's female creations were far better, vivid, delightful, and capable of surprising action—just not in *Noah's Compass*. Some even saw Liam and the irritating Eunice as older versions of Macon and Muriel from *The Accidental Tourist*—although not Anne, when asked. She also refused to acknowledge that her male characters were any different from her females, or to make generalizations about the sexes. "Men and women can do anything the other sex can do," she had always insisted. "Macon isn't passive because he's a man."

But at the same time there was plenty of praise: for the *Boston Globe* her writing was as "lovely and transparent as ever," for the *Washington Post* the work was sensitive and witty, for *The Oprah Magazine* an "offbeat delight." The *Baltimore Sun*, loyally, dubbed the work masterly—noting local references such as Liam shopping at a branch of Eddie's grocery, and how he makes a list of grammatical errors found in that very paper. Imperfect, said the *Times Literary Supplement* in Britain, but the *Times* deemed it as bright and witty as her best work, despite her weakness for "borderline-autistic men." For the *Observer* it was "beautifully subtle." In Canada, for the *Globe and Mail* this was writing "inspired by passages of such divine loopiness you flip the book over, look long and deep at the author photo and suspect you've underestimated her all along."

In the end, Liam remains alone, living sparsely in his small apartment, content enough with a book to read and with his new job as a helper in a kindergarten. He considers his position: he has a good enough place to live, is solvent, and very healthy.

Then he switched on the lamp beside his favorite armchair. He sat down and opened his book...He leaned back against the cushions with a contented sigh. All he lacked was a fireplace.

But that was all right. He didn't need a fireplace.

(Noah's Compass, 2009)

When Judith Jones retired from Knopf in 2011, Anne lost her sole editor for the past forty-seven years. By then, senior editor Judith was also vice president of Knopf, and had worked not only with Anne but with other big names like John Updike and the famous cook Julia Child; she had also published a memoir and a number of her own cookbooks, including a 1998 edition of a work on bread baking that was illustrated by Anne's daughter Mitra. So important a figure was Judith Jones in the career of Julia Child, in fact, that she became a character in the 2009 film *Julie and Julia*, starring Meryl Streep as Julia and Erin Dilly as Judith. (The scene in the film in which Judith cancels a dinner because of rain was stupid, Anne commented, something the gourmet editor would never have done in reality. "Judith Jones would go through a blizzard...She's the most indomitable person.")

But, despite their long association, Anne confessed to visiting the Knopf offices in person only twice. Former editor-in-chief and president of the company Robert Gottlieb described Anne as responsive, efficient, completely without ego and "a total charmer," but he could only remember seeing her at Knopf once in his twenty years there. She met Judith in person only four times over the whole relationship (including a meal for Judith and her husband hosted in Anne's home early on), but even with the back-and-forth required for each book and various other matters—Judith's friendly, jokey little letters to Anne usually scrawled in green ink—the two spoke on the phone just once or twice a year. There were no lunches. "Oh no, no," said Anne emphatically. "What would we have to say?" She appears to have been a little more forthcoming with her agent Timothy Seldes, welcoming him at her home for dinner on at least one occasion in 1982, and inviting him out for a meal in late 1984 when the family was in New York for Mitra to interview at two prestigious art schools. She and Taghi had also attended a dinner party thrown by Timothy for Eudora Welty in

Washington in 1993, Anne in a lovely long white dress looking "just *wonderful*," in Eudora's words. Eudora was very impressed and touched that Anne had made the effort to come. (She thought Anne a beautiful woman, loving her "kind of Chinese look," as she put it.)

There are hints that Anne may not always have welcomed Judith's suggestions: she freely admitted that the editing process raised her hackles. Asked if she would ever phone her editor if she needed to talk about a work in progress, the answer was again no. For Anne the role her editor played in the process of writing had to be "as little as possible...I don't want to know about anything that goes on in New York."

Nevertheless, she believed herself extraordinarily fortunate to have had the same publisher and editor for so long; for all that time, they had "jogged along together without much incident of any sort." She described Judith, diminutive both in her person and in terms of her editing, as "very delicate and graceful, almost weightless." Judith in turn had nothing but good to say of Anne, whom she dubbed a great social observer. "There's something very special about her...She has a wonderful sense of humor but it's never mean. It's always very sympathetic and understanding, and she takes risks that an established writer often doesn't." Judith declared that the most important thing an editor could do was be a diplomat. She believed her editorial suggestions (always using her green pencil) had usually ended with writers expressing themselves much more clearly. She died in 2017 at the age of ninety-three, Anne praising her as both an astute and gifted editor and a remarkable human being.

Anne's subsequent editors included Sonny Mehta, Chairman and Editor-in-Chief at what had by then become the Knopf Doubleday Publishing Group. She described him as elegant in appearance and, with his precision and deft assurance, even more elegant when working on a manuscript; for Anne, he was the "Fred Astaire of editing."

§

Time was passing for Anne too. October 2011 was a milestone birthday.

I often have the feeling that I'm seven, which seems to be the age of reason, when you first start saying, Oh, I'm me and there's the world there. I turned seventy on my last birthday, and I thought, just looking out through my own eyes, not at myself in the mirror, I'm seven, how did this happen?

That year Anne had been one of thirteen international finalists for Britain's Man Booker International Prize, a £60,000 accolade honoring an entire body of work and picking just one winner out of all living authors of fiction writing in English. She lost out to American writer Philip Roth, author of the shocking 1969 novel *Portnoy's Complaint.* One of the panel of judges, publisher Carmen Callil, resigned from the panel in protest at the decision, describing Philip Roth as going "on and on about the same subject in almost every single book. It's as though he's sitting on your face and you can't breathe." As might be expected, Anne made no comment. "I'm not an angry or competitive person, even underneath," she once remarked.

Hard as *Noah's Compass* had been to write, and despite daily musing about retiring, Anne did of course start another book, but this time with the thought that she did not have to finish it if she decided she didn't want to. "I find that I love the act of working too much just to walk away from it." Her essential reason for writing, apart from the love of it, remained the same: to live lives other than her own.

I do that by burrowing deeper and deeper, quarter inch by quarter inch, till I reach the center of those lives. But I'm not content to do it alone; I want other people to come into that center with me. It's something like when a child finds a secret spot in the woods and immediately wants to show her best friend.

She always used to tell herself that the next book was going to be bigger and more eventful, that it really was going to be *War and Peace*, just set in Baltimore. And then when it was finished she would think,"Uh-oh, it's the same book as the last one." She seemed to herself to be "constitutionally committed" to looking through a microscope rather than a telescope.

The setting for Anne's next was certainly Baltimore, and again Roland Park (the no less attractive "wrong" side of Roland Park with the slightly smaller houses where most of her characters tended to live, according to Anne). The time was the present, if not very much reflected. Anne admitted to inserting "a rather clumsy reference to the war in Iraq and Hillary Clinton...so we'd know what era we were in." She just didn't want any more than that, herself averse to finding, even in a historical novel, that every dinner conversation involved Napoleon and his doings. "That's not the way the world works."

Her subject in *The Beginner's Goodbye* in 2012 was again grief, the storyline a familiar one: a reserved, passive male narrator with a slightly eccentric job; an uneasy marriage between opposites; and an event that propels the hero toward self-knowledge and change. (On the subject of her characters' offbeat jobs Anne pointed out that she could not create a character in a vacuum who did no work, and that she enjoyed having them create their various odd businesses. "If you just had them sitting in a cubicle in an office what would I do with them?")

This time, instead of Anne waiting for one of the cards in her index box to have ripened enough to use, it started with the main character speaking directly to her—the thing that usually happened only much further along. She had still been at the very beginning, that miserable month of looking at her sheet of white paper and asking herself what she could possibly do, when in her brain she clearly heard a male voice saying, "The strangest thing about my wife's return from the dead was how other people reacted." A few minutes later the voice added: "I have a couple of handicaps. I may not have mentioned that."

Anne found it all baffling and decided to ignore it, but a while after that, when the same voice added that he also had a little speech problem, she began to pay attention. She recognized "how insane" it was to say that characters spoke to her, and guessed it was really her subconscious letting thoughts surface that she didn't know she was thinking. She loved the slight duplicity of the man's tone—that he may have been trying to hide his disabilities, with the "I may not have mentioned" such a dead giveaway. This told her it had to be a first-person narrator, something she usually considered a bit of a cheat. In this way the subject of grief was "sort of visited" upon her, although at the same time Anne consciously drew on her feelings after Taghi's death fifteen years previously. "When it happens you think this is unbearable, and it *is* unbearable. But of course everybody bears it...I miss him still." Being widowed was unbearably sad from start to finish, she observed sadly; no one part was more painful than any other. She included in the novel her old reflection that no couple buying wedding rings wanted to be reminded of the inevitable future, the fact that someday one of them would have to receive the other one's ring from a nurse or an undertaker.

The experience of losing Taghi had included a sense of bewilderment:

The main thing I thought after my husband died was "Where did he go?" You can't have that much vitality and exuberance and joyfulness and it just comes to nothing. No! It's got to be somewhere. I'm not religious, but I really did sit very still and think, say something to me. He never did.

All this was being mulled over for ten or twelve years before she started the book, Anne reported. For her, writing did not help to process an experience, it was the other way round: "I think I have to process it before I write it." As she did not believe in people living after death or coming back from the grave she did not want to write a ghost story, and could not have been more surprised to discover that this was what her next book would be. The idea just would not go away and so she created Aaron, whose dead wife keeps appearing to him. But every step of the way, as she mapped the work out, Anne's reluctance continued. She kept thinking, "I don't want to be doing this. How will I get out of this?" She wrote it so that it was not, in fact, a ghost story, being very clear in her mind that only Aaron can see his wife. "She's not there. Or more accurately, she's there only for him." What Aaron interprets as his friends' awkwardness in acknowledging his dead wife's presence is really their awkwardness at speaking to someone bereaved, she explained. But because Aaron is the narrator, the reader has to see events through his slant of vision, even if that vision is flawed.

Aaron Woolcott works in the family firm, a vanity publisher specializing in terrible amateur war memoirs and a Beginner's series: *The Beginner's Wine Guide*, *The Beginner's Monthly Budget*, *The Beginner's Cancer*. He has recently lost his stern young doctor wife Dorothy in a freak accident (based on the anxiety Anne used to feel about a huge oak tree that leaned over the girls' bedroom when they were young). Bereft, Aaron moves in with his spinster sister, brushing off people's well-meaning attempts at consolation and trying to lose himself in his work. Then Dorothy begins to appear to him in random locations. As they talk, and bicker, Aaron finally gets a chance to tell the seemingly no-nonsense Dorothy what she always wanted to hear, and to come to terms with his loving but misfit marriage (as were all marriages, Anne said again when discussing this latest work; for a writer, the post-marriage stages were so much more interesting, grating along together and adjusting to each other's foibles and flaws).

A wise, gently funny, charming novel, decided the *Australian Women's Weekly*, while for the *Sydney Morning Herald* it was a touching and gently humorous study in grief, its main achievement the virtuoso feat of characterization achieved through Aaron's narrative voice: while telling us about the other people in his life, he unwittingly reveals the wide range of things that he doesn't know about himself. The *New Zealand Herald* declared that Anne Tyler was an observational writer with an ear for the small details that convey the most poignant messages. She unwrapped emotions and laid them bare, showing how people sleepwalk through life's tragedies until they can cope again. And although her ending could be seen as over-neat and tidy, the paper added, it had the ring of truth about it.

In Britain the *Times Literary Supplement* noted Anne's tendency to set her books in a sleepy middle-class enclave of Baltimore that was "more Charm City than Bulletmore, Murderland," but found the new work very funny. Anne's ability to look head-on into her hero's loneliness also provided the pinch of gravitas to offset her "pervasive sweetness and kookiness, which might otherwise begin to cloy." For the *Times* the novel was as "tight and as well-tuned as the BBC Philharmonic," confident and utterly compelling, the work of an artist at the peak of her powers—and an unsentimental examination of the emotional arc of grief.

But British journalist Lisa Allardice, mirroring the similar complaint from New York reviewer Michiko Kakutani, charged that Aaron was another in a long line of male characters lacking in testosterone, just drifting along until jolted out of their passivity. In a parallel list to Kakutani's she cited Macon Leary in *The Accidental Tourist*, reluctant to step out of his front door; Ian Bedloe in *Saint Maybe*, spending twenty years atoning for a teenage mistake and renouncing everything from sex to sugar; and poor old Ezra, who spends his life trying to get his family to finish one meal together in the Homesick Restaurant. Barnaby Gaitlin in *A Patchwork Planet*, Jeremy Pauling from *Celestial Navigation*, and the hero of *Noah's Compass* could all be added to this list, Allardice suggested, and now Aaron, "with his leg-brace, stutter and bossy sister," was no exception.

Anne did not agree that her men were weaklings—or that her characters were offbeat:

Oh that always bothers me so much. I don't think they are wimps...People are always saying we understand you write about quirky characters, and I think, isn't everybody quirky? If you look very closely at anybody you'll find impediments, women and men both.

Musing about her male characters in general, she wondered if her novels had such a strong male following because it came across that she really liked them—pointing out again that after all those amazing men in her family she felt more comfortable with them. She had been granted a very positive view of men,

Anne repeated, and had gotten to know them well because she was so interested in them, and liked them. She felt confident adopting a male perspective and as a novelist was also attracted to the challenge posed by a society that almost forced men to hide their feelings:

> *When I'm writing from a man's point of view, particularly if it is first-person, all of a sudden I'm aware of how confined I feel, how I can't use that word because it is emotionally charged, too gushy. I feel I'm walking this narrow path with high walls on either side of me. The first time I realized I was so surprised, I thought, well here we are always worrying about women's liberation, but how about men?*

Canada's *Globe and Mail* carped at the novel's lack of realism, calling for some acknowledgment of life as it really was, "or what we have is Disneyland." Anne Tyler fans—most of the known universe, the paper's reviewer Kathleen Byrne conceded —would find just what they were looking for in the novel, all the loose ends tied very tightly indeed with a pretty pink bow. When, near the end, Aaron announces that he wants the jolts and jogs of ordinary life, realness even if "flawed and pockmarked," Byrne knew just how he felt.

At home, Michiko Kakutani in the *New York Times* saw Anne as "doggedly" following her usual formula in her "tepid" new novel but adding a supernatural twist borrowed from old movies. In Anne's more powerful work, sympathy had lofted the reader up over whatever was clichéd or cloying about their stories, she proclaimed, but the characters in *The Beginner's Goodbye* were irritating stick figures, insipid and emotionally uptight. The new book was "arguably this talented author's tritest and most predictable novel" (yet another damning judgment from the ferocious Kakutani, although damning judgments of beloved and respected authors—including John Updike and Nick Hornby—were so much her stock in trade that the verb "Kakutanied" was coined to describe the experience).

When another *New York Times* reviewer, Julia Glass, noted the novel's mention of an Apple store but otherwise found little evidence in Anne's work of the technological innovations now radically altering modern life, a woman wrote in to respond. She agreed that the characters were too removed from the larger world and that, after years of finding Anne Tyler's works lovely, funny, and insightful, she had begun to wonder why Anne's characters never used obscenities and were able to leave a marriage or abandon their children without any real repercussions. Of Anne's many books this reader often couldn't remember which was which, and suggested that it was probably because of the similar plotlines and facile resolutions.

But a world without Anne Tyler novels struck her as a sadder one.

Sometimes when you're looking at a snow globe, which Glass uses as a metaphor for the Tyler "cosmos," you wish you could just move in.

Emergence

At the age of seventy, Anne suddenly emerged from the self-imposed isolation of some thirty years.

For all that time she had refused any live, face-to-face interviews or appearances. (When Joe Donahue of National Public Radio's *Book Show* in the US proudly boasted to his mother that he had secured an interview with author Philip Roth, she replied: "Let me know when you get to interview Anne Tyler." It was to be a long wait.) Reporters had regularly shown up on the doorstep, or attempted to corner Anne at the few social events she attended, or called up her old high-school teachers; one was even rumored to have invented a sick baby in order to get to her through Taghi. But Anne had remained resolutely cloistered.

Her reasons for the long seclusion were, of course, mostly to do with the damage that might be done to her writing. When queried about her work it was as though the book in question was being ripped open and exposed, Anne explained, and any time she had previously spoken at length in an interview she really couldn't write for a long while afterward. Her mental image—fey, she admitted—was that the Writing Elf had gone off in a sulk. Even an email interview could make her uncomfortably aware of the process for the ensuing few days, but at least with email there was a manageable time period involved and so the effects tended not to last as long. The secret of writing for Anne was still to pretend to herself that no one would ever see it, an illusion that of course was shattered by talking about it. She had continued to maintain that asking a writer to go public was like telling a baker that, since they baked bread, they should perform a ballet.

There was also her strong sense of privacy: "By nature, I just prefer to be private, and having written a novel doesn't alter that." A national book tour with publicity and book signings would destroy her, she believed.

Her agent at this point, Jesseca Salky, suggested yet another reason for Anne's unwillingness to talk: that it was not detachment but, paradoxically, kindness. Anne hated to say no to anyone, and got so many requests that she felt overwhelmed; rather than refusing selectively it was easier to set a blanket policy, Jesseca stated. A close friend of Anne's also made clear that her reticence did not stem from aloofness or haughtiness or being puffed up by her own reputation, as people who did not know her tended to think. Instead, said the friend, she was humble, soft-spoken, and a very good listener. Friends like these were very protective of Anne's privacy, closing ranks to questioners, although Anne denied ever presuming to dictate to them what they could or couldn't say: "After all, I'm not guarding state secrets here; I'm just trying to keep the focus on what's important."

Now, it would seem, she had reversed her decision to keep herself to herself. Acknowledging the apparent whimsicality of it, Anne explained the complete turnaround as just her usual oh well, why not? way of thinking (long ago claimed as the reason for her decision to marry Taghi)—even while continuing to give voice to all her usual reasons for not talking:

> *The more I talk about writing, the more self-aware I become as I sit down to write, and it doesn't go so well. So I just think it's probably better not to blather on about writing forever.*

In fact she was interested to see, now that she was beginning to talk more, how long it would take her to write: "I'm curious to know. Will the Writing Elf understand?"

But there was more to Anne's sudden emergence from the shadows, a very practical reason for breaking her long moratorium on public appearances. She had been getting hints from her publisher that, with all the new technological competition to books, she was not pulling her weight in terms of promotion. A few years later, talking live to broadcaster Diane Rehm on National Public Radio, Anne confirmed that it had been explained to her how very different the book world had become. Previously, people only heard about a book through reviews in newspapers, and that had been sufficient; now, there were fewer newspapers, and she could see it did make sense to talk to people more directly about what she thought and to publicize her books that way. This was the reason for the end of her hibernation, she revealed, despite never being very good at doing things like book tours and still insistent that promoting books was "completely unrelated" to writing them (this time using the analogy of a roller skater getting asked to become a pastry chef). But Anne saw it almost as a duty to engage the next generation of readers:

I am still reluctant, to be honest, but the world has changed so much. I used to think it was my publisher's job to get people interested in my books and persuade them to buy copies, but books are suffering. We need to do all we can to encourage people to see books and reading as part of their lives. If we don't, then someday kids will stop reading and that will be the end.

With Diane Rehm
(Photo credit: American University Radio (WAMU))

Anne's first forays back into the public eye were naturally awkward. Talking to a Canadian journalist she invited into her home in 2012, she explained that she had agreed to a handful of interviews to promote *The Beginner's Goodbye* but that she was out of practice: "I don't know how these things work." The two started the interview seated opposite each other on two long couches across a vast expanse of Persian rug but, at the journalist's request, they ended up perched at either end of the same couch as more conducive to conversation. By the time of the live interview with Diane Rehm it had become easier. She was "unexpectedly" enjoying the interview, Anne admitted.

From 2012 onward, Anne was thus no longer the "Greta Garbo of the literary world," as once dubbed by a critic—although, despite her reputation as a recluse, she had never actually maintained absolute silence. She had frequently responded by letter or email to questions sent to her by journalists and academics, sometimes at length and occasionally very frankly, as when she mentioned her breast cancer and Tezh's brain tumor in an emailed contribution to a profile in the *Baltimore Sun* in 2001. She now made herself far more available, not only for face-to-face interviews but also for radio and personal appearances both at home and abroad—perhaps most notably at her first public event in Britain that April, where she was just as popular as in her own country, if not more so. Her novels sold extremely well there and a great many of them—*Earthly Possessions*, *Dinner at the Homesick Restaurant*, *Breathing Lessons*, *Saint Maybe*, *Ladder of Years*, *A Patchwork Planet*, *Back When We Were Grownups*, *The Amateur Marriage*, and *The Beginner's Goodbye*—had been adapted, dramatized, or read aloud on BBC radio. Anne herself had been interviewed by the BBC way back in 1982, just before the publication in Britain of *Dinner at the Homesick Restaurant*. She found an avid audience awaiting her.

The occasion for this long-anticipated personal appearance was a one-to-one interview before a packed audience at the Sheldonian Theatre in the ancient university city of Oxford, where Anne was to receive the Sunday Times Award for Literary Excellence—an accolade bestowed in recognition of a lifetime's achievement in books. She was described in the press as "tall and elegant, with smooth silver hair in a pioneer chignon, a straight back" and an endearing appearance of instant lively engagement, responding to questions like a "charming guest at a good dinner party, with wit, grace and an apparently transparent honesty." She received a standing ovation from the 850 people crammed into the theater. Many other writers were in the audience (including the author of this biography): one told a reporter later that she was almost in tears several times during the event, and that the whole thing had felt "quasi-religious." Another said he had never sensed that amount of love in a room for an author. Writer Annie Lyons was particularly moved, feeling the "jittery panic" experienced on meeting someone long admired — in this case, the person who had expressed everything she felt herself and made her want to be a writer too. When Anne remained behind to sign a strictly rationed one book per member of the audience, men as much as women lined up to say how much her books meant to them, and after an hour in line Annie Lyons finally met her heroine. Hearing that her books had been such an inspiration, Anne smiled "in a no-nonsense, kind way, like a favourite aunt," told her to keep going and wished her luck with her future work. On reaching outside, Annie burst into tears.

(Photo by kind permission Annie Lyons)

As for Anne, although clearly nervous, she appeared to have enjoyed herself. The event had been held as part of Oxford's Literary Festival and Anne professed to find the whole festival a "kind of literary heaven," both listening to the other attendees talking to each other about books at breakfast and her own appearance before such a fervent audience. During the interview Anne talked of her writing life and methods, how she was happiest when writing and how she continuously drafted and redrafted. To a question from the audience about what she liked to read, Anne replied that she read a great many contemporary novels, particularly first novels. She confessed to coming quite late to Jane Austen, having first read *Pride and Prejudice* only in her thirties (after attempts when she was younger at her mother's urging, Anne said elsewhere, but thinking the famous English author "very fusty and old fashioned" when she did so). When she finally did read Jane Austen properly, she fell in love—and was later to be compared to the great writer herself.

A Beginner's Goodbye might be her last novel [in view of her age], Anne declared to the audience, but she loved being in the throes of writing one. Her idea of heaven was to be in the middle of a book and to have an eleven-year-old daughter—because they were at an age to still think their mother wonderful, she had observed on another occasion—and a new puppy. (It was a statement she was often to repeat, sometimes wishing for a new cat instead of the puppy.) Her plan now was to start a big, sprawling family saga and work backward a generation at a time; going backward, when she died nobody would ever know whether she had reached the end she planned or not, and she would just be in the middle of the book forever —which was what she now wanted, having tired of finishing a book and being forced to see it from an outsider's point of view. Her daughters could then publish it if they chose.

The remark that *A Beginner's Goodbye* might be her last novel was picked up by the press out of context and reported, wrongly, to be a declaration that Anne Tyler would never write again.

Author Nick Hornby was also in the audience, still obsessed with Anne's writing. He described her during the interview as hesitant in manner and laughing nervously a couple of times when, in his view, she was revealing the extent of her commitment to her art. He recalled that a gasp went up from the audience when she mentioned that she wrote out a second draft of each novel in longhand, leaving Nick in a state of shame that he imagined himself a professional author. She was a genius, he wrote later, one who made writing seem effortless but whose seriousness and craft were so user-friendly she still did not always get the credit she deserved. He saw Anne as a living American great whose sympathy for her characters, and determination to find redemption for even the most hopeless of them, sometimes led to her being patronized by the type of critic who needed writers to make a song and dance about their profundity and worth.

But although with this event and others she had finally emerged from the cocoon, Anne still continued to avoid book tours and book signings if she could. Her own feeling as a reader was that she had no particular interest in meeting the writer. If she were told that Tolstoy could come to dinner with her tomorrow, she would say well, why don't I just sit here and read *Anna Karenina*?

I don't think writers are particularly exciting people. And I know that, in fact. I see it sometimes in people's faces. I'll be in the grocery store and somebody will stop me and say, are you Anne Tyler, and I feel as if almost from the beginning I'm disappointing them because I don't say anything beautifully worded or witty or dramatic. I just say, how are you? And that's like a disappointment for them. So it doesn't make me want to go out and meet readers.

§

Throughout her long seclusion, however, Anne had naturally remained available to her few close friends, who at this period included about five women (perhaps former fellow members of a classics-only book group she had belonged to back in the 1980s). They all met regularly for a glass of wine and binge viewings of *The Wire*, the cult TV series about Baltimore law enforcement. She loved the way that in the middle of something brutal going on there was also something poignant happening, and loved many of the show's other subtleties too:

You feel for both sides in what should be a black and white situation in terms of the law and the lawbreakers. Half the time the law seems like the bad guys. And you get so attached to people, and they keep dying...and I love the language, it's almost like poetry sometimes.

It was beautifully acted, she felt, with real character. At first she and her friends had used subtitles because they couldn't understand what the drug dealers were saying, but eventually they learned the lingo. Even years later, if one of the friends texted her with a question, Anne's answer might be a Baltimore drug dealer's "most def!" The group had watched all five series twice, Anne confessed, and were considering another run (she ended up watching it again on her own). She disagreed with the way Baltimore's mayors had decried the show, and saw the series as very insightful. "It's very true to Baltimore," she insisted. "It is a very pocketed city. We walk the same streets, the drug dealers are doing their business and I'm doing mine, and we almost don't see each other." She herself felt perfectly safe walking down such streets because as an "old, white lady they basically don't see me," but acknowledged that if she were a young black man wearing the wrong color scarf she would be taken for a gang member and would be in danger of her life. "We inhabit the same space but there's a lot going on that's complex."

One old friend of Anne's was fellow writer Robb Forman Dew, prizewinning author of several novels. They first got to know each other in the early 1980s when Anne was asked to review Robb's first work *Dale Loves Sophie to Death*, which she said bowled her over. One of its many virtues, she observed—and mentioned in the review—was its respect for the significance of food; like Robb, Anne still believed that someone's attitude to food revealed "reams about character." Responding to the review Robb instantly sent Anne the full recipe for shish kebab that had appeared in a shortened form in the novel, and which Anne had praised; later, when they were both serving as judges for a fiction prize, they had the first of their many, sometimes daily phone conversations, although not meeting in person until about 2002.

Robb loved Anne's novels and was to say that over the years of reading them she had taken up dual citizenship of both the real world and Anne's fictional world. But it was never work they talked about in their calls. What surprised Anne when she looked back on their exchanges—often about books, just never their own—was how seldom they directly discussed writing (although whenever she ended a phone call with Robb she somehow felt that was what they had really been talking about

234

all along). Once they spent a solid half hour analyzing a bathing-suit model in an Orvis catalog, both interested that a model Anne described as "actually a bit dumpy, with the beginnings of a tummy," had posed so confidently:

It called up all kinds of questions about where our attitudes about ourselves come from—why one person with a less-than-perfect figure would be strutting while another shrinks.

Perhaps this was why their meandering conversations might really be about writing after all, Anne conjectured: character preoccupied both of them, and dominated their fiction.

Anne claimed that other, presumably less intimate friends were unaware she was a writer (a little hard to believe after selling more than ten million novels). "It's not a big deal...I mean, writers don't walk down the street and get people asking them for autographs. It's not something that affects my daily life." One friend who certainly did know she was a writer was the director John Waters, fellow famous citizen of Baltimore. They met up only every so often. "I don't go to biker bars with him. Once a year, he comes to mine for dinner and once a year I go to his. He's a very sweet man." She would laugh about a lunch they once had with one of her daughters who, then a teenager, wanted a tattoo. The generally transgressive John, surprisingly, advised her not to do it: "Think how it will look on your wrinkled skin when you're sixty-five."

(Photo licensed under CC BY-NC-ND 2.0)

John read Anne's books way before they first met; his favorite was *Ladder of Years*, which he judged a perfect description of what it was like to be a Baltimorean—unpretentious, impervious to the outside world and layered in eccentric family traditions. They never agreed on the kind of books they liked, but he believed they were similar in both concentrating on eccentrics in their work. He was interested in people who thought they were normal and yet were totally insane; Anne, he said, wrote about people who thought of themselves as normal and were normal, but also eccentrics who didn't know it. He believed that the public fixation on Anne's connection to Baltimore obscured her achievements as a fiction writer, because she could write about any city. "She beautifully captures regular people who are not trying to be noticed. She writes about real life." As a filmmaker, he wanted to see her books adapted by an outsider, "a European art film director, someone with a fresh eye."

John once told Anne it would be nice to have somebody in his life, but he thought that after maybe two days any potential partner might say something like, "How about I hang this one picture of mine over on that wall?" That would have done it for John, whoever it was would have to go. Anne felt much the same way, although she knew she would be in trouble if she decided to just stay home and commune with herself. But while acknowledging that it was important to interact with others, that was still as far as it went:

I don't want to move over and make room for somebody else. I'm good on my own. I have good friends and daughters and sons-in-law and grandchildren. It seems like a full life to me.

§

Anne by now had written a total of nineteen novels, which worried her a little. When she looked at someone else's book and saw a long list of previous titles she tended to think less of the author, that they must be just "spewing them out." But at least she would always be beaten by Joyce Carol Oates, she joked. (The two knew each other and had corresponded.)

Anne's view of her earlier novels was, in her words, the way a mother cat feels about her grown kittens: she never thought about them again, they were gone. Those initial works seemed very distant to her, although she still nourished a special affection for *Dinner at the Homesick Restaurant*. She no longer read any of them, having done this a decade or so previously and found it very painful, like lying in bed staring at a ceiling she had painted herself and seeing all the mistakes. She did occasionally check through some of them to avoid repeating herself, however, spotting a number of recurrent motifs in the process:

I've read small parts of my past books from time to time because when I'm writing, I'll occasionally think, "Wait, didn't I say that in an earlier book?" It always surprises me to see how the same themes and observations seem to pop up over and over in my work, completely unintentionally.

She continued wanting to buy up every copy of her first four books and destroy them, still aware that she did not yet know what she was doing when she wrote them: "I just wanted to write a novel, and it shows." She saw again her early need to tell people something, to put her world across to a larger audience. "What arrogance, really!" The first four were basically only rough drafts, Anne now knew, having learned that in the rewriting process things developed and got layers, with more elements of a character emerging than she had ever realized the first time around. What she did differently now was to try and step inside a situation instead of just pronouncing on it, and try to listen more to her characters—or even to become them, for a while.

A Spool of Blue Thread, the sprawling family saga Anne had written backward so that it could still be published if she died in the middle, emerged in 2015. Now that she was older and tired more quickly, she had cut down from six hours' work or so a day to around three, and was continually surprised to find that she achieved about the same amount. Aging had done only good things for the creative part of her life, Anne felt: she had continued to grow ever more trustful of her characters, more willing to take risks, and more patient with herself. She was less enamored of the change in people's attitude toward her as an older person, on the other hand—being called "dear" by flight attendants and feeling dismissed when looked at, although recognizing that she had probably dismissed a lot of old people herself in her time. Inside, Anne felt she was still looking out at the world through seven-year-old eyes.

The new work was the story of three generations and their beautiful house, constructed by founder of the clan Junior Whitshank, and inherited by his son Redcliffe, wife Abby, and four children. The story delves into the troubles experienced over the years by Red and Abby with their wayward son Denny, who suffers from a lifelong jealousy of his adopted brother Stem. When the house is sold and the family scattered after a tragic death, the tale moves back in time to when Red's father Junior and his country mother Linnie Mae first meet and move into the lovingly built house; the novel ends as their grandson Denny starts life again on a more positive path—maybe.

It was hugely enjoyable for Anne to write, the characters just taking over. To begin with, as usual, she had the uncomfortable sense of making it up and merely ordering the characters about willy-nilly:

Oh, what a silly, artificial business novel-writing is, I'll think. Who am I kidding, here? And I glance at the John Updike poem that I keep above my desk, "Marching Through a Novel" where he likens his characters to meek foot soldiers blindly following his orders. Poor dears. I pity them.

But gradually, as ever, new layers developed and things started to happen by themselves. She had planned for Denny to marry, but didn't know exactly whom, and remembered that she smiled when his wife first made her appearance. She felt intrigued by Stem's wife Nora, who was as mysterious to Anne as she was to the rest of the family, and made Anne perk up whenever she entered a scene. Then she found out, to her surprise, that Abby as a teenager used to have a bad-boy boyfriend; she had to go back to an earlier section to drop in a couple of references to him. This was why Anne loved

238

rewriting: each new draft revealed extra layers that she had not initially foreseen.

She also didn't know till she got there that the earlier members of the family were such "limited" people. The glimpse she received of Junior's father showed her that he probably had no interior at all and was just living a very hard-scrabble life. Unable to imagine what to do with that generation, she decided she would have to end the book after all.

There were a number of ideas that Anne had wanted to explore in the novel. She gave the Whitshanks a few stories they liked to tell about their family history because, prior to writing, she had been mulling over how families always seemed to have a couple of anecdotes, picked out of hundreds, to pass down and make a big deal of; she wanted to know why people chose that one or two to focus on, and what it said about their family. In her own case, the stories were her grandfather's tale of running for coffee for his dying mother, and one her father Lloyd used to tell about a birthday gift of miniature carpentry tools as a boy that were confiscated and given away to another child. She wondered why those two stories, in particular — why the note of pride in her family's voices as they were told and retold? Why did her family view them as so special? Why did they half imagine that they made the family itself special, by extension?

She remembered, too, the Modarressi stories relayed to her on that first visit to Taghi's family in Iran in 1964 as a newlywed. Like her own family, they singled out a certain few tales to tell again and again, in Anne's words "to examine from every angle and to polish and reflect upon." How one of the aunts had fiercely rebelled against an arranged marriage and at long last, to everyone's amazement, persuaded her iron-willed father to let her marry the man she loved instead. How another aunt had not rebelled, but then after being widowed many decades later, had finally married the man *she* always loved (which did not turn out to be a happy ending). These stories were very different from those Anne had heard at home, and yet once again there was that undertone of pride, that sense of specialness. She believed that families liked to have "a sort of mythic understanding of themselves," to think they are exceptional, and closer than other families are—although at the same time they would be casting sideways glances when they went to the beach "to see if they're really doing it right and if there's another family thinking that they're a happy family."

I may not agree with Tolstoy's statement that happy families are all alike, but I do believe that families in general, whether they're happy or unhappy, cling to the notion that they are in some way remarkable...And I suspect that all of them are absolutely right.

When she was beginning to "manufacture" the Whitshanks—a word Anne deliberately chose in order to express her usual "dishearteningly mechanical act" of manipulating characters like toy soldiers until in the end they took charge, turning bossy and opinionated and coming up with their own plot twists and stretches of dialogue—what arrived first were their stories. These seemed to her, in this instance, to have the common theme of envy. Abby's was about how she fell in love with Red, and Red's sister's was about how she stole her husband from his first fiancée. "Once you know a family's favorite stories, you're pretty much on the way to knowing the family itself," Anne believed.

As well as the telling of family legends, Anne was fascinated by what she called "makeshift" families—loving the idea of a household blended through divorce and remarriage, or adoption, or by someone somehow drifting in and joining: "It shows the us and themness of a family, it points up what's going on inside the circle to have this outsider come in." (If given a choice about her own family, Anne once said, she would always choose the makeshift, surrogate kind formed by various characters unrelated by blood.) The outsider in the Whitshanks is Stem, taken in as a tiny child when his father dies and brought up as one of their own.

Families clearly remained Anne's eternal preoccupation :

Friendships don't particularly interest me. Lots of interesting things can happen, but you don't have to get along just to get together. The compromises people make for [one] another and the lifelong wounds and all that stuff is just fascinating to me.

Anne's fascination with craftsmen also fed into the story. When writing and editing with the usual windows open to hear ordinary life outside, she particularly liked to listen to them—the way they talked and worked, their solid capability. She always felt happy and contented when some handyman was puttering around her house, as though disaster could not then strike. She was a great eavesdropper on workmen, she admitted: their concerns, their artistry. She made both Junior and Redcliffe Whitshank dedicated carpenters. Their beautifully built house becomes almost another character in the book because Anne was trying to think like the builders they both were. She figured that if they themselves were telling this story they would want readers to notice the integrity of their dwelling place, how they scorned shortcuts and synthetics.

But there were also far more personal elements to *A Spool of Blue Thread*.

The story was directly inspired by something that really happened to Anne: after her mother died, she was mending a shirt for her father when, opening a closet, a spool of blue thread rolled into her hand. "It was almost as if she handed me the spool," Anne recalled. In the novel she has this happen to Denny after the death of *his* mother. When her publishers wanted to change the title, Anne fought back bitterly. She thought the rolling of the spool into Denny's hand "such a small moment" that if it were not the title, it might just pass people by. The incident clearly meant a great deal to her, and this time she won the fight: the title remained as she wanted it. In the novel, Denny wonders if the rolling spool is a sign of his dead mother's forgiveness, but then realizes it might also mean that she knows *he* forgives *her*. "We sometimes get mixed up about who's supposed to be forgiving whom," Anne commented, "and the fact that it has to go in both directions."

She chose too to use another very personal memory in the novel. On their annual beach holiday, the Whitshanks' rental is next door to a family who has been renting theirs as long as they have, thirty-six years. Over all this time the Whitshanks have watched these temporary neighbors from a distance as the slim young parents grow older and grayer, and their daughters become young women. Then something happens:

One summer in the late nineties, when the daughters were still in their teens, it was noticed that the father of the family never once went down to the water, spending the week instead lying under a blanket in a chaise longue on their deck, and the summer after that, he was no longer with them...they continued to come, the mother taking her early-morning walks along the beach alone now, the daughters in the company of boyfriends who metamorphosed into husbands, by and by, and then a little boy appearing and later a little girl.

(A Spool of Blue Thread, 2015)

This was Anne and Taghi and their family, Anne revealed. Before, she had given Tezh and Mitra only cameo roles in her novels, but now she included all of the expanded family:

It might be one sentence, you might see a young woman walking by looking for her cat or something, but it's them, and then of course they got married so I had to add the sons-in-law in, and then one had two children and they were added, so this is all of them—plus for once Taghi and I too, because that of course is the father.

Yet more of Anne's life and surroundings was woven through the work. The setting is Roland Park and the family has a charge account at Eddie's grocery. Baltimore train station is depicted on a gray day, its skylight, ordinarily "a kaleidoscope of pale, translucent aquas," this time opaque from overhead clouds; outside looms the modern sculpture, erected in 2004, which Red thoroughly dislikes: "It's embarrassing! Other cities' train stations have fountains...We have a giant tin Frankenstein with a heart that pulses pink and blue."

Like Anne, the Whitshanks have a genetic predisposition to lying awake for two hours in the middle of the night. Linnie Mae comes from a poor family in Yancey County, the location of Anne's childhood commune in North Carolina; like Anne, as a girl she picked galax to make money. Abby—who hasn't believed in angels since she was seven—is a social worker who used to picket for civil rights and marched against the Vietnam War with her youngest astride her hip. Now she is beginning to suffer from Alzheimer's, like Anne's mother (which Anne herself was currently fearful of, worrying that every passing lapse might herald the onset of the disease).

A Spool of Blue Thread was shortlisted for two British prizes: the Man Booker Prize, the leading literary award in the English-speaking world, and the Baileys Women's Prize for Fiction (now the Women's Prize for Fiction), awarded for the best novel written in English by a woman of any nationality. The work enjoyed six-figure sales, despite the inevitable poor review from Anne's seemingly now fiercest critic, Michiko Kakutani of the *New York Times*. While still lauding what she saw as Anne's best work in the 1980s, Kakutani felt the lesser books stumbled into predictability and cliché, and that *A Spool of Blue Thread* unfortunately fell into that category, recycling virtually every theme and major plot point used in the past and doing so "in the most perfunctory manner imaginable." The Whitshanks were just Tyler types, she pointed out: Abby a caring busybody with a zany streak that embarrasses her children, husband Red a typical Tyler male—self-employed, practical-minded, convinced that simple cold logic could solve all of life's problems and wondering why he is married to someone over-sympathizing and pitying. It was hard to care about either them or their family, she complained, and their author seemed to be coasting on automatic pilot.

But for another reviewer in the same paper, Anne had "a knack for turning sitcom situations into something far deeper and more moving," and the *Washington Post* also had a different take on the over-familiarity of characters and plot: what was familiar from other works seemed here transcended, "infused with freshness and surprise—evidence, once again, that Tyler remains among the best chroniclers of family life this country has ever produced." In Britain, the *Guardian*, while acknowledging Anne's mining of the same seam throughout her career, wrote that her power derived from the "restless depths beneath its unfractured surface." In Australia, the *Sydney*

Morning Herald found the switch at the end to the story of Red's parents' marriage unbalancing, and the novel therefore structurally flawed, but still declared that Anne's description of the house made it "a thing of substance, real and solid and like her books—a beautiful thing."

A Spool of Blue Thread supplanted *Dinner at the Homesick Restaurant* as Anne's favorite novel. For her, *Homesick* featured a fundamentally unhappy family, but *Spool* was about a functioning, happy one.

§

A Spool of Blue Thread was published just after the 2015 terrorist massacre of twelve people at the offices of the French satirical paper *Charlie Hebdo* in Paris. Anne found herself feeling hopeless.

I've never quite agreed with that Anne Frank line "I still believe that people are truly good at heart." I'm not so sure they are. I'm very distressed about the way the world is going.

She had never been comfortable about using her fiction (or interviews, those that she permitted) as a platform to express her political beliefs, Anne once stated. But of course she had her views—in 2012 she donated to the Obama for America reelection campaign under her married name Anne Modarressi. But now, it seemed, she was feeling freer to vent in the media. She was worried about human beings and the state of the world, she remarked, and in broad terms was not optimistic, but took comfort and escape for herself "in creating a tiny world where things work a little better, a sort of alternate universe" where people always mean well and try to stay hopeful. For Anne there had been a turning point after 9/11 when the US could have taken the high road, but instead did everything wrong and "set monsters loose." What she would have liked to do was sit down with the perpetrators and say, "I just don't understand. Can you tell us exactly what went wrong and what's going through your minds here?" She had wanted to write a profile of Osama bin Laden and ask him the same questions, hoping that after the expected rant he would quiet down a bit and tell her what the issue really was. Nobody did any of this, to her regret. There was a pause where she had hoped it would happen, followed by "a lot of bombing of people who weren't even involved."

Meanwhile life had to go on, which for Anne meant writing, still somewhat unreal as an occupation, and trying to stay positive. She liked to walk a couple of hours every morning to get her groceries—buying further afield to prolong the exercise —and then get down to work, writing in her eternal longhand and listening to everyday life outside: car doors slamming, people talking, workmen. She especially liked to hear children playing. "There is a scarcity of children on my street, but I'm always hopeful." Other than these outside sounds, she needed silence.

Anne still missed Taghi, particularly reading to him after their evening meal. He had been her best friend—"a cliché, but true….it's still unbearable, but I've gone on." She was even sadder for him now, not seeing his two grandchildren growing. She had her group of friends, and perhaps still enjoyed an occasional evening out at a movie theater as she had done in the past. Her heart lay with movies rather than plays, "maybe because they're so up close that they can more easily convince me I'm actually inside the lives they're showing." She would throw the occasional dinner party, although nothing pretentious:

I can't imagine myself hosting a literary dinner party. What on earth would a bunch of writers talk about? I'd rather just curl up with a sandwich and read some favorite book over again on my own.

At night she did not read to get to sleep, finding that she became too caught up in it and read till she was too tired, and would then forget half of it by morning and have to go back to the beginning. The exception was the *New Yorker*, which Anne kept on her nightstand and did her best to eke out over the space of an entire week. She was sorry that there were only forty-seven issues a year, which made the eking-out process a mathematical challenge. To get to sleep Anne now entertained herself with a time travel fantasy: that she had been invited into a time machine to take a trip to a different era, with a well-worked-out reason for a seventy-plus novelist being asked aboard: "Because they have to have everything observed, not just in scientific terms, right?...Naturally, they'd come to me." There were a few specific destinations she would like to visit:

I'd like to go to the part of human development when language first started emerging; caveman days, if that's what that was. I'd like to go to Jesus's time and see what was going on there. I'd like to go to Shakespeare's time and see him rehearse a play.

Then she would like to end up in 1910, as probably the ideal year to be alive: before the two world wars, hot and cold running water, nice clothes. Time remained a fascination, one that Anne still cheerfully admitted was the only plot device she had going for her. Everything that happened in her books was "totally because of time."

As for real travel, Anne remained uninterested, but was amused to find that even now, living alone, her children grown, her husband dead, she still sometimes thought about running away from home. She didn't even have anybody to run from— and preferred home anyway:

The funny thing is, now I don't seem to be thirsty for the broader world. I always thought, when I was a child, that I would travel. Then it turns out I'm kind of like the accidental tourist about traveling. I'll do it, I don't complain, but it's just I want my own bed at night.

She had had a "brief spurt of adventurousness, then retreated," she said in reference to her unusual choice of major at college and marriage to a foreigner, and was conscious of now living a quite restricted life. One of Anne's great fears when Tezh and Mitra left home was what to do with no one to "bring the outside world in." When they were teenagers in the late 1970s and early '80s, the girls used to turn on the radio in the dining room and blast rock out all over the house. "Listen to *this*," they would say to their mother. Then the door bell would ring and off they would go, leaving Anne with the rock. (Blondie's "Heart of Glass" would always remind her of that time.) When their daughters left for college she told Taghi she wasn't sure she could write any more, because there was no one telling her what was going on. How was she going to find out?

For the present, she was really "in my shed in the woods, so to speak, but I keep trying."

§

To be nearing her mid seventies was to see her career receding, Anne felt.

I'm not the hot new young thing...I used to be about the youngest novelist around; now I'm one of the oldest. It's like other people's sense of me as a writer is fading away but I'm still here, doing what I was doing when I was three, which is telling myself stories.

A new story was of course underway: *Vinegar Girl*, the slim, very funny account of obstreperous twenty-nine-year-old Kate, who works as a preschool assistant in Baltimore and keeps house for her widowed father and flibbertigibbet younger sister Bunny. Although loved by the children in her class, Kate does and says what she likes and gets into trouble for being rude to the parents. Her scientist father, desperate to keep his Eastern European lab assistant Pyotr from being deported, tries to persuade a reluctant Kate to marry him; Kate, half interested in Pyotr but also smitten by a colleague at school, slowly comes to understand that doing what her father wishes, instead of her usual balking, might lead to independence and even happiness.

Vinegar Girl, published in 2016, was actually part of a group project with other authors. A collection of famous writers, amongst them *Handmaid's Tale* author Margaret Atwood, had been invited to recast Shakespeare plays as modern novels. Anne's was *The Taming of the Shrew*, which she hated in the original—in fact hated all Shakespeare's plays—seeing it as "totally misogynistic" and unfunny, although meant to be a comedy. "People behave meanly to each other, every single

247

person." But the new version was very entertaining to write, she discovered, just the experiment of taking on a plot about taming a woman that didn't feel at all like something she would ever have chosen to write, and trying to make it her own. The first time she realized she was enjoying herself was when she wrote the line: "Kate had nothing to say, so she said nothing."

Women in general, we're sort of raised to smooth things over all the time, and to natter on if there's a silence and say nice things to people if they seem to need it. She's totally clueless and doesn't bother. I sort of liked that. I liked being rude to people, vicariously.

Anne saw Shakespeare's shrew Katherina as insane—"just spouting venom...shrieking at Petruchio from the moment she meets him"—and decided the character needed to be toned down. When the book came out several people then told her that Kate didn't seem like much of a shrew, leaving her feeling that perhaps she had toned her down too much. She made the plot depart considerably from the original, and very deliberately from Shakespeare's ending, with Katherina's speech on why wives should always obey their husbands. Anne's Kate, instead, delivers a lecture on how hard it is for men always having to hide their emotions.

Anne had to sign a contract beforehand that specified a minimum number of words, and for once she actually activated the word count function on her computer to make sure she had enough. There was, but only barely—a few more "very verys" had to be stuck in, she admitted.

Having a foreigner in the novel allowed Anne another opportunity to depict Americans as seen from outside: seemingly friendly but hard to get to know, and given to speech mannerisms annoying to Anne herself, such as starting sentences with "So" when, as Pyotr remarks, "there has been no cause mentioned before it that would lead to any conclusion." Kate's teenage sister Bunny—good at heart and ultimately revealed as not the airhead she appears to be—ends most of her sentences on an upward note that makes them sound like questions, another fad that clearly drove Anne crazy. (In her next novel, the main character abhors young men in suits discussing "asks" and "reaching out" and "taking a meeting.") Other of Anne's personal likes and dislikes were donated to Kate and family: like Anne even now, Kate has a soft spot for goats, her father hates merging onto expressways, and she likes to read time-travel novels and fantasize about traveling back to the Cambrian Era whenever she has trouble sleeping.

In Britain, land of Shakespeare, the novel was fortunately well received. Anne's deepest purpose was to challenge the premises of Shakespeare's comedy, wrote the *Times Literary Supplement*; her gentle, funny novel "insists that it is possible, in spite of our customarily blind perversities, to find unexpected ways of breaking free from self-destruction." For the *Guardian* it was fun, accomplished, readable, and enjoyable; for the *Daily Mail*, knockabout comedy at its best, genuinely laugh-out-loud funny and possibly Anne's funniest book to date.

Australia thought otherwise. A critic at the *Sydney Morning Herald* was "crestfallen." Anne Tyler had genius in everyday observations but such splashes were not enough to more than momentarily halt the unfunny trudge through the novel, wrote the reviewer; not one of the characters unfastened from the pages to take on a life of his or her own and the male characters, Pyotr and Kate's father, were mere slapstick. "Is this what happens when a great novelist, a novelist of genius (threaded with occasional glibness), is confined to a commission where her flutey, organic imagination is necessarily straitjacketed? Must be. This is Tyler tamed." *The New Zealand Herald* found the novel an easy and relaxing read, but too short and too easy to put down. The country's *Otago Daily Times* enjoyed Anne's "usual slyly perceptive observations of people," her clever attempt to broadly match the original play, and the occasional stretch of wonderfully humorous dialogue, but felt that the plot constraint had a limiting effect on her ability to make the story absorbing or to get the reader personally involved with her characters.

At home, however, it was another *New York Times* Bestseller. Shakespeare would be pleased, wrote author Jane Smiley in the *New York Times Book Review*. It was clear that Anne had had fun with *Vinegar Girl* and readers would too, said National Public Radio: "A fizzy cocktail of a romantic comedy, far more sweet than acidic, about finding a mate who appreciates you for your idiosyncratic, principled self—no taming necessary." For the *Washington Post*, the work was better than Shakespeare's original, "an ingenious resetting…with considerably more humor and gentleness than in the Bard's version."

§

The following year new paperback editions of *The Accidental Tourist*, *Breathing Lessons*, and seventeen other Anne Tyler novels were issued by Vintage Books. Anne's worth was now estimated in the millions. Still the books kept coming, because she just couldn't stop:

> *What happens is six months go by after I finish a book...I start to go out of my mind. I have no hobbies, I don't garden, I hate travel. The impetus is not inspiration, just a feeling that I better do this. There's something addictive about leading another life at the same time you're living your own.*

But the world was changing, and Anne decided that her next work would be a closer reflection of at least one current reality. Violent crime was again rising in Baltimore; there had been a spike after the 2015 death in police custody of a young black man, Freddie Gray, which sparked riots and a subsequent increase in the murder rate. But Anne had never wanted to attempt any depiction of the black experience, however, recognizing that it would be "very presumptuous" and indeed "disrespectful" to write from that point of view and there would be much for her to get wrong. She believed she had the right as an author to do so if she wanted to, and had no patience with those who cried cultural appropriation—what else was writing? she asked. To her mind if a writer was writing fiction then he or she wanted to be someone else, and so did the reader: that's why they were reading. However, she knew she would be open to justified accusations of messing it up if she tried it. All the same, the strong feelings that had driven her involvement in the civil rights movement as a young woman had never gone away: when asked around this time which living or dead Baltimorean she would like to have a conversation with, Anne replied that she'd like a word with Edward Bouton, the man who conceived Roland Park in the late nineteenth century. She had recently learned that he asked his lawyers if there were a way he could legally ban black people from living there. "Somehow, the fact that he was so calculating makes it all the worse. Definitely worth having a little talk about." But her decision remained not to try any reflection of the black community in Baltimore.

She was particularly concerned about the growing presence of guns, both in Baltimore and in the country as a whole: it was becoming more and more difficult to ignore, Anne commented. Shortly before starting to write the new novel she had read in the *Baltimore Sun* of yet another random shooting victim—this time a toddler, fortunately not killed, who was sitting in her father's lap on their front porch when she was shot. Nothing came of police inquiries, and eventually the whole subject just disappeared from the news.

I was struck by how we all moved on from it—not that we didn't care, but that we'd grown accustomed to such things, in the same way that we're no longer shocked by school shootings. Once you give that any thought, it seems almost surreal.

Anne realized later how strongly she had been affected by the fact that she left it behind so easily, and she made a gun incident pivotal in the upcoming work. As for politics, though, Anne preferred to leave well alone. She did not want to write a novel that was a tract, although she believed it was getting harder and harder, and more miserable, to live in her country. A part of her said she should be putting certain things in, while another part felt that it would mean veering off from the story. When Donald Trump then became president, Anne wondered how she could ignore it, but in the end decided that her central character Willa would probably just have ignored it herself.

Clearly, though, Anne simply did not want to write about the new incumbent:

I think of writing as a visit to a thoughtful, reasonable world where people try to be kind to one another. I can't imagine how I could ever fit Trump into that world.

President Trump may not have appeared in her fiction, but in 2017 Anne was one of sixty-five writers and artists to sign an open letter to him from the writers' organization PEN America, of which Anne was now a longstanding member. The document criticized his executive order banning citizens from seven Muslim countries from entering the US, and urged against further measures that would impair freedom of movement and the global exchange of arts and ideas. It was not the first time (and would not be the last) that Anne had lent her name to a PEN crusade for artistic freedom. An earlier petition to both Donald Trump and Hillary Clinton had pushed them to uphold the freedom of the press enshrined in the US Constitution, and denounce journalist intimidation tactics. Following in the footsteps of her campaigning parents, Anne also signed protests against American involvement in Syria, nuclear waste recycling, and no doubt others.

The story Anne was working on was *Clock Dance*, her twenty-second novel, published in 2018. It consists initially of what seem like rapidly whisking episodes in the life of Willa at successive stages: as a child (dreaming of living somewhere with sidewalks), as a college girl, as a young wife and mother, then widow, and finally married for the second time and thinking she is at the end of her journey. (They were all pivotal moments, Anne was to explain, although her character doesn't know it). Then Willa receives a call at home in Arizona to come and take charge of Cheryl, the young daughter of her son's ex-girlfriend. The girl is not her son's child but when Cheryl's mother is shot and taken to hospital, Willa is summoned in the mistaken belief that she is the grandmother. Willa impetuously obeys the summons anyway and finds herself in a quirky, working-class Baltimore neighbourhood unexpectedly enjoying her novel responsibilities. There are new friends and new relationships that seem to bring out the original Willa—as opposed to what she has become, a polite, conciliatory woman in expensive clothes married to a fussy lawyer—but should she stay and make her life in Baltimore when her husband is waiting for her at home?

Anne deliberately made Willa passive and conventional, "not very contemplative or reflective," but she has her fall in love with Arizona's saguaro cactus because of its power and reserve and dignity, qualities that she felt Willa would instinctively long for. (Anne herself had never seen a saguaro till she made a trip to Arizona when in her 50s, perhaps during her travels with Mark Furstenberg. She was struck by them in the same way Willa is: "I didn't know why, but they gave me a kind of physical ache.")

She initially began the book at the point Willa is sixty-one, thinking to refer only in retrospect to the significant moments in her life. She didn't know when she started writing what those pivotal moments were going to be, or that this was what the book was going to be about.

The plan was to drop back during the novel to these earlier events and say this probably had something to do with...then I remembered I really don't like reading flashbacks as a reader. I think they're kind of a cheat, and I didn't really want to do it that way so it's as if the book took over and said no, we've got to do it this way.

She opted to present the moments as widely separated episodes, "leaping across great spans of time," because as a reader she always felt a sense of relief when the author trusted her to imagine the intervening years for herself. (In general Anne now very deliberately avoided telling readers "every little thing, things they could work out for themselves"—if she ever made a mistake in her books, she reflected, it was around over-explaining and not trusting the reader.)

Anne chose too to revisit certain painful episodes in her life: her difficult mother, and dealing with grief.

Willa as a child suffers because her generally loving, fun mother sometimes goes on rampages: "Nothing terrified Willa more than an angry woman." She sometimes disappears from home for days at a time, leaving Willa and her little sister in the care of their father, hating the bleak and empty house while they wait for her return. As for their mild-mannered, forgiving father, it was "marry such a person or *be* such a person," the young Willa figures, just as Anne had done about Lloyd Tyler. The adult Willa tries to be a good mother to her own children, which to her means a *predictable* mother—exactly as Anne had determined to be, when still a child under the yoke of the tempestuous Phyllis. One of Anne's brothers once told her as an adult that his memories of childhood were of tip-toeing to their mother's bedroom door each morning, and opening it a crack to see what kind of a day it was going to be; in the novel, Willa promises herself that her children will never have to do this. Anne still remembered childhood very clearly, including the stage where her mother was the absolute center of her world, the source of all that was good; if a mother was also the source of what is bad, she commented—although never suggesting that Phyllis had either absconded or been physically abusive like Willa's mother—then a child has to overlook it and turn to her anyway. As she ages, Willa's feelings for her now-dead mother grow far kinder, more accepting, as Anne's seem to have done. "A certain sense of acceptance creeps in with age," she remarked, "and I wouldn't have known that if I'd tried to write about a sixty-one-year-old when I was a young woman."

When widowed, Willa, like Anne, consoles herself by looking at other people and knowing that they had suffered losses but still managed to put one foot in front of the other and even smile. Willa's father takes a different approach to bereavement, trying to just enjoy whatever moment he is in—a coping technique Anne herself had arrived at:

I remember when my husband died, having the thought that Willa's father talks about, when he was talking about his wife's death. I thought, I don't know how I'm going to get through the rest of my life without him. And then I thought, well, okay, but at least right now, I'm drinking this cup of coffee, and it tastes good, and it's a nice sunny morning, and I'll just get through this...and I do think that most people who lose a wife or a husband stumble across that approach to it.

She was still investigating how her characters managed to endure, Anne said. Nobody was leading an adventurous or a particularly successful life; they just kept on keeping on and were pretty cheerful about it. "They do it in different ways and I like to study how they do it." For as long as she could remember, she had been impressed by how gracefully "so-called ordinary people" managed to endure tedious or difficult or even tragic lives—how they still got up every morning, no matter how disappointing yesterday was or the day before. That seemed to her far more admirable than the conventional, swashbuckling type of heroism. And it was certainly more of a challenge to make interesting to readers, who she was aware had their own first-hand experience of exactly this sort of daily fortitude.

For the *Independent* in Britain, the novel got off to a jerky start and the ending came as no surprise, but the critic found himself rooting for Willa all the same. Not Anne's best book, wrote the *Evening Standard*, the second half drawn out and labored and the twist—"such as it is"—coming almost too late. "An unexpected treat from an immensely funny writer," judged the *Telegraph,* on the other hand; for the *Sunday Times* it brimmed with all the qualities that had brought Anne her legions of fans and high critical acclaim. "Characters pulse with lifelikeness. The tone flickers between humorous relish and sardonic shrewdness. Dialogue crackles with authenticity. Beneath it all is an insistence that it's never too soon to recognize how quickly life can speed by and never too late to make vitalizing changes."

At home, the novel was again a *New York Times* Bestseller. The paper wrote that Anne Tyler was sometimes dismissed for her books' readability and deeply familiar pleasures, but her novels only seemed simple because she made the very difficult look easier than it was. Her books were "smarter and more interesting than they might appear on the surface." For the *Boston Globe* it was a "psychologically astute study of an intelligent, curious woman...A triumph." The *Washington Post* found in it some stock Tyler characters—including errant mother—and the usual lack of the erotic, but appreciated Anne's constant exploration of what people find to live for. Exquisite, said *O, The Oprah Magazine*: "What keeps us glued are the lovely, intricate details; the depiction of human emotion as odd and splendid; and the tiny flickers of hope that feel like bursts of joy." Anne Tyler was the most dependably rewarding novelist now at work in our country, declared the *Wall Street Journal*.

But the *Chicago Tribune* charged her with being old-fashioned, even anachronistic, her books centering on family dynamics and ignoring all the outside forces that now felt so menacing: "While many of us can't stop thinking about politics, government overreach, climate change and gun violence, characters like Willa seem oblivious." An unjust accusation, given Anne's conscious choice to build her plot around a gun injury and make it a prominent issue. Willa is caring for Cheryl precisely because the child's mother has been randomly shot, and Anne spells out that because in Baltimore gun crime is so common, young men with gunshot wounds arrive at the hospital already knowing what type of wheelchair they want. Cheryl's mother complains that her daughter acts so unconcernedly "you'd think mothers get shot all the time." They do, actually, replies a doctor friend.

Anne did not respond to this particular injustice, or perhaps was unaware of it—still maintaining that, while she was "very apprehensive" when a book was coming out, she never read her reviews. However, she admitted that while not reading them, she knew if "a stinker" had come out because friends would nervously say something like: "There, there, Anne, I don't think you're sentimental."

What can I say? I probably am sentimental. There is such a thing as feeling as you go through life and I write about it. I am not excusing my limitations. I feel as if I will never be Tolstoy. I have my little, tiny world that I seem to have to deal with.

In this tiny world she was very interested in the things that sometimes seemed trivial, and how there were things underneath that meant more. For Anne it was "almost a challenge to have someone wash the dishes and find something to say about it that would mean more than just washing the dishes."

§

Anne had now lived in Baltimore for over half a century and, contrary to her original opinion on first moving there, she had come to consider it a Southern city:

For me, raised in the South, Baltimore originally seemed Northern, but now that I've been here for fifty-odd years, I have to say it strikes me as more Southern.

In *Clock Dance*, the city finally achieves something like a eulogy: the warehouse roofs and factory smokestacks of its outskirts are described as "suffused with a leftover, pale-yellow glow that made them look eerily beautiful." Clusters of brightly dressed people amble happily toward the Orioles stadium with their babies, diaper bags, seat cushions, and homemade posters; the community Willa finds herself in is neighborly and caring. In an interview Anne now ventured a firm opinion about her city, although still harboring the old fear that true Baltimoreans knew she was not really one of them ("the grandmothers are whispering, she doesn't know a thing about Baltimore!"). People didn't know, she said, that in spite of its reputation it was a good place to live:

Baltimore is a very kind-hearted city. People are genuinely warm to each other, they mean well always. It's not what people imagine. And you learn this after you've been here a long while…It also has a lot of color and grit, we have to say. Things going on in it—I always wonder if I could set a novel in another city and have it be the same kind of writing, and I'm not sure I could.

She had never consciously decided to write only about Baltimore, and part of it was "just laziness"—it was simply a lot easier to set a story in the place where she lived, Anne admitted. But part of it was also admiration. She believed Baltimore had immeasurably added to her work, with its strong sense of self and its people "just so distinctly Baltimorean." It was a tough place sometimes, she acknowledged, feeling that songwriter Randy Newman's description of Baltimore as a hard city by the sea had got it right.

257

But for Anne as a writer, the value of Charm City lay in the fact that it was a character, "with its own distinctive quirks and foibles that color every story set there." It made writing a lot easier if your characters lived in a place that had its own sense of itself, she said. "I don't travel very much these days, but when I do, Baltimore always seems so staunch and dear when I come back to it." She was still a loyal customer at Eddie's market and had always loved stocking up at the celebrated Greg's Bagels for the annual journey to the beach with her young family. A few years earlier she had said of Penn Station that she loved its size —spacious but not self-vaunting, like Philadelphia's station— and the way the sunlight slanted through the tall windows onto the mix of passengers lining the benches, the peace that fell after they left. "Sometimes, if I'm not in a hurry, I'm actually pleased to learn that my train's delayed and I'll have a reason to sit there longer."

She felt that just about everyone in the city, across all classes and cultures, behaved with grace and patience. She only had to observe some trying episode in, say, a supermarket checkout line—a customer taking too long counting coins or an inept cashier. Baltimoreans stood by quietly, or tried to help out if they could, without even an eye-roll. It was a kind-hearted city, in Anne's opinion, where downtown you never heard angry traffic horns the way you would in New York. All across Baltimore people smiled at each other in the street, and helped each other. "I think this has an influence on my writing. In such surroundings, how could I possibly invent a mean-spirited character?" Hearing two women talking there in the market, she would be making notes in her mind (she was an "eavesdropper's writer," she once remarked). "It's a very catchy way of speaking, the way Baltimoreans speak." In *Clock Dance* Willa, unused to the accent, thinks that someone is named Sir Joe until she finds out his name is actually Sergio.

But Anne was a realist, all the same. She was all too aware of the violence in her city, some that had personally affected her: in 2018 an old friend, the journalist Rob Hiassen, was gunned down along with four others by a local man angered by what he considered defamatory reporting on him in Rob's newspaper. Anne joined Rob's family and colleagues at his memorial service. "I loved him dearly. I thought he was smart and funny and wise," she said sadly beforehand. She knew about the poverty, both in the city and in the rest of the state, and was a regular contributor to the Fuel Fund of Maryland, which provided assistance to people needing help with their utility bills or buying food and filling prescriptions; in 2015-2016 she was listed among those donating an unidentified sum over $500 (which she still did as "Taghi and Anne Modarressi"). The following year she donated at least $25,000 to the Maryland Food Bank, again as Anne Modarressi. There were many, many such contributions, always under her less visible married name, particularly to organizations seeking to improve the lives of those in her home city: the Baltimore Community Foundation, Aids Action Baltimore, Health Care for the Homeless, the Women's Housing Coalition, the Woodbourne charity for children, the American Civil Liberties Union of Maryland, the House of Ruth Maryland refuge for battered women, the Associated Black Charities of Maryland—as well as donations to beloved institutions such as the Baltimore Museum of Art and the Enoch Pratt Free Library, where Anne had taken her daughters for their books as children. In 1991 she and Taghi had bought tickets to a Phantom Ball in support of a Baltimore literacy campaign, donating a sum of money that brought them into the "Gold Donors" category (the phantom ball no doubt a type of event appealing to Anne as she did not need to turn up). Other, wider-ranging organizations also received Anne's help: the National Association for the Advancement of Colored People, American Near East Refugee Aid, the Vietnam Veterans of America Foundation, the Carter Center for the alleviation of human suffering, Médecins Sans Frontières, the Mercy Corps humanitarian aid organization.

But because her novels did not as a rule directly address the issues in her city, and because she maintained a very low profile about her giving, Anne was often perceived as willfully blind to the actualities of Baltimore. In 2019 came a personal attack in *White Flights: Race, Fiction, and the American Imagination,* a book of essays about whiteness in modern American fiction by a professor of English, Jess Row. In reference to Anne's frequent setting of Roland Park, he declared that she was a writer "rooted in a place that is so comfortable, unthreatening and familiar that it becomes almost featureless." According to Row, the area was a site of timeless normalcy where the white world would never be significantly altered, and this normalcy depended on the general absence of black people. He suggested that if Anne Tyler were to give them a voice, they might tell stories like the one he used to hear from a colleague of his who grew up in Baltimore. "When I was young, our name for Roland Park was Hang-a-n*****," the friend had recounted. "My parents made sure I knew never to go up there, not for any reason."

Prior to the book's publication Jess Row had already blogged that while he was not labeling Anne Tyler an overt, intentionally racist writer, she still typified a "posture of racial silence: not talking about race, and likely, for the most part, wishing that conversations about race didn't have to happen." What was remarkable about Anne in particular, he went on, was that Baltimore had such an extreme, obvious, seemingly unavoidable history of racial discrimination and violence, and yet one would never know it from reading her novels. She evoked white characters who mostly lived claustrophobic, narrow lives, subsumed by their own quirks and their imperfect or unhappy experiences in life. Witness the convulsions that had gripped Baltimore in the five decades of Anne Tyler's career, he pointed out: the riots of the late 1960s, the economic collapse and emptying-out of entire sectors of the city, the bankruptcy of the city's largest employer, Bethlehem Steel, the crack wars and soaring murder rates that still persisted to this day. For Row, Anne Tyler's response to these events had been absolute silence. Her work was "probably the most important illustration of how the world has seen Baltimore over the last half century: by not seeing it."

Anne's response, if she read the review of Row's book in the *New York Times* that mentioned some of the criticism leveled against her, was again silence.

She continued to make her own choices about subject matter and to remain quiet about her decades-long support of the black community in city and state. She continued to be truly fond of Baltimore, even to say that she loved it. Baltimore in its turn was proud of Anne. After her latest novel came out, the *Baltimore*

Sun ran a full-page piece about real locations in the city that evoked a similar feel to the book's invented ones, explaining that while some places might be instantly familiar to residents, most minor venues were in fact made up: no one would ever find the "Café Antoine" where Willa ate with her son. But perhaps some of the locations in the novel were still based on real places, they suggested—maybe modeled on this area of older homes running small businesses, maybe that lushly landscaped apartment block, or that elementary school with its colorful picket fence. Baltimoreans were invited to send in their own ideas about where Anne might have been thinking of, with a promise to publish the cleverest.

Final Chapter

Another "refilling" period was now due for Anne, her usual space of about six months to a year.

I always said if you asked a woman who's just given birth, "When are you going to have your next baby?" she'd say, "Whaaat?"

In these non-writing times Anne would accept more invitations (as ever, in order to have something to write about), become what she called "more outdoorsy" and putter in her yard, throw some dinner parties or small suppers, clean out all her dresser drawers, and read non-stop. Mostly it was a matter of just paying more attention to the real world again. "It's as if I've been off on a long trip—even, let's say, a space voyage." Her house might need attention, although generally spotless and comfortable, kept in order not by a fleet of cleaners but by Anne herself. Mess in other people's houses was "interesting and kind of cozy"—she always gravitated to strange kitchens to learn about their lives from the notices and pictures plastered to refrigerator doors—but not in her own. Her cleaning schedule divided the house into sections: one day for all the bathroom fixtures, another for dusting, her least favorite because there was nothing to show for it. This was the day Anne would imagine she was getting Alzheimer's because of trying to remember whether or not she had already done the coffee table: it was such a boring job her mind would have shut down. She truly believed that nobody should spend more than thirty minutes a day cleaning (and called herself "the accidental housekeeper").

Somebody would still occasionally arrive unannounced at the house wanting to meet her. Being a writer was not like being a movie star, Anne observed, and being famous was not what you imagine it to be. "To have somebody ring your doorbell and say, I have to talk with you, may I come in? It hasn't happened very often, but it's unsettling." Others would approach her very politely and non-intrusively, though Anne still believed she could never be anything but a disappointment when she came out with something not sounding like her books. Reporters visiting by arrangement were always met with great friendliness, some even getting hugged on departure—although Louise France from the *Weekend Australian Magazine* recalled being told by Anne's editor that she would have no idea what Anne was actually feeling: if she was put out or ruffled, she would not show it.

She still battled the occasional impulse to abscond from home, loving the idea of packing her two favorite sweaters and hitting the road. Instead, she would travel to see her daughters, frequently making the trip to Philadelphia to visit Tezh, now married to a "fine Donegal man," in Anne's words, and to the West Coast to see Mitra and the nearly adult grandchildren. They would sit around and talk about Taghi, even about his foibles, which made them laugh and lessened the sadness. He was "always sort of explosive," Anne related:

I remember once he told one of my daughters she ought to go to medical school and she said well I'm not interested in medicine and he said well what does that have to do with anything? We like to quote that.

He also once asked Anne, who had a very poor sense of direction, if it had ever occurred to her that if only she would turn right when she thought she should turn left, she was more likely to be correct.

Her grief for Taghi never changed: she still thought about him every single day.

Eventually the fallow period would work itself out. One day Anne would wake up and, as usual, feel that something was missing in her life. Then it would start all over again—"bare desk, large window, total lack of inspiration..." For about thirty days she would sit hour after hour in her study, looking at her pictures and gazing at her Richard Wilbur poem *Walking to Sleep*, with its line on stepping off assuredly into the blank of your mind. "I see those words as about getting an idea and making a book...I don't get anxious. It will come to you, let it come in." (Her own novels were not on the shelves in the study: "too weird," Anne felt, although there was still a paperback set in the house for reference in case she started repeating herself, which did happen because of forgetting a book as soon as she finished it.) She would again go through her box of index cards —some now decades old, some passed over myriad times but which might suddenly mean something—and ponder how to fit them all into a novel. So many observations and overheard phrases, like the grandmotherly saying Anne had heard that if something is lost, just put an onion out on the kitchen counter and then you will find it. "How can you not write that one down? You start to think, how can I use that?" (On other occasions she would think, why can't I just use up the cards in the box and be done? But she knew that wasn't going to happen.)

The cards also stored lists of first and last names from years of overhearing somebody being called and making a note of the interesting ones. When Anne was trying to think what a character's name was, she always knew what the first letter would be, if nothing else. "It's got to be a name beginning with N," she would think, and then go down the list. Sometimes she turned to a baby name book she kept for the same purpose.

When she was ready, Anne embarked on her twenty-third novel, *Redhead by the Side of the Road*. Each book still began with a one-page outline but her methodology had now evolved a little: first, the usual drafting in longhand (these days with a Pilot P-500 black gel pen), then revising again and again, still in longhand, until she had a section she was satisfied with and could type it up into her computer. Then came more editing and a final print before rewriting the entire draft in longhand for a second time and reading the whole thing out loud into a dictaphone (eventually replaced by an iPhone), to hear what didn't sound right, what seemed wooden or strange. She had been "flabbergasted" to discover how much recording the text helped her writing. All of a sudden she could say, oh, that is such a wrong word there, or he would never say that, he wouldn't put it that way. Sometimes she would have written the same word three times on one page, and could now catch it. The next stage was making additions and final editing. Every so often it was difficult to call a halt to the revision, Anne feeling she could go on forever. But the rewriting process was one she loved: "...that's when I can relax and play around, knowing that at least the bones of the story are in place."

Nights were still difficult, with little sleep. She did not want to read or get up, and spent many hours just listening to the BBC news—a bad idea, she admitted, with so few good tidings. "I got my heart broken," she was to say after the storming of the Capitol building in 2021, "when I saw the US constitution wasn't really very well defended." Global warming was another anxiety, making Anne almost wish she had never had children, and to feel that her grandchildren might not thank her.

Her day began early, because these days "my mind sort of goes after one pm." After a nice long amble through the woods —now carrying her cell phone, in a tiny hanging wallet around her shoulder, after several arguments with her daughters and friends—she would reluctantly enter her study to start work, still hating to "break through the crust of the morning." During her walk she would not have been thinking about the book but usually found on arriving back at the house that the solution to some issue had presented itself:

...although I may begin my walk thinking about a recipe or a house-maintenance problem, by the time I'm on the homeward loop my characters are all at once talking in my mind, and I go directly upstairs and start writing down what they've said.

Anne had long ago learned how to deal with the occasional writer's block, which she knew arose from a subconscious realization that she had taken a wrong turn—forced a character into something he would never do, or cheated somehow in the storyline. If she did not spot where she had gone wrong after a day or two, it helped to go back to the start of the problem and painstakingly rewrite those pages by hand, a process slow enough to discover the misstep.

When working, she needed a silence in the room so total that she kept away from her computer so as not to hear the "little ding" of emails. Sometimes things went badly but more often she would be swept away by what her characters were saying to her, enjoying the amusement and adventure of it, before suddenly looking up to find it was lunchtime. In the afternoons Anne had been persuaded by friends to just sit and read, which at first had felt like drinking in the daytime. Her best place to do it was in a particular easy chair in the living room that overlooked her backyard. She had migrated to mostly reading on a screen, relishing that she could have a book instantly, more cheaply, and in a downsized format. If she was really taken with an ebook she would then buy the paper edition, if possible at a small bookstore. There was something almost holy about stepping into an independent store, Anne believed, and seeing how much true booksellers know and understand, what dedication they showed in sharing their knowledge with their customers. (Audiobooks did not appeal: "I seem to take more in through my eyes than my ears.")

Fiction remained Anne's strong preference. "I'm so uncomfortable with memoirs that I don't read them. I just think, I'm going to be really nice to you and not read your memoir." (She thought it would be better if biographers wrote a novel about the person instead.) She still enjoyed different types of new fiction but always looked for a story that evolved from character, feeling not the slightest bit interested in murder mysteries or adventure. The books were chosen on the basis of reviews rather than suggestions from friends, as Anne tended to disagree with their tastes; the best of what she read she would then recommend to them to disagree with as they saw fit.

If she did not enjoy a book, she put it down—"too many books, too little time." And there *were* many she did not enjoy. She took a "really strong dislike" to the quartet of novels by the hugely popular Italian author Elena Ferrante, having lost count of how many people told her she was going to love them and then finding that she was unable to finish even one, let alone carry on:

A couple of times I was rude enough to say so to a friend and we came practically to blows. People feel very strongly about those books. But I just felt everything I was reading was fake. And there are so many other things to read.

266

What Anne hoped for from a book—her own or someone else's—was transparency, for the story to shine through without any hint of the writer. When reading, she was purely a reader:

I just want to be told a story, and I want to believe I'm living that story, and I don't give a thought to influences or method or any other writerly concerns.

But as well as new fiction there were longstanding favorites that Anne always returned to: most recently, Elizabeth Strout, because every sentence of hers was "so exactly right that it seems to have been born rather than created." If she could write like one other author, Anne said, it was Elizabeth. Another standby, frequently mentioned over the years, was Australian author Christina Stead's 1940 work *The Man Who Loved Children*, a novel that had shocked Anne with its stark, troubling picture of family life but that somehow rang true (and caused passionate arguments amongst readers, with Anne recognizing that no one could ever be neutral about it). She would return to Jane Austen, following her late discovery of the classic writer, and mentioned also that she had been "subtly influenced" by more books than she could count, often wishing that she had been the one to come up with some pivotal moment in a plot or some leap of language—and then eventually, "in my own different way," trying it herself. But top of Anne's list of favorites, of course, was Eudora Welty, whose *The Golden Apples* gave her comfort because it reminded her of the "many kinds of crazy, funny, touching ways people interact with each other." She recommended it as a good book to read when sitting home alone. She had first read it as a teenager in 1950s North Carolina, she wrote:

The linked stories about the inhabitants of a small town in Mississippi made me feel right at home; I recognized these people, and none of them surprised me. Rereading the book now, though, I'm struck by their great distance from everything that preoccupies me in 2020. They still make me smile, but their innocence breaks my heart. Why I should find this a comfort, I can't explain, but I thank them for it.

267

If she could only read one book for the rest of her life, Anne felt, this was the one. She could not think of a better demonstration of how writers should behave toward their characters.

As for her own novels, she still started each one thinking that this one would be different, and it never was. Even at this late stage of authorship, Anne continued to remain fascinated by all her old obsessions: how families work, endurance, how people get through life. People could not leave their families without enormous upheaval, she observed, and she had to keep circling the subject of how they continue to live together after inflicting pain on one another:

> *We're endlessly striving and keeping going. How many times we hurt each other in families or drift apart or do harm—and then we come back together and try over again. It's very heartening and touching.*

The setting for *Redhead by the Side of the Road*, inevitably, remained north Baltimore, around the now-familiar streets and venues so often featured in works gone by. The central character is the fortyish Micah Mortimer, owner of a one-man mobile computer repair service, who is living for free in the basement of his building in return for maintenance. He leads a highly regulated life, with a specific day for cleaning the kitchen counters and appliances, another for mopping the floors, another for vacuuming. He has written a basic computer how-to book called *First, Plug it In* (published by Woolcott Publishing, the vanity publisher from *The Beginner's Goodbye)*, but spends most of his time visiting his customers and doing odd jobs around the apartment block. His undemanding, kind-hearted girlfriend Cass is a teacher at the underprivileged Linchpin Elementary (Cheryl's school in *Clock Dance*); she breaks off the relationship after Micah fails to ask her to move in with him when she is possibly in danger of eviction from her apartment. He is in any case distracted by a surprise visitor, Brink, a runaway rich-kid college student who mistakenly believes Micah may be his father. Micah in helping to sort the situation out unexpectedly reconnects with Brink's mother, the woman he loved but drove away back in college, and after she has been to fetch her son he is left feeling alone and unhappy. As the novel ends, he suddenly finds himself making an unplanned visit to Cass at her school.

At the start of the writing process, Anne had been racking her brains in her usual way for something to write about when a single sentence popped into her head:

"You have to wonder what goes through the mind of a man like — —." (I didn't have a name for him yet.) I was baffled. Why should I have to wonder? I thought, and then up popped the next sentence: "He lives alone; he keeps to himself..." The rest of the book was up to me, but at least I was on my way.

She had no idea what he would do next, a thrilling point for Anne until a character opened up. She still thought, as always, that when writing a book the happy part was when the characters began talking, because then she was being told a story. Nothing was more important to humans than story, Anne declared, even above music or art—or at least for her. If she were disabled on her death bed she wanted to listen to story, not music.

The voice she had heard was the sort of neutral, neuter tone employed by the mind when it thinks in actual words, she explained; it was as though when she was really inside what she was working on, her mind's voice sometimes began rolling ahead of its own accord, especially with dialogue or with a character's internal monologue. It was not in any way mystical or even, strictly speaking, a matter of "inspiration"—just momentum.

Her writing involved "a kind of sinking" into an event rather than orchestration, Anne further explained about her methods at around this time, so much so that she had jokily wondered if sinking deeper and deeper might get her to the inner truth of the universe (although by now she had learned to stop at the point of feeling she would throw up if she read the book one more time). Because of this slow sinking she never considered the technical aspects of a scene but just proceeded inch by inch, getting her characters in the door, figuring out who arrived first, and who next, and what it would be logical for them to say to each other. Then, coming back from her morning walk (not having given the scene a single conscious thought), she would suddenly think, "Wait! That brother who just showed up—his family hasn't seen him in ages. It's only natural that the sister who's observing this should have some thoughts about what he looks like now."

So I'll go back and insert an extra chunk to cover that. If the passage were a picture it would be a collage, with rags and tags and bits of string pasted on to it here and there. But eventually I'll have the great happiness of rewriting the whole thing, from beginning to end, and seeing it come together as a single whole. This is why I worship the notion of a subconscious.

The title of the new novel came from Micah's mistaking a fire hydrant for a redheaded child or a very short adult while out on his daily run, something that had happened to Anne several times on her morning walk. Her brain never learned the lesson: she kept having the same thought every time she saw the hydrant. The experience started her thinking about how many other mistakes, more serious mistakes, were repeated in the course of our lives. "How often do we fail to realize that they were mistakes, even?"

She admitted giving Micah her own rigid housekeeping schedule, which she saw as a way for him to exert control in a chaotic world; for Anne he was a man who was worried about having his boundaries transgressed, making him in her view quite close to Macon in *The Accidental Tourist*. (Micah also shares Anne's continuing irritation with statements that sounded like questions.) There is a surprising amount of computer speak in the novel although Anne denied doing much research, fearing as always that knowing actual facts might cramp her style, but owned up to cribbing from YouTube on how to remove porn sites from a teenager's laptop so she could get Micah to do it. She liked to add one detail "so ridiculously precise that readers start assuming I must know what I'm talking about over all."

The novel is suffused with a sense of loneliness, a consciousness of how a person can become set in their ways and lead an isolated life. Micah is nevertheless abreast of current events, with Anne again bringing in topical references in a way she had for so many years eschewed (and been criticized for not doing): this time, a news report covering a mass shooting in a synagogue, families dying in Yemen, and immigrant children torn from their parents in Trump's America. She commented that she had found it easy to "be" Micah throughout the book, but especially in that particular passage. The events that he was reflecting upon weighed so heavily on her own mind these days, Anne felt, that even Micah would have to be affected by them. While she had always disliked topical novels and had never tried to write anything about political or historical events, in this case it had seemed almost dishonest not to at least lightly mention these things because they should weigh very heavily on everybody and should at least cross Micah's mind: they were things he was "unhappy really hearing, even if he's not out there being an activist in any way." America now had what she called a "feral toddler" in the White House, and she believed that the world had become so harmed by everything that it would be wrong for a character to not notice, and also (perhaps as a consequence of some of the criticism leveled against her) that it would be "immoral to pretend life was just la la la." Despite this observation, she deliberately made Micah a very kind person — if wrongheaded in his relationships — in order to offset what she saw as a depressing new mean-spiritedness in America. "I think I needed to create this other world to take refuge in because the real world is a mess," she said again, although trying to remain optimistic in principle. "Up close you'll always see things to be optimistic about."

Micah was the latest in a line of male characters in Anne's work who fail at college — prevented from going in the first place, or called home in the middle, or held back later by family duty and inherited hardship. Anne wondered if all these men unable to realize their dreams might have to do with her sense that it must be very hard to be a man, "hard to *become* a man, when you're young and not very sure of yourself but you're expected to be in charge." She thought the novel's rich kid Brink, for instance, would probably turn out to be a nice guy when he had grown out of his self-centeredness, and was aware that a "little bit of prejudice" had emerged in her depiction:

I'm not particularly sympathetic to spoiled rich kids. I mean, this just clearly is somebody who's kind of slid through life, and he has all the trappings of it. You know, he sort of dresses in that way, and I'm aware that I'm stereotyping and I shouldn't. But anyway, I couldn't help just having him be that way. I thought it would be fun.

She had worried a little about the book, fearing it was too short, but the novel was generally well received. For the *Washington Post* the characters were a series of moderately eccentric poses presented without much wit or psychological insight, but not for the *New York Times*, who wrote that Anne Tyler had every gift a great novelist needs: "intent observation, empathy and language both direct and surprising...unembarrassed goodness." Slighter and more bittersweet than some of her recent novels, said the *Guardian* in Britain, "but, like all her work, it tenderly opens an ordinary life and shows us the universal truths hidden inside." For the *Sydney Morning Herald* in Australia, if there was a flaw in this "sweet story" it was the suggestion that everyone was swimming like salmon toward the norm of family life, but Anne Tyler's writing was so expertly nuanced and honest that she carried the reader into fictional strangers' lives as if they really mattered. Published in 2020, *Redhead by the Side of the Road* was an instant bestseller and longlisted for the Man Booker Prize—a shock to Anne, who felt the novel covered "such a narrow sliver of a life" that she had not expected it to garner much attention. (Her own favorite Booker-winner was *The Remains of the Day* by Kazuo Ishiguro, because she loved "the quiet thud of realization that fell over the main character at the end of his story. To me it felt as cataclysmic as a bomb.")

By now Anne had already sold more than eleven million books worldwide, with fans everywhere leaping on the latest Tyler. According to her publisher, every time a new Tyler manuscript arrived—always immaculately presented, without any anxious calls beforehand from the author—all their other celebrated writers would get wind of it and start clamoring for advance copies.

§

Redhead by the Side of the Road was completed long before the arrival of the Covid-19 virus, but was published at just about the time the pandemic was gaining strength. Curiously, the novel seems almost to predict it: when Micah goes for his early-morning run, he briefly fantasizes that the empty streets are due to some cataclysm and that he's the last person left alive; he is relieved to come across two women talking, and gazes at them like a starving man staring longingly at a feast.

When the virus struck in early 2020, a planned appearance in March for seventy-eight-year-old Anne at the British Library in London had to be canceled and, along with everyone else, she was obliged to go into lockdown. Anne confessed to feeling "kind of relieved" about the cancellation, apparently having secretly hoped for something that might put the trip off. Naturally she then felt bad that people were suffering from the virus, which was like when she had prayed for the school to burn down before a math test as a girl, while knowing how guilty she would have felt had it actually happened.

Anne and her circle had "no confidence in our government" as regards their dealing with the pandemic. Initially, she was unfazed about staying at home even more than usual, generally needing to be much alone in any case because of exhaustion if too long in company. "You could almost say that I live a quarantine life anyway," she declared, if aware as always that her tendency toward self-isolation was not very healthy. She watched streamed series on TV (when Taghi died she had given herself the present of never again watching live TV, which made her feel passive and not in control of what was on the screen), and did a lot of cooking—complicated recipes to keep her busy. Through the open window in her study she began to hear "more and more birds and fewer and fewer humans," and eventually started wanting more contact with the outside world.

First I thought, "Oh, well, never mind; I basically shelter in place anyhow, and I already know about working from home—how you have to be sure and change out of your pajamas." But then after a few days I thought, "Oh. Wait a minute. I'm surprised at how often now I feel the need to step out on my front stoop and start a conversation with a passing neighbor."

The pleasant tenor of her life had changed. The two friends that had still regularly turned up for what they all called their vinotherapy could no longer come, and on her morning walks in the woods Anne felt sad not to see all the children on their way to school. She could not make her frequent trips to see Tezh and her husband in Philadelphia or Mitra and her family in San Francisco, grandson Taghi now a college student and granddaughter Dorri a high school student, neither happy to be suddenly stuck at home and seemingly back in childhood. Anne was concerned about her family and knew it was going to be a hard time.

For her own part, she had suffered a general feeling of distractedness in the first few days of lockdown, unable to read when she picked up a book, although eventually finding fiction a source of company and hoping that everyone would start reading anything they could to console themselves. When she tried to work she seemed to write the same three pages over and over, although able in the end to sink back into it (and to write an introduction to a new edition of *Delta Wedding* by Eudora Welty, who had died in 2001). A new novel was in progress and, when Anne found herself describing an Easter dinner where the people were behaving "a bit snarkily" with each other, she thought, as she so often had, oh, now I remember why I write: because it makes me happy.

As for whether the virus would ever feature in her work, Anne continued to maintain that generally she did not think current events made for very good literature.

They have to mellow for a while. We need a little distance to see them for what they are.

This time she was proved wrong: the pandemic did feature in her next novel, *French Braid*.

§

On 18 September 2020, an exhibition celebrating a century of women writers opened at the Smithsonian's National Portrait Gallery in Washington, DC. An arresting oil portrait of Anne, painted by the Australian artist Ralph Heimans in 2015, hung side by side with images of twenty-three other world-renowned American authors like Alice Walker, Joyce Carol Oates, Maya Angelou, and Willa Cather. The label on Anne's portrait quoted from *The Taming of the Shrew*: "Sit by my side, and let the world slip." (The rest of the quote, "we shall ne'er be younger," is perhaps left to the viewer to supply.)

(Photo by kind permission Ralph Heimans)

Asked in old age what life had taught her, Anne replied: to be still and listen. In matters of love she knew she had been very lucky in her life, and she did think it was luck. With her wonderful father, brothers, and grandfathers, to love men had been less fraught for her than for some people: she still saw them as innately kind and well-meaning. Her husband Taghi had been her best friend. "I know everyone says that, but it's true." Although she spent a great deal of her time with "incompatible husbands" as part of her work, her own marriage had been supremely happy.

Watching her grandparents get older, Anne in her youth had imagined it must be awful to be approaching the end of life. Now, in her late seventies, it seemed natural. She did not want to go on living forever and it was not an upsetting idea. When Abby dies in *A Spool of Blue Thread* Anne had written simply: "And then no more." She still thought that must be what dying was like: that you saw the car coming at you and then nothing, that was the end. She might be in the middle of a book when it happened, but the nice thing for Anne about getting to old age was thinking, well, what if I never finish it? The world will go on without another of my books.

What she wanted as a legacy was for readers to have been fully immersed in her novels, so that after reading them they would feel they had actually stepped inside another person's life and come to feel related to them. The whole purpose of her books was to sink into other lives, and she would be delighted if others sank along with her:

> *I would love it if readers said, "Oh, yes, I was once an accidental tourist," or, "I once owned the Homesick Restaurant," and then recalled that in fact, that hadn't really happened; they had just intensely imagined its happening.*

The word she would choose to characterize her work would be "truthful."

The book started after *Redhead by the Side of the Road* was one "totally dictated to me by my characters" (who became another source of company in lockdown). She allowed herself to plan only a very little, preferring to see where it went—even if, "Surprise, surprise. It's about a family in Baltimore." She said she wanted to investigate, again, the humdrum surface of things and what lies beneath, the old challenge of having somebody wash dishes and trying to figure out something to say about it that would mean more than just that mundane task. She could not really envisage ceasing to write, because it continued to make her so happy, although retirement did still occasionally beckon. She had contemplated going to live near one of her girls, but preferred to stay where her support group was. For Anne, the shape of an average person's life was the shape of a human eye: starting from a small point, widening as more happens when you move out into the world, then narrowing again. She was now back at the small point, in Baltimore, and it felt "right" that she should end up there.

Perhaps her memories were enough. Appearing in February 2022 on the British radio show "Desert Island Discs," where guests choose eight music tracks they would take to a desert island, Anne's choices included "This is My Father's World," the hymn that reminded her of her Quaker childhood in the commune; Blondie's "Heart of Glass," the song that took her back to her daughters' teenage years; "Baltimore," as sung by Nina Simone; and, of course, Taghi's much loved "Sheep May Safely Graze." The single book she would take would be Eudora Welty's *The Golden Apples*, and, requested to choose just one luxury item, she opted for a giant supply of puppy chow so she could make friends with any animals on the island. If she could take only one piece of music, it would be Taghi's old favorite. "I could listen to that forever."

French Braid was issued to its eagerly awaiting audience in March 2022. The story of the Garrett clan from 1959 through the pandemic of 2020, the work is another deeply moving exploration of the family, with all its love and flaws and ructions. At the center of the tale is artist Mercy, who only wants to paint, but waits until her children are grown before gently detaching herself from her devoted husband Robin (whom she still loves). There is little more in the way of plot. It is time, again, that provides the arc of events: people marry—not always choosing whom you might be expecting—and have children, sometimes surprising ones. Grandchildren connect with grandparents, then lose them. The Garretts do not always like each other or choose to be close; as Mercy's daughter says to herself on a family holiday, watching her parents and siblings at the beach, "A passerby would never guess the Garretts even knew each other. They looked so scattered, and so lonesome." But through it all, happinesses and hidden wounds alike, unbreakable links are forged—even if nearly everything is left unsaid. When Mercy moves, in stages, out of the marital home to her studio, her adult children politely maintain the fiction that their parents still live together. A gay member of the family

277

is completely accepted, and protected, without anyone feeling the need to bring up the subject if he doesn't want to. The bonds binding them all together are inextricable, the braid of the title (and not just a regular braid, the more complex French kind). Even those members of the family who have purposely drifted away cannot fully untangle themselves. That's how families work, Mercy's son tells his wife. "You think you're free of them, but you're never *really* free; the ripples are crimped in forever."

The story had been sparked by Anne's memory of the time she had learned about the death of two aunts from a friend compiling a genealogical chart. The aunts were elderly, but the random way the news reached her had left Anne feeling shaky and bewildered, shocked by the way they had all lost touch. She had always liked the aunts and there had been no falling-out, they simply lived further away. How could a family just drift apart? she asked herself. Her opening scene in *French Braid* is of one cousin uncertain whether she has recognized another at a busy train station.

Baltimore features less than usual, although the Orioles baseball team gets a mention, and Anne took the opportunity to repeat Ira Moran's opinion in *Breathing Lessons*—presumably her own—that the city's refurbished harbor area was a "glorified shopping mall."

It is tempting to see something of Anne in Mercy, whose art is at the core of her being, and who sometimes entertains mostly unserious fantasies of leaving home:

> *She enjoyed picturing what disguise she might choose—dyeing her hair a vivid black, for instance, and switching to tailored black slacks with creases ironed down the front, and perhaps even taking up cigarettes...She could sashay right out of the neighborhood, blowing smoke rings all the way to Penn Station, and no one would give her a glance.*

(French Braid, 2022)

In the end Mercy does escape to a new life (with shades of Delia's flight in *Ladder of Years*). But Anne did not agree she was like Mercy, seemingly back to insisting that she herself did not feature in her novels. "We all have private, negative feelings we don't talk about but I don't think I have secrets." For her, *French Braid* was again all about endurance. People really do live lives of "quiet desperation," she commented, quoting Thoreau, and, as always, families were basically the only group that could not easily split up. It was her version of a disaster movie, said Anne, putting people in a burning building and watching how they behaved under duress.

She was not too interested in the book's critical reception. "I'm not particularly rooted in the outside world," she told journalists. Reviews of the often rather bleak *French Braid*, however, were stellar, critics perhaps appreciating the fact that this beloved writer was still in their midst. Vintage Tyler, wrote the *Sunday Times* in Britain: "accessible, comforting, driven by humanity." Her novels might feel repetitive—the same kindly middle-class families grappling with the same old puzzle of how to live a decent life in a confusing world—but Anne got away with it because she had a genuine streak of genius. The *Sydney Morning Herald* in Australia saw Anne as a novelist of the "diffuse and the trivial" whose genius lay in reading the imperceptible signs of drama behind the surface, and in *French Braid* she had done it once again; but she had just written a few too many books that all merged together and failed to stay in the memory. Her "relevance, that beautiful attentiveness to the trivial, might be getting rickety."

For the *New York Times* Anne was at heart a 20th-century realist, interested in the tension between freedom and intimacy, personal fulfillment and the demands of family life. In this latest novel, however—her 24th—she had bypassed the domestic detail of the earlier work to supply something "subtler and finer, the long view on family: what remains years later, when the particulars have been sanded away by time." *French Braid*, said the review, was about what is remembered, what we are left with when all is said and done. It was a "moving meditation on the passage of time." Brilliant and captivating, wrote the *Washington Post*. If Anne Tyler isn't the best writer in the world, who is? demanded the BBC.

A critic in Britain's *Spectator* spied something larger and more ambitious in the novel: a portrait of a nation at a time of crisis, something essentially American and entirely resilient in the very awkwardness and angst of Anne's archetypal family. The *New York Times* had seen feminism in it too, with Mercy's actions the consequence of stifled female ambition. As usual, Anne made no comment about the varying interpretations, but as part of the necessary publicity accompanying the book she did take the opportunity to express her views about the way the world was going. She was horrified by "cancel culture"—disliking even the very term—and its implications for writing. The appropriation issue astonished her; she still asserted her right to write from the viewpoint of a black man if she so wished, although conceding that it would be "very foolish." And, for Anne, if something deleterious were to be discovered about an incredibly talented novelist he should certainly be condemned for it, but not have his works withdrawn from publication. "We couldn't look at Gauguin's paintings, could we? They would have to be destroyed or put away." Anne's views were relayed in the media, sparking the inevitable comment from those on either side of the debate.

After *French Braid* was finished Anne found she was unable to start another novel, though she kept trying. The distraction she had experienced at the start of the pandemic had continued a little, although it was hard for her to understand why, as she had no real fear of the virus. Perhaps losing the superficial encounters of daily life had dried up her sources of inspiration, she mused: movie nights with her friends, running into somebody on the street, eavesdropping at the grocery store. The extent to which she relied on these "random brushes with humanity" had surprised Anne; without them, she felt deprived. Covid had taught her that she wanted a little more human connection than she thought.

She hoped the writer's block would ease when things returned to normal. But, because not writing was not an option, she went on putting pen to paper with a series of short stories "just for the drawer," as she put it. She couldn't just sit home all day.

I get in and out of my characters' lives for three weeks, and then I'm done. I'm not going to send these stories to my agent.

§

Anne's stated "preferred mode of death" was something quick and relatively painless, like a heart attack, but with about half an hour's warning so that she could phone both of her daughters first and tell them how much they had added to her life. If she was remotely religious, Anne said, she would believe that a little gathering of her characters would be waiting for her in heaven when she died. Then what happened? she would ask them. How have things worked out, since the last time I saw you?

I am a lifelong fan of Anne Tyler and really enjoyed finding out more about her life. If you have enjoyed this book too, please consider leaving a review on Amazon. Thank you.

Also by Anne Wellman

BETTY
The Story of Betty MacDonald, Author of *The Egg and I*

In 1945 Betty MacDonald published *The Egg and I*, a lightly fictionalized, very funny account of her life as the wife of a chicken farmer in the remote American Northwest in the 1920s. The book was an immediate success, selling a million copies in less than a year, and was eventually translated into over thirty languages. A Hollywood movie of the book appeared two years later and at least eight further movies based on the popular *Egg and I* characters Ma and Pa Kettle were to follow.

In the next decade Betty wrote a number of highly popular children's books (*Mrs. Piggle-Wiggle* being the best known) and three more semi-autobiographical works. Her four comic memoirs of a life in the West and Northwest range from a rough mining community in Montana to the lush Olympic Peninsula and the bright lights of big city Seattle, and her life may even be viewed as a paradigm of early twentieth-century American experience: pioneering, homesteading, the Great Depression, war, and finally prosperity.

This is Betty's true story.

Available from:

In the UK: https://www.amazon.co.uk/dp/1493662422

In the US: https://www.amazon.com/dp/1493662422

Also available in other Amazon markets

MONICA
A Life of Monica Dickens

"All I have ever done is to report the experiences of my life."

So said Charles Dickens' great-granddaughter Monica Dickens, author of twenty-five novels and many classics for children, and one of the most popular writers of her day. Born into the upper classes, as a bored and unhappy debutante in the 1930s she took the incredible step of going into domestic service. *One Pair of Hands*, the book Monica wrote about her exploits, sold in the millions and has never been out of print since. Her subsequent works, calling on her rich experience as a wartime nurse, Spitfire factory worker, GI bride and more, sold in similar numbers but are now largely forgotten.

Often dismissed as a "light" writer, and her widespread appeal deflecting serious recognition, Monica Dickens was nevertheless highly praised by some of the most respected authors of the twentieth century, and indeed beyond. Far from writing lightly, in her middle period she addressed issues such as child abuse, suicide, and inner city deprivation. After becoming a volunteer for the Samaritans in England, this deeply compassionate woman went on to found the first branch of the organization in America and hence to save countless lives. Her name is engraved on a marker near the soaring bridges over the Cape Cod Canal, where she campaigned for the erection of higher barriers to stop desperate people jumping to their deaths.

Available from:

In the UK: https://www.amazon.co.uk/dp/B07HLM73WS

In the US: https://www.amazon.com/dp/B07HLM73WS

Also available in other Amazon markets

Angry Young Women
six writers of the sixties

A Taste of Honey, The L-Shaped Room, The Pumpkin Eater, Up the Junction, Poor Cow, The Millstone, and *Georgy Girl*: works that are seen as defining radical female literature in 1960s Britain. All of the authors were young. Their writing spread beyond their native shores to be just as eagerly consumed in America, Canada, Australasia and indeed around the world. Every one of these iconic works was made into a film, most of them equally iconic, if not more so.

Each of the writers, at one time or another, was labeled an "Angry Young Woman." Shelagh Delaney, author of *A Taste of Honey*, was the first, on that occasion by a theatre critic reviewing the play's opening performance in 1958. "She knows what she is angry about," the programme for the production likewise declared. But what was it?

Shelagh's writing almost at the start of the decade, and that of the other young women as the 1960s played out, was about the realities of being female at the start of the second half of the twentieth century. A new excitement was in the air: the economy was thriving, the class system was beginning to splinter and there was a growing realization that women had a right to the same things as men, including in matters of sex. But real life was a different affair, and the consequences of sex the same as they ever had been. Women knew very little about their own bodies and contraception was a word too explicit and rude even to be mentioned. The pill was available on the NHS health service from 1961, but for many years doctors and clinics would prescribe it only to married women. Abortion remained illegal until 1967 but nevertheless took place, frequently and dangerously. The actuality was therefore that despite the new era, young women were far from free, still in thrall to biology and liable to become pregnant. Pregnancy, abortion, childbirth, and motherhood: still the realities of life, and the subjects these "Angry Young Women" chose to write about—plus the added new possibility of raising a child alone.

The central parts in the movie versions were played by the decade's rising young stars as well as established favorites. All the directors were men, who for the most part distorted the original intention of the play or novel and produced films different in tone and detail but in some cases almost more celebrated.

This is the story of these pivotal works: how they came to be written by those women at that time, what was meant, how they were received and translated into film—and how some of these writers ultimately viewed their work across the span of years.

But were they really "Angry Young Women"?

Available from:

In the UK:

https://www.amazon.co.uk/dp/B088P574CW

In the US:

https://www.amazon.com/dp/B088P574CW

Also available in other Amazon markets

Sources

Allardice, Lisa, "Anne Tyler: A Life's Work," *Guardian*, 13 Apr 2012

Allen, Brooke, "Anne Tyler in mid-course," *New Criterion*, May 1995

Australian Women's Weekly

Bahari, Maziar, "Inside Iran," *New Statesman*, 11 Sept 2008

Bail, Paul, *Anne Tyler: A Critical Companion*, Greenwood Press, 1998

Baltimore Magazine

Baltimore Sun

Binding, Paul, *Separate Country: A Literary Journey through the American South*, Paddington Press Ltd, 1979

Bookseller, 2015

Brooks, Arthelia, *The Backside of Yesterday: My Life and Work*, Celo Valley Books, 1994

Bush, Lyall, review of *The Amateur Marriage*, *Books in Canada*, 2004

Canberra Times

Chanticleer yearbooks, Duke University

Chicago Tribune

Cook, Bruce, "New Faces in Faulkner Country," *Saturday Review*, 4 Sept 1976

Cook, Bruce, "A Writer—During School Hours," *Critical Essays on Anne Tyler*, Ed. Alice Hall Petry, G. K. Hall, 1992

Croft, Robert W, *Anne Tyler: A Bio-Bibliography*, Greenwood Press, 1995

Daily Mail (UK)

Draughn, Kelly Elizabeth, *Harvard of Celo*, Blue Ridge Parkway: Agent of Transition, Longleaf Services on behalf of UNC – OSPS, reprint edition, 1 July 2017

Duke University calendar 1974/75
https://catalog.hathitrust.org/Record/100123292

Ebert, Roger, review
https://www.rogerebert.com/reviews/the-accidental-tourist-1989

Encyclopaedia Iranica
http://www.iranicaonline.org/articles/modarresi-taqi

Evans, Elizabeth, "Early Years and Influences," *Anne Tyler as Novelist*, Ed. Dale Salwak, University of Iowa Press, 1994

Evans, Elizabeth, *Anne Tyler*, Twayne Publishers, Inc., 1993

Evans, Elizabeth, "'Mere reviews': Anne Tyler as Book Reviewer," *Critical Essays on Anne Tyler*, Ed. Alice Hall Petry, G. K. Hall, 1992

Good Housekeeping, "Writing is an Adventure," 1 May 2020

Gottlieb, Robert, *Avid Reader: A Life*, Farrar, Straus and Giroux, 2016

Guardian (UK)

Guy, David, "Ardent Spirit, Generous Friend: remembering the novelist Reynolds Price," *The American Scholar*, 3 June 2011
https://theamericanscholar.org/ardent-spirit-generous-friend

Globe and Mail, Canada

Hicks, George L, *Experimental Americans: Celo and Utopian Community in the Twentieth Century*, University of Illinois Press, 2001

Hinde, Natasha, "Anne Tyler, Author Of *A Spool Of Blue Thread*, On Writing Her Prize-Winning Books 'Completely Without Inspiration,'" *The Huffington Post UK*, 29 May 2015

Hornby, Nick, "A Good Read," BBC Radio 4, 1 Jan 2018
https://www.bbc.co.uk/sounds/play/b09kb2m6

Hornby, Nick, "Stuff I've Been Reading," *The Believer*, 1 June 2012

Independent (UK)

Kline, Karen E, "The Accidental Tourist on Page and On Screen: Interrogating Normative Theories About Film Adaptation," *Literature/Film Quarterly*, vol. 24, no. 1, 1996, pp.70–83. *JSTOR* www.jstor.org/stable/43796701 Accessed 17 July 2020

Latipac yearbooks, Needham Broughton High School, 1957, 1958

Lockyer, Joshua Peter, *Sustainability and Utopianism: An Ethnography of Cultural Critique in Contemporary Intentional Communities*, University of Georgia, 2007
https://getd.libs.uga.edu/pdfs/lockyer_joshua_p_200708_phd.pdf

Los Angeles Times

Lueloff, Jorie, "Authoress Explains Why Women Dominate in South," *Critical Essays on Anne Tyler*, Alice Hall Petry, G. K. Hall, 1992

Macleans, Canada

Mail on Sunday (UK)

Michaels, Marguerite, "Anne Tyler, Writer 8:05 to 3:30," *New York Times*, 1977

Montreal Gazette

Morgan, Ernest, *The History of Celo Community*

Nesanovich, Stella Ann, " The Individual in the Family: a Critical Introduction to the Novels of Anne Tyler" (1979), *LSU Historical Dissertations and Theses*. 3454
https://digitalcommons.lsu.edu/gradschool_disstheses/3454

Nesanovich, Stella Ann, "The Early Novels, A Reconsideration," *Anne Tyler as Novelist*, Ed. Dale Salwak, University of Iowa Press, 1994

New York Times

New Yorker

News and Observer (Raleigh, North Carolina)

Observer (UK)

O'Neill, Patrick, "'Beautiful Lofty' column writer remembered," *Indyweek*, 15 Feb 2006
https://indyweek.com/news/phyllis-tyler-1917-2006/

Palaemon Press Limited, works published, Rubenstein Library, Duke University Libraries
https://library.duke.edu/rubenstein/collections/palaemon

Petry, Alice Hall, *Understanding Anne Tyler*, University of South Carolina Press, 1 Dec 1990

Petry, Alice Hall, "Tyler and Feminism," *Anne Tyler as Novelist*, Ed. Dale Salwak, University of Iowa Press, 1994

Philadelphia Inquirer, interview with Mitra Modarressi, 12 Dec 1993

Price, Reynolds, *Ardent Spirits: Leaving Home, Coming Back*, Scribner Book Company, 2009

Rahimieh, Nasrin, Translator's Preface, *The Virgin of Solitude* by Taghi Modarressi, Syracuse University Press, 2008

Rich, Barbara, review of *The Accidental Tourist*, *Women's Review of Books*, 1985

Ridley, Clifford A, "Anne Tyler: A Sense of Reticence Balanced by 'Oh Well, Why Not?,'" *National Observer*, 1972

Saturday Review

Shivers, Frank R, *Maryland Wits and Baltimore Bards: A Literary History with Notes on Washington Writers*, Maclay and Associates, Inc., 1985

Smartt Bell, Madison, *Charm City: A Walk Through Baltimore*, Crown, 2007

Sunday Times (UK)

Sydney Morning Herald

Telegraph (UK)

Time magazine

Tyler, Anne, conversation with Robb Forman Dew, c. 2012 https://www.penguinrandomhouse.com/books/215139/the-beginners-goodbye-by-anne-tyler/9780307969156/readers-guide/

Tyler, Phyllis Mahon, interview, *Southern Oral History Program Collection* (#4007), 10 Oct 1988 https://docsouth.unc.edu/sohp/html_use/C-0080.html

Updike, John, "Family Ways," *New Yorker*, 29 March 1976

Updike, John, "On Such a Beautiful Green Little Planet," *New Yorker*, 5 Apr 1982

Updike, John, "Loosened Roots," *New Yorker*, 6 June 1977

USA Today

Variety, "TriStar to make plans for 'Dinner'," 6 Nov 1997 https://variety.com/1997/film/news/tristar-to-make-plans-for-dinner-111637179/

Washington Post

Washington Star

Willrich, Patricia Rowe papers, David M. Rubenstein Rare Book & Manuscript Library, Duke University

Willrich, Patricia Rowe, "Watching Through Windows: A Perspective on Anne Tyler," *VQR magazine*, summer 1992

Selected stories by Anne Tyler

"The Galax," *Freshman Writing, Duke University*, 1958-59

"Laura," *Archive* (Duke), Mar 1959

"I Never Saw Morning," *Archive* (Duke), Apr 1961

"The Saints in Caesar's Household," *Under Twenty-five: Duke Narrative and Verse, 1945-1962*, Ed. William Blackburn, 1963

"The Baltimore Birth Certificate," *Critic*, Feb 1963

"A Street of Bugles," *Saturday Evening Post*, Nov 1963

"Nobody Answers the Door," *Antioch Review*, 1964

"A Misstep of the Mind," *Seventeen*, 1972

"A Knack for Languages," *New Yorker*, 1975

"Your Place is Empty," *New Yorker*, Nov 1976

"Uncle Ahmad," *Quest*, Nov–Dec 1977

"Linguistics," *Washington Post Magazine*, 1978

"Laps" (published in the UK as "Sometimes You Wonder"), *Parents* magazine, 1981

"Teenage Wasteland," *Seventeen*, November 1983

"C.C. Mulvaney," *Woman's Own* (UK), Dec 1983

"Hidden Dangers," *Washington Post Magazine*, Aug 1984

"A Woman Like a Fieldstone House," *Louder Than Words*, New York: Vintage Books, 1989

Children's works by Anne Tyler

Tumble Tower, Orchard Books, 1993

Timothy Tugbottom Says No!, Putnam, 2005

Novels by Anne Tyler

1. *If Morning Ever Comes*, Knopf, 1964
2. *The Tin Can Tree*, Knopf, 1965
3. *A Slipping-Down Life*, Knopf, 1970
4. *The Clock Winder*, Knopf, 1972
5. *Celestial Navigation*, Knopf, 1974
6. *Searching for Caleb*, Knopf, 1976
7. *Earthly Possessions*, Knopf, 1977
8. *Morgan's Passing*, Knopf, 1980
9. *Dinner at the Homesick Restaurant*, Knopf, 1982
10. *The Accidental Tourist*, Knopf, 1985
11. *Breathing Lessons*, Knopf, 1988
12. *Saint Maybe*, Knopf, 1991
13. *Ladder of Years*, Knopf, 1995
14. *A Patchwork Planet*, Knopf, 1998
15. *Back When We Were Grownups*, Knopf, 2001
16. *The Amateur Marriage*, Knopf, 2004
17. *Digging to America*, Knopf, 2006
18. *Noah's Compass*, Knopf, 2009
19. *The Beginner's Goodbye*, Knopf, 2012
20. *A Spool of Blue Thread*, Knopf, 2015
21. *Vinegar Girl*, Knopf, 2016
22. *Clock Dance*, Knopf, 2018
23. *Redhead by the Side of the Road*, Knopf, 2020
24. *French Braid*, Knopf, 2022

Anne Tyler correspondence and papers

Alfred A. Knopf, Inc. Records (Manuscript Collection MS-00062). Harry Ransom Center, The University of Texas at Austin

Anne Tyler papers, David M. Rubenstein Rare Book & Manuscript Library, Duke University

Anne Tyler Letters (MS 550), Sheridan Libraries, Johns Hopkins University

Anne Tyler letter to Jay Neugeboren, 25 Apr 1985

Anne Tyler letter to Robert Fink about *Searching for Caleb*, 1993

Anne Tyler letter to Franklin Mason, 9 May 1997

Anne Tyler letter to Rani Paul Ukkan, 11 Feb 2002

Elizabeth Evans papers, Southern Historical Collection, Louis Round Wilson Special Collections Library, University of North Carolina at Chapel Hill

Russell and Volkening Records, Manuscripts and Archives Division, The New York Public Library

Anne Tyler interviews

With George Dorner, "Anne Tyler: A Brief Interview With a Brilliant Author from Baltimore," *Rambler 2*, 1974

With the *Washington Post*, 1980

With Sarah English, "An Interview with Anne Tyler," *Dictionary of Literary Biography Yearbook*, 1982, Gale Research, 1983

With Lucinda Irwin Smith, *Women Who Write: From the Past and the Present to the Future*, Julian Messner, 1989

With Wendy Lamb, "An Interview with Anne Tyler," *Iowa Journal of Literary Studies 3* (1981): 59-64 and *Critical Essays on Anne Tyler,* Alice Hall Petry, G. K. Hall, 1992

With Jennifer Morgan Gray, 2007 https://www.penguinrandomhouse.com/books/181364/digging-to-america-by-anne-tyler/

With *Writer's Digest*, "Anne Tyler's Tips on Writing Strong (yet Flawed) Characters," Sept 2009

With *Goodreads*, Apr 2012 https://www.goodreads.com/interviews/show/662.Anne_Tyler

With Lynn Neary (National Public Radio), 30 Mar 2012 https://www.npr.org/2012/03/30/148926821/the-art-of-the-everyday-the-alchemy-of-anne-tyler

With the *Beacon*, June 2012
https://issuu.com/thebeaconnewspapers/docs/june2012balt

With Mark Lawson, "Front Row," BBC Radio 4, 2013

With Diane Rehm, National Public Radio (WAMU), Feb 2015

With Mariella Frostrup, "Books and Authors," BBC Radio 4, Feb 2015

With the *New York Times*, 5 Feb 2015

With Tim Teeman, "Anne Tyler: 'I am not a spiritual person,'" *Guardian* (UK), 15 Feb 2015

With Eleanor Wachtel, CBC (Canada), 22 Feb 2015 https://www.cbc.ca/player/play/2654907260

With Harriett Gilbert, "World Book Club," BBC Radio 4, Mar 2015

With Richard and Judy (UK), 10 Aug 2015 https://blog.whsmith.co.uk/richard-and-judy-ask-anne-tyler/

With *Baltimore Magazine*, 12 July 2018 https://www.baltimoremagazine.com/section/artsentertainment/anne-tyler-talks-gun-violence-inspiration-and-clock-dance/

With the *Weekend Australian Magazine*, "After 22 Novels US Author Anne Tyler Finally Gives an Interview," 21 July 2018

With the *New York Times*, July 2018

With "Woman's Hour," BBC, July 2018

With Rebecca Jones, "Why Anne Tyler Won't Be Writing About the Coronavirus," BBC News, 2 Apr 2020

With Sarah Gilmartin, *Irish Times*, 11 Apr 2020

With Hadley Freeman, *Guardian* (UK), 11 Apr 2020 https://www.theguardian.com/books/2020/apr/11/anne-tyler-up-close-youll-always-see-things-to-be-optimistic-about

With New Zealand public radio (RNZ), 14 Apr 2020
https://www.rnz.co.nz/audio/player?audio_id=2018742561

With Irish Radio (RTÉ Arena) 15 Apr 2020
https://www.rte.ie/culture/2020/0413/1130207-pulitzer-prize-winning-author-anne-tyler-talks-to-rte-arena/

With Jane Garvey and Fi Glover, "Fortunately," BBC Radio 4, 29 May 2020 **https://www.bbc.co.uk/sounds/play/p08fk5j5**

With *New Statesman*, 6 July 2020

With *Kinfolk* magazine, September 2020

https://www.kinfolk.com/anne-tyler/

With "Desert Island Discs," BBC Radio 4, February 2022
https://www.bbc.co.uk/programmes/m0014p3b

Articles by Anne Tyler

"Will This Seem Ridiculous?" *Vogue*, 1 Feb 1965

"Olives Out of a Bottle," Duke University Archive, 1975, and *Critical Essays on Anne Tyler*, Ed. Alice Hall Petry, G. K. Hall, 1992

"Because I Want More Than One Life," *Washington Post*, 15 Aug 1976

"Please Don't Call it Persia," *New York Times*, Feb 1979

"Still Just Writing," *The Writer on her Work*, Ed. Janet Sternburg, Norton, 1980

"The Fine, Full World of Welty," *Washington Star*, 26 Oct 1980

"A Visit with Eudora Welty," *New York Times Book Review*, 2 Nov 1980

Introduction and editing, *The Best American Short Stories*, Houghton Mifflin Harcourt, 1983

Introduction, *In Black and White*, Eudora Welty, Lord John Pr, 1985

"Miss Cone, Miss Cone, Thank You, Thank You," *Art and Antiques*, Nov 1985

Introduction and assistance with selection, *The Available Press/PEN Short Story Collection*, NY: Ballantine Books, 1985

"Why I Still Treasure 'The Little House'," *New York Times*, Nov 1986

Introduction, *Best of the South: From Ten Years of New Stories from the South,* Workman Publishing, 1996

"Reynolds Price: Duke of Writers," *Critical Essays on Reynolds Price*, G. K. Hall, 1998

Introduction, *Best of the South: The Best of the Second Decade,* Shannon Ravenel Books, 2005

Foreword, *Midstream: An Unfinished Memoir*, Reynolds Price, Scribner Book Company, 2012

Miscellaneous

https://www.imdb.com/title/tt0168156 /
https://wamu.org/story/14/01/24/mark_furstenberg_prepares_for_new_adventure_in_baking_with_bread_furst/
https://annielyons.com/2015/05/10/the-anne-tyler-book-club/
http://www.mitramodarressi.com/biography.html
https://the-talks.com/interview/nick-hornby/
https://bandofthebes.typepad.com/bandofthebes/2012/04/john-waters-on-anne-tyler.html
https://baltimorefishbowl.com/stories/anne-tyler-you-are-a-baltimorean/
https://www.christies.com/lotfinder/books-manuscripts/tyler-anne-dinner-at-the-homesick-5847737-details.aspx?from=salesummery&intobjectid=5847737
http://loucksgallery.com/tezh-modarressi-1
https://fuelfundmaryland.org/file/annualreport2015-16pdf
https://mdfoodbank.org/wp-content/uploads/2018/02/pubs-2017-AR-Donor-Listing.pdf
https://bookpage.com/interviews/8232-anne-tyler-fiction#.XxsOk3uSlhg
https://global.penguinrandomhouse.com/announcements/sonny-mehta-receives-maxwell-e-perkins-award-from-the-center-for-fiction/
https://www.smithsonianmag.com/smithsonian-institution/twenty-smithsonian-shows-see-2020-180974093/
https://blog.libro.fm/author-interview-anne-tyler/
https://thebookerprizes.com/news/interview-longlisted-author-anne-tyler
https://medium.com/@rowjess/want-to-understand-racism-and-neglect-in-baltimore-read-anne-tyler-b1a55dc05e83
https://metrograph.com/an-interview-with-frederick-wiseman/
https://www.upi.com/Archives/1982/03/12/Babies-are-just-as-liable-to-suffer-from-depression/1738384757200/
https://crosscut.com/2020/01/iranian-america-immigrants-share-their-hopes-fears-and-frustrations

Printed in Great Britain
by Amazon

14847768R00173